Development and the Right to Education in Africa

A. C. Onuora-Oguno

Development and the Right to Education in Africa

palgrave
macmillan

A. C. Onuora-Oguno
University of Ilorin
Ilorin, Nigeria

ISBN 978-3-030-07994-9 ISBN 978-3-319-90335-4 (eBook)
https://doi.org/10.1007/978-3-319-90335-4

Cover image: © traffic_analyzer
Cover design: by Ran Shauli

Printed on acid-free paper

This Palgrave Macmillan imprint is published by the registered company Springer International Publishing AG part of Springer Nature
The registered company address is: Gewerbestrasse 11, 6330 Cham, Switzerland

To God for the ability to add a voice to the quest of realising access to education on the African continent

Foreword

The right to education is one of the most important human rights of our time. It is a 'multiplier' or an important tool for the realisation of other rights. The denial of the right to education 'leads to compounded denials of other human rights, and continuation of poverty and underdevelopment'. In fact, the right to education is an important instrument for human development as well as for the development of Africa. Yet, millions of children are still deprived of this right. As observed by Kishore Singh, the Special Rapporteur on the right to education (2013), 'the enjoyment of the right to education is often least accessible to those who need it most—disadvantaged and marginalized groups and, above all, children from poor families'. This volume establishes the nexus between development and the right to education. To this end, it demonstrates the importance of education for development. In unpacking challenges to the right to basic education, Dr. Onuora-Oguno provides a comparative analysis of these challenges in African states. Similarly, the author explores the development of regulatory framework to achieve the right to basic education. Furthermore, in examining the extent to which the courts can be useful in securing the right to basic education, Dr. Onuora-Oguno provides a comparative analysis of the jurisprudence on the right to basic education in Nigeria, South Africa, Uganda, Ghana. In the same vein, he also studies the Indian Jurisprudence known for its judicial activism. Still in an attempt to open the doors to school to all, the author explores possibilities for strategic ligation. This is followed by an insight on how the African human right system responds to the challenges of access to basic education and how institutions can turn the right into reality. This volume offers a thorough examination of the right to basic education and as such is suitable not only for academics and students interested in this right, but also for practitioners advocating or litigating the right to education.

Pretoria, South Africa
January 2018

Prof. Serges Djoyou Kamga
Associate Professor at the Thabo
Mbeki African Leadership Institute
UNISA, South Africa

Preface

The motivation to write this book was informed by the years of research during the course of my LLD in International Human Rights Law at the Centre for Human Rights, University of Pretoria. During this period, participation in conferences, research findings and the reality of the lack of development in Africa was sparked in me. Discovering the place of education appropriate and well applied in driving development increased my desire to join the noble course of advocating for the realisation of the right to education in Africa. In this book, I have identified possible challenges that may influence access to education; means of overcoming the challenges and the role the law via the judiciary can play in realisation of this aspiration. I am optimistic that the impact of this book would be felt within countries in Africa and that the state of access to education would be enhanced to influence the development of this great continent.

Ilorin, Nigeria

A. C. Onuora-Oguno, LL.D.
Senior Lecturer, University of Ilorin;
Researcher, Centre for Human Rights,
University of Pretoria

Acknowledgements

To my wife Blessing and my lovely children: Ifunanya, Onyedika and Ebube.

To my research assistants in the course of preparing the final manuscript; Emmanuel G., Hibatullahi K., Udemadu R., Adeosun M. and Adekunmbi A.

To Prof. Michelo Hansungule, Prof. Frans Viljoen, Prof. Wahab Egbewole, Prof. Serge Kamnga and all staff/colleagues at the Centre for Human Rights, University of Pretoria for all the support during the period of writing up my LL.D. thesis that formed the main stay of this book, I appreciate you. To Professor and Mrs. F. O. C. Nwonwu, I appreciate your role during the quest and my stay in Pretoria. Finally my siblings, Prof. N. C. Onuora-Oguno, Ifeoma Nduka-Obiora, Oby Onuora-Oguno and Ndidi Okoro I say thank you for standing by your kid brother to aspire and develop his academic prowess. To my fellow comrades in the academic struggles, Godwin Odo, Engr. Ewim and Dr. (Mrs.) Ngozi Chuma-Umeh, I appreciate you and trust that we all shall make our indelible marks on scholarship. Finally, I appreciate members of the Dennis Memorial Grammar School, Class of 1994 World-Wide for your support and drive towards excellence (Your scholarship scheme and support of our alma mater) is a true representation of my desires to see non-governmental involvement in enhancing access to education and development.

Contents

About the Author

Dr. A. C. Onuora-Oguno LL.B. (Ilorin), NLS (Nigeria), LL.M. (Pretoria), LL.D. (Pretoria) is a senior lecturer with the Jurisprudence and International Law Department at University of Ilorin. He is also a researcher with the Centre for Human Rights, University of Pretoria where he obtained his LL.D. in 2015. Azubike is an international human rights law scholar with a passion for socio-economic rights, minority rights and disability studies. Azubike is a Solicitor and Advocate of the Nigeria Supreme Court with over ten years post-call experience, he was a former clerk in the Office of the Prosecutor, International Criminal Court.

Abbreviations and Acronyms

ABEK	Alternative Basic Education for the Karamoja
ACHPR	African Charter on Human and Peoples' Rights
ACRWC	African Charter on the Rights and Welfare of the Child
ADMHCDS	Anglican Diocese of Mbamili Health and Community Development Services
AI	Amnesty International
AIE	Alternative and Innovative Education
APRM	African Peer Review Mechanism
BEA	British Education Act
BH	Boko Haram
CC	Constitutional Court
CESA	Centre for the Study of Economies in Africa
CFRN	Constitution of the Federal Republic of Nigeria
CHRAJ	Commission on Human Rights and Administrative Justice
CLE	Continuing Legal Education
CLU	Clinical Law Units
COE	Colleges of Education
CRA	Child Rights Act
CRC	Convention on the Rights of a Child
CRM	Country Review Mechanism
CRPD	Convention on the Rights of People with Disabilities
CSO	Civil Society Organisation
CWD	Children with Disabilities
DFID	Department for International Development
DRR	Disaster Risk Reduction
ECHR	European Convention of Human Right

EFA	Education for All
EGS	Education Guarantee Scheme
ESCR	Economic, Social and Cultural Rights
FCT	Federal Capital Territory
FG	Federal Government
FME	Federal Ministry of Education
GAJE	Global Alliance for Justice Education
GC	General Comments
GDR	German Democratic Republic
HOD	Head of Department
ICCPR	International Covenant on Civil and Political Rights
ICESCR	International Covenant on Economic, Social and Cultural Rights
ICPC	Independent Corrupt Practices Commission
IEA	India Education Act
IHRC	India Human Rights Commission
KHRC	Kenyan Human Rights Commission
LDC	Language Development Centre
LEGA	Local Government EducationAuthority
MDG	Millennium Development Goals
MEC	Member of Executive Council
MoE	Ministry of Education
NBA	Nigerian Bar Association
NCE	National Certificate of Education
NEDS	National Education Data Survey
NEMA	National Emergency Management Agency
NERDC	National Education Research and Development Council
NGO	Non-governmental Organisation
NHRC	National Human Rights Commission
NHRC	Nigeria National Human Rights Commission
NLS	Nigeria Law School
NOUN	National Open University of Nigeria
NPE	National Policy on Education
NPEC	National Primary Education Commission
NPEF	National Primary Education Fund
NTI	National Teachers Institute
NUC	National University Commission
NUT	Nigerian Union of Teachers
NYSC	National Youth Service Commission
OAU	Organisation of African Unity
PAJA	Promotion of Administrative Justice Act
PIL	Public Interest Litigation
PLWD	Persons Living With Disabilities

PTA	Parents–Teachers Association
RTE	Right to Education
SACC	South African Constitutional Court
SAHRC	South African Human Rights Commission
SAN	Senior Advocate of Nigeria
SAP	Structural Adjustment Programme
SEN	Special Education Needs
SERAP	Socio-economic Rights and Accountability Projects
SGB	School Governing Board
SMoE	State Ministry of Education
SPEB	State Primary Education Board
SUBEB	State Universal Basic Education Board
TEP	The Education Partnership
TMLI	Thabo Mbeki Leadership Institute
TRCN	Teachers' Registration Council of Nigeria
UBE	Universal Basic Education
UBEA	Universal Basic Education Act
UDHR	Universal Declaration of Human Rights
UNESCO	United Nations Education Scientific and Cultural Organisation
UNGA	United Nations General Assembly
UPE	Universal Primary Education

CHAPTER 1

Right to Development and Education: An Introductory Note

Establishing the nexus between education and development is fundamental to appreciating the core purpose of this book. In attempting to establish this nexus, the book examines the concept of the right to education and its impact on development. It would resolve if the later is dependent on the former and the situation in Africa as regards both concepts. Considering that Africa is generally accepted to be the least developed in the equation of continental statistics, the need to examine the factors that influence the poor state of development is fundamental vis-a-vis the role that education plays. For the purposes of this, low access to basic education is identified as playing a major role in this seeming underdevelopment. This situation is all the more disturbing as the government continues with political rhetoric: mainly insincere and pretentious commitment s to curbing poor access to basic education and developmental issues in Africa. In the human rights discourse today, the role of education is important as it forms the basis on which other rights are built. The government is required by national legislation and international law to protect, promote and fulfil human rights. African governments are under an obligation to ensure the elimination of all challenges capable of depriving the African child access to basic education.

In analysing the state of education in African countries, the lived realities present a situation in dire need of urgent revival. For instance in Nigeria, the level of illiteracy has reached an alarming rate and has

A. C. Onuora-Oguno, *Development and the Right to Education in Africa*,
https://doi.org/10.1007/978-3-319-90335-4_1

consequently jostled all spheres of the national existence.[1] The situation in Ghana, Zambia and South Africa all present the same challenges ranging from issues of access to education to poor quality of the accessed education. In Nigeria, with a population of about 180 million,[2] an estimate of about 10 million children are out of school and almost the same number are forced to drop out of school because of an inability to sustain the requirements of the basic education system, most often occasioned by poverty, cultural and religious affiliations of parents.[3] Issues of access, acceptability and quality today confront the education industry in Africa, providing a basis for poor development of the continent.

Some scholars have blamed the advent of the European colonialists on the African continent as a major contributor to the underdevelopment of Africa.[4] Scholars like Mandela and Fafunwa opine that education has a central basis in ensuring and driving development thus aligning with the theory of both Mandela and Fafunwa the book advances the need to drive development in Africa by relying on the place of an enhanced access to quality education. The poor access and poor completion of basic education remain a major challenge. For instance in Nigeria statistics show that, at present, access to basic education in Nigeria is poor, especially in the northern part of the country, with quality below an acceptable threshold in the nation as a whole.[5] Apart from the challenge

[1] Chinelo O. Duze, "Falling standards of education in Nigeria: An empirical evidence in delta State of Nigeria," *LWATI: A Journal of Contemporary Research* 1 (2011): 3; Action Aid, "Transforming education for girls in Nigeria: Baseline research summary report," http://www.actionaid.org/sites/files/actionaid/aategintbaselinenigeriafinal.pdf; "Happening now: OAU students protests the state of education in Nigeria," http://www.nigeriadailynews.com/news/206343-happening-now-oau-students-protest-state-of-education-in-nigeria.html (accessed 15 October 2017).

[2] http://www.population.gov.ng/images/Priority%20Tables%20Volume%20I-update.pdf (accessed 7 November 2017).

[3] See generally statistics on state of education available at http://data.uis.unesco.org/Index.aspx?queryid=120 (accessed 30 November 2017); http://data.worldbank.org/topic/education (accessed 30 November 2017).

[4] Walter Rodney, *How Europe underdeveloped Africa* (Bolge L'Ouverture, 1972).

[5] A state-by-state literacy status compiled by the commission covering 2008–2010 shows that very few states have done well. Most of the states in the north-east and north-west zones have not done well at literacy level. Borno State has only 14.5% of literate population; Gombe has 39%; Jigawa has 24%, while Katsina has 21%. Those doing well are Lagos with 92%; Anambra has 75.1%, Abia has 72.5% while Ekiti has 74.7%; FCT has 61.4%. See http://nigerianpilot.com/index.php/-other-section/-features/

of access, quality is another huge challenge in the realisation of basic education. The African Peer Review Mechanism (APRM) to Nigeria noted that, despite the legislative provisions and policies in place in Nigeria, the quality of education is substandard, with many schools ill-equipped and lacking qualified teachers.[6] The APRM, in addition, noted the impact of corruption and poverty as challenges hampering access to quality education in Nigeria.[7] This example from Nigeria clearly finds

4085-the-challenges-of-mass-illiteracy-in-nigeria (accessed 27 December 2017). As already stated in the introduction, UNESCO statistics also show the poor state of out of school children in Nigeria. This position effectively forecloses the political argument on the basis for the reliance on the statistics of UNESCO as the dismal situation is captured in both national and international statistics. Furthermore to the UNESCO statistics, UNICEF in a separate research have also found that 'Forty per cent of Nigerian children aged 6–11 do not attend any primary school with the Northern region recording the lowest school attendance rate in the country, particularly for girls. Despite a significant increase in net enrolment rates in recent years, it is estimated that about 4.7 million children of primary school age are still not in school…Even when children enrol in schools, many do not complete the primary cycle. According to current data, 30% of pupils drop out of primary school and only 54% transit to Junior Secondary Schools. Reasons for this low completion rate include child labour, economic hardship and early marriage for girls'' see generally http://www.unicef.org/nigeria/children_1937.html (accessed 20 December 2017). In 1998, UNESCO found the number of out of school children in Nigeria to be 7 million, the recent estimate of 10.5 million further reiterate the depreciating turn of events in the basic education industry in Nigeria, see http://www.unesco.org/education/efa/global_co/policy_group/children_out_of_school.pdf (accessed 30 November 2017).

[6]African Peer Review Mechanism (2008) Report No 8 para 347. In a UNESCO research, the state of literacy for Nigeria basic education was found to be below 50%. It was found that '[T]he mean percent scores on the literacy, numeracy and life skills test were 40.8, 43.1 and 43.1 respectively for private schools; while the mean percentage scores for the public schools for literacy, numeracy and life skills tests were 22.2, 30.1 and 30.6 respectively' see generally R Aderinoye Literacy Assessment Practices (LAP) in selected developing countries Nigeria case study Discussion Document Prepared for ILI/UNESCO LAP 2nd Experts' Meeting UNESCO Paris, 18. In buttressing the quality challenge the former Supervisory Minister of Education in Nigeria, lamented the poor state of teacher–pupil ratio in Nigeria. According to records it is put at '1 teacher to 350 Pupil' see generally Nigeria to address shortage of qualified English, Maths teachers, http://www.premiumtimesng.com/news/164561-nigeria-to-address-shortage-of-qualified-english-maths-teachers-wike.html (accessed 15 December 2017).

[7]This situation leaves yet unanswered the issue of acceptability. As stated in the case of the Anambra West local government area, the predominately fishermen and farmers sometimes decry the obstruction of their means of livelihood by having to let their children go to school. The situation in the north, where the Boko Haram has emerged, is also another case worth investigating. It is important, therefore, that the government must evolve a workable legal framework to take care of all interests to ensure that not only access is guaranteed but also acceptability.

expression in other situations across the African continent. With the menace of corruption leading to a lack of access to and, consequently, the non-availability of basic education, the problem deepens. Cultural and religious undertones, coupled with the non-adaptability of the curriculum content of basic education in Nigeria, further leads to the rejection of education.[8]

In understanding the nexus between education and development, it is equally important to take into cognisance the role institutions would generally play in ensuring a sustainable synergy. Smith[9] and Heyns[10] adumbrate the role of institutions in realising rights be it development or education *vis-à-vis* their relationship with the state. In this regard, Heyns projects the possibility of a struggle approach, which may arouse people towards realising their fundamental rights when the institutions fail to do their work. Laure-Helene,[11] while providing a rights-based insight into social protection, discusses the mandate of the state to ensure the promotion, protection and fulfilment of rights. McLean and Mbazira[12] explore the issues of litigating socio-economic rights, Olowu[13] deals with the issues of justiciability of socio-economic rights and human development in Africa. Woolman and Fleisch[14] provide insight into law and education. Veriava and Coomans in their treatise, 'the right to education', identify core issue that is important to the focus of this book.

[8]A new conundrum is the rise of the Boko Haram, a supposed Islamist group which in 2012 alone has 'burnt down 14 schools in Maiduguri, the capital of Nigeria's Borno state, forcing over 7000 children out of formal education and pushing down enrolment rates in an already ill-educated region,' http://www.protectingeducation.org/news/nigeria-school-attendance-down-after-boko-haram-attacks (accessed 13 November 2017). This has led to a reduction in access to basic education in the region.

[9]Jackie Smith, "Exploring connections between global integration and political mobilisation," *Journal of World System Research*, B. Podobnik and T.E. Reifer (eds), X(1).

[10]Christof Heyns and Kareen Stefiszyn (eds), *Human rights, justice and peace in Africa: A reader* (2006).

[11]P. Laure-Helene, "Rights-based approaches to social protection," http://www.gsdrc.org/go/display/document/legacyid/1617 (accessed 30 November 2017).

[12]Christopher Mbazira, *Litigating socio-economic rights in South Africa: A choice between corrective and distributive justice* (Pretoria: PULP, 2009).

[13]Dejo Olowu, *An integrative rights-based approach to human development in Africa* (Pretoria: PULP, 2009).

[14]Stu Woolman and Brham Fleisch, *The constitution in the classroom: Law and education in South Africa, 1994–2008* (Pretoria: PULP, 2009).

I argue that 'denial of the right to education is a denial of the full enjoyment of other rights that enable an individual to develop to his or her full potential and participate meaningfully in the society'.[15] They advance that denial of access to education is a tool that can be employed to ensure the continued discrimination of a people and ultimately their underdevelopment. This is argued to influence the South African situation showing how education was used by apartheid to ensure that the black South African remained at the lower end of the ladder.

The right to a basic education is described as been a priority right above other socio-economic rights. It is an 'unqualified right that necessitates a determination of the scope and content of basic education'.[16] This approach requires the state to ensure that comprehensive measures must be adopted, well-articulated and co-ordinated towards realising the right to basic education.[17]

The work of McConnachie and McConnachie[18] also support the views adopted in this book that the right to basic education is an unqualified right. They, however, advance reasons on which the right to education may be reasonably limited[19] while also identifying the increasing impact of litigation in the quest to enhance the realisation of the right to basic education.[20] McConnachie and McConnachie work provides a valuable guide as it examines the interpretation of the right to basic education in both India and South Africa amidst the

[15] Faranaz Veriava and Fons Coomans, "The right to education," in Danny Brand and Christof Heyns (eds), *Socio-economic rights in South Africa* (Pretoria: PULP, 2005), 60.

[16] Brand and Heyns, "Socio-economic rights in South Africa," 60; See also the dictum of Nkabinde J as reproduced in Cameron McConnachie and Chris McConnachie, "Concretising the right to a basic education," *SALJ* 561 (2012): 129.

[17] Brand and Heyns, "Socio-economic rights in South Africa," 47, 49.

[18] Cameroun McConnachie & Chris McConnachie, "Concretising the right to a basic education."

[19] This position is in contrast to the views of Viljoen on the immediacy of the meaning and concept of basic education. See also the views of Veriava and Coomans above. Importantly also, the CFRN does not contain a limitation clause as obtainable in Section 36 (1) of the South African Constitution. It is therefore important to draw this distinction in applying the approach to the application and execution of the laws and policies and laws on the right to basic education in Nigeria. See McConnachie and McConnachie as above 564.

[20] Cameroun McConnachie and Chris McConnachie, "Concretising the right to a basic education".

challenge of resources while yet demanding and imposing 'extensive range of obligation on the state to provide an education'.[21] They explore the role of the courts by finding[22]:

> The unqualified right will require courts to give content to the right to a basic education and to assess the impact of poor school facilities on learners and teachers to determine whether the right has been limited.

Thus for development to be achieved via education, the approach of the state must be 'effective, indicative and hold the real prospect of providing relief to the individuals whose rights have been violated, even if the relief cannot be immediate'.[23]

Another aspect touched by the book is on the role the judiciary can play in this regard. The challenge facing the judiciary and the anticipatory role that they can play in enhancing the realisation of the right to basic education is well explored by Skelton when she interrogates the extent the courts can go[24] and the roles they can play in the realisation of basic education.[25] Also instructive are the pragmatic suggestions on how the state could be held responsible in the face of claims of a progressive realisation of the right to a basic education.[26] Aoife Nolan's work on the socio-economic rights of children further provides an insight into the circumstances and situation that the right of children should be subject to judicial protection.[27] Thiruvengadam lauds the impact of PIL,[28]

[21] Cameroun McConnachie and Chris McConnachie, "Concretising the right to a basic education," 557.

[22] Cameroun McConnachie and Chris McConnachie, "Concretising the right to a basic education," 579.

[23] C. Cameroun McConnachie and Chris McConnachie, "Concretising the right to a basic education," 589.

[24] Ann Skelton, "How far will the courts go in ensuring the right to a basic education?" *SAPL* 396 (2012): 27. See Generally Aoife Nolan, *Children's socio-economic rights, democracy and the courts* (Oxford, UK: Hart Publishing, 2011).

[25] Ann Skelton, "The role of the courts in ensuring the right to a basic education in a democratic South Africa: A critical evaluation of recent education case law," *De Jure* 46 (2013): 3.

[26] Ann Skelton, "Leveraging funds for school infrastructure: The South African 'mud schools' case study," *International Journal of Educational Development* 59 (2014).

[27] Aoife Nolan, "Children's socio-economic rights, democracy and the courts."

[28] Arun R. Thiruvengadam, "Swallowing a bitter PIL? Reflections on progressive strategies for public interest litigation in India," in Oscar Vilhena, Upendra Baxi, and Frans Viljoen (eds) *Transformative constitutionalism: Comparing the Apex Courts of Brazil, India and South Africa* (Pretoria: PULP, 2013).

and 'urge progressives to increase-rather than abandon-engagement with the law and courts'.[29] The work provides further insight into the challenges that may confront the reliance on PIL as a means of realising economic rights. This position brings to the fore the role the judge should play in engaging with PIL and economic rights. While criticising the role of judicial activism as advanced by Baxi,[30] it is advanced that social actors, organisations, lawyers should be all major players in the quest. In addressing the identified issues, the book is divided into ten chapters.

Chapter 2 embarks on a conceptual framework of grounding that education at the basic level is a fundamental right; establish also that development under the new human rights discourse is also a fundamental right. In Chapter 3, obstacles to the right of access to basic education are examined from a developmental perspective. In Chapter 4, I consider the debate surrounding the issue of inclusive education and special education. In Chapter 5, I argue that there is need to reconceptualise the African perspective to education if development would be realised. Chapter 6 engages the debate of the human right or human capital concept to education and canvases for the need to adopt a human rights approach. Following an examination of the role of the judiciary, Chapter 7 explores a comparative analysis of jurisprudence governing basic education. In Chapter 8, I highlight the response of the African human rights system in addressing the challenge of education on the continent. Two chapters are dedicated to two important concepts of quality and inclusive education, representing conference presentation at the International Association of Constitutional Lawyers and the Global Alliance for Justice Education.

The book concludes on the note that education is pivotal to the development of Africa and that an intersection of law, individuals, state apparatus are all required in the quest to ensure an enhanced access to education for the development of Africa.

[29] Arun R. Thiruvengadam, "Swallowing a bitter PIL? Reflections on progressive strategies for public interest litigation in India."

[30] Baxi as cited by Thiruvengadam places a lot of importance on activist judges to aid the realisation of socio-economic rights, despite the disagreement, it is advocated that 'judges can lend support to PIL without appearing to act in partisan or ideologically motivated ways'. Arun R. Thiruvengadam, "Swallowing a bitter PIL? Reflections on progressive strategies for public interest litigation in India," 527.

CHAPTER 2

Theoretical Framework and Benefits of Basic Education

2.1 Introduction

In establishing the core content of the right to education, it is noted, according to Coomans, that the term 'core content' should be regarded as an aid to identification though not without challenges. However, he identifies that:

> With respect to the right to education as laid down in international documents, two aspects can be distinguished. On the one hand, realisation of the right to education demands an effort on the part of the state to make education available and accessible. It implies positive state obligations. This is the social aspect. On the other hand, there is the personal freedom of individuals to choose between state-organised and private education, which can be translated, for example, in parents' freedom to ensure their children's moral and religious education according to their own beliefs.[1]

The purport of the chapter's analysis of the relevant provisions is to ground the arguments in support of a strong link between basic education as a human right and its fundamental human rights nature as opposed to a mere social obligation or human capital development component.

[1] Fons Coomans, "Clarifying the core elements of the right to education," http://www.aihr-resourcescenter.org/administrator/upload/documents/core.pdf (accessed 12 January 2018).

A. C. Onuora-Oguno, *Development and the Right to Education in Africa*,
https://doi.org/10.1007/978-3-319-90335-4_2

2.2 Conceptual Analysis of Education: An African Perspective

Education has different connotations for different groups of persons, either varying according to their religious, social or cultural perspectives. Education is a broad concept and can be viewed as a cycle which makes it an unending process in life. The claims of the advent of education acknowledge the Jewish, Greek and Roman origins, with little or no recognition of the African perspective of education. However, these positions may not be correct, as Africa also lays claim to its own concept of education. Despite the claim by some scholars that the African style of education was on a different paradigm from the style of education brought by colonialism in Africa; literature shows that the African concept of education was one that was acceptable and adaptable to the people; slowly but gradually leading to its emancipation.[2] On a generalised basis, the education cycle should be one in which everyone has a role to play: 'The child, parents, teachers and government must get involved so as to ensure that education achieves its set out aims and objectives'.[3]

In Nduka's analysis, education is all about expressing, conveying and receiving of information and ideas. In this regard, no one must be stopped from expressing views and opinions. Education represents a process of cultural transmission in three tiers. This includes inheriting a culture, changing the culture for better or for worse, and passing it on to the younger generation.[4]

[2] Michelo Hansungule and Azubike C. Onuora-Oguno, "African perspective of education: A catalyst for the desired Africa of tomorrow?" Paper presented at the Thabo Mbeki Leadership Institute Symposium on Finding Solutions to Africa's Development, University of South Africa, August 2013. It is also worthy to note that Northern Nigeria which is predominantly Muslim has Islamic basic education which is regulated by the Islamic law. The discourse on Islamic basic education is beyond the scope of this present research but points to the need to ensure that curriculum of education developed must uphold and respect the belief of individuals.

[3] James Bowen and P. R. Hobson, *Theories of education studies of significant innovation in Western education thoughts* (Brisbane: Watson Ferhuson, 1974), 8.

[4] Otonti A. Nduka, *Western education and the Nigerian cultural background* (Ibadan: Oxford Press, 1975), 12.

The African perspective on education entailed two primary realities: that of African cultural traditions and political/economic environments.[5] Ayodele and Adedokun are of the opinion that 'education is not only a social service but a transformative act which is fundamental to social and personal development because when there is access to education, there is an increase in social and political awareness and heightened aspirations, self-assurance and self-assertiveness'.[6] The purport of this perspective leads to a generalisation that education encompasses a whole lot that deals generally with the well-being of people and how they can be better entities to both society and themselves as individuals.

According to Kwame Nkrumah, 'human history has been dominated by the quest for bread and human rights'.[7] The analysis of human rights in this sense includes the various attempts to lay claim to ways of life of African people prior to colonial experiences. Various philosophies and attributes of the African society were lost in the distorted historical perspectives that have graced the academic circles on various issues like education, medicine and so forth.

Kolawole describes education in Nigeria 'not just as a medium for cultural transmission, but also as the main vehicle for ensuring individual, community and national development towards its survival and sustenance'.[8] Tomasevski opines that 'education traditionally must treat children as objects of education specifying the rights of parents, teachers and the state'.[9] Tomasevski's perception draws the trilogy of the key

[5] In Bowen and Hobson's commentary on the biography of Plato, it is stated: 'The cycle of educational development as shown in Plato's view was not well developed in the late 5th century BC and that generally the privileged boy only went to school with the girl not given any schooling'. The view of training only the 'guardians' of the state represents another discriminatory stance of early education styles absolving African traditional society of the blame of not educating the girl child.

[6] Joseph B. Ayodele and Mary O. Adedokun, "Towards achieving functional adult literacy in Nigeria," *European Scientific Journal* 8(5) (2012): 1.

[7] Kwame Nkurumah's address on education and nationalism cited in Ama Biny, *The political and social thoughts of Kwame Nkrumah*, https://libyadiary.files.wordpress.com/2011/09/pdf-2011-the-political-and-social-thought-of-kwame-nkrumah.pdf (accessed 12 January 2018).

[8] Kazeem Kolawole, "Redressing the growing of concern of the education sector in Nigeria," *Edo Journal of Counselling* 3(1) (2010): 41.

[9] Katrina Tomasevski, *Removing obstacles in the way of the right to education*. Primers No. 1 (2001), 44.

stakeholders in education. The state therefore has a vital role to play in ensuring that education is advanced, while acknowledging the role of the parents and the best interests of the child. It is pertinent then to include the views of parents and communities in an attempt to draft the curriculum and to determine the scope of the type of education that must be delivered to learners in order to ensure the development of every society.[10] The consequences of this are that education must be adaptable to make a meaningful impact the development of any community. The above perspective brings to the fore the central place of education in enhancing the capacity of an individual and aiding the individual to realise his full potential while playing a definite and defined role in the society towards a society's development. Besides the African description of education, other descriptions of education also exist. For instance, according to the Latin jurisprudence, the word 'education' was derived from the Latin word *educare*, meaning 'to bring up, to lead out, to raise up and to educate...in its original sense, to educate means acting in order to lead out fully all the potential of individuals'.[11]

In his analysis of the African and European perspectives of education, Kenyatta found that 'the striking thing in the ...education and the feature which most sharply distinguishes it from the European system of education, is the primary place given to personal relations'.[12] In addition, Kenyatta opines that '[t]o the European individuality is the ideal of life, to the Africans the ideal is the right relations with, and behavior to, other people'.[13] Africans were educated in the 'way thought fit, a policy that has been carried out without due regard for the ideals and aspirations of the people concerned'.[14] 'The fundamental nature of personal relationships in the scheme of education shows clearly how these things are

[10] W. Bray, *Human rights in education* (Pretoria: Centre for Education Law and Policy, 2008), 59.

[11] Alice A. Jekayinfa and D. O. Kolawole, "Conceptual background to education," in J. O. O. Abiri and A. A. Jekafinfa (eds), *Perspective on the history of education in Nigeria* (Ilorin: Bamitex, 2010), 3.

[12] Jomo Kenyatta, *Facing Mount Kenya. The traditional life of the Gikuyu* (London: Secker and Warburg, 1979), 121.

[13] Jomo Kenyatta, *Facing Mount Kenya*, 122.

[14] Jomo Kenyatta, *Facing Mount Kenya*, 126.

valued...prosperity depends on the joint activities of all the members of the society'.[15]

In addition, the 'first and most obvious principle of educational value which we see ... is that the instruction is always applied to an individual concrete situation...the child is left free to develop his own initiative by experiments and through trial and error to acquire proficiency'.[16]

The main purport of advancing the fact that Africa had a concept of education does not proceed on the footing to discredit Western education wholly, but to underscore the importance of inculcating the African perspective of education. An application of this will ensure that proper education planning in line with the ideological leaning of various communities in Africa will lead to a more acceptable notion of education and assist in eliminating cultural and religious obstacles to the realisation of the right to basic education,[17] and consequently development.

2.2.1 Various Perspectives on Education

Plato opines that education is no less than a 'philosophical assumption linking the cosmos and the operation in nature of harmony and balance'.[18] Plato's view insinuates the relevance of education in ensuring that the likelihood of achieving harmony in the world will be achieved with the proper style of education. It is on this premise that Plato canvassed for the education of the guardians in his era, stressing the importance of a quality curriculum.[19] This position of Plato is not acceptable, because it could possibly form the basis of discrimination in society. It is argued that each individual has the right to be educated, irrespective of a perceived intellectual disability. Plato's position is[20]:

[15] Jomo Kenyatta, *Facing Mount Kenya*, 113.

[16] Jomo Kenyatta, *Facing Mount Kenya*, 121.

[17] See generally Hansungule and Onuora-Oguno, "African perspective of education: A catalyst for the desired Africa of tomorrow?"

[18] Bowen and Hobson, *Theories of education studies of significant innovation in Western education thoughts*, 27.

[19] Bowen and Hobson, *Theories of education studies of significant innovation in Western education thoughts*, 65–67.

[20] Bowen and Hobson, *Theories of education studies of significant innovation in Western education thoughts*, 28.

> Little can be done for the lower levels of society beyond seeing that their lives are reasonably comfortable and secure… lacking the capacity for high level of intellectual life the laboring masses should be protected from disturbing ideas by having their myths and legends maintained; shielded from intellectual challenges because lacking the ability to solve them, they can only become disturbed and frightened and perhaps liable to stampede… they should be helped to pursue their daily activities by being provided with vocational skills, learned by community involvement and the traditional method of direct apprenticeship.

The above position is faulted because a criterion for the selection of different curricula for different groups on the basis of perceived intellectual ability is discriminatory. While I argue on the need for the adaptability of education curricula, it is not advanced because of the reliance on the basis of perceived intelligence, but on the basis of choice and relevance to suit the specific needs of groups and individuals. It is important that education is inclusive.[21] Consequently, education must be provided not only for the perceived 'guardians' of the state, but also for every individual irrespective of the learning capabilities of the individual.

As accounted by Bowen and Hobson, Ivan Illich opines that '[e]ducation involves essentially a process which intentionally transmits what is valuable in an intelligible and voluntary manner which creates in the learner a desire to achieve it'.[22] As opposed to Plato's 'discriminatory selective' criteria, the process of education, since it involves several stakeholders, should be a democratic one with all the stakeholders playing a role, development as its end point.[23] Thus, for an act to be described as education, it must fulfil certain basic functions from the interdependence of all stakeholders. According to Bowels and Gintis[24]:

> These functions are broadly classified as integrative, egalitarian, and developmental. To be integrative, education must help organise youths into various occupational, political, economic and stable polities. To be egalitarian

[21] The use of the term 'inclusive' in the thesis relates to education of the children with disability discussed later in Chapter 4.

[22] Bowen and Hobson, *Theories of education studies of significant innovation in Western education thoughts*, 398.

[23] Bowen and Hobson, *Theories of education studies of significant innovation in Western education thoughts*, 170.

[24] S. Bowels and H. Gintis, "Broken promises: School reform in retrospect," in S. F. Semel (ed), *Foundations of education: The essential texts* (2010), 61–65.

> education must ensure that each individual gets an opportunity to escape from the limitations of social groups in which he was born and to come into living contact within a broader environment. To be developmental, education must act as a major instrument in the psychic and moral development of the individual.

One important characteristic of any style of education that may be advanced is the underlying factor that education is important for emancipation and the enjoyment of life. The concept of education, when used, is linked to various activities that take place through several institutions: formal, non-formal and informal existing in the social strata.[25] For the purpose of this book, more attention is paid to education at the basic level which, to a large extent, excludes colleges and universities. Education can also be seen as the acquisition of knowledge, attitudes, beliefs and values learned by getting involved with society in general.[26] The link between education and development cannot be separated as the 'education process is one of continual reorganising, reconstruction and transforming'.[27]

According to Peter, as stated in Bowen and Hobson, whatever the style or concept of education that is advanced, it is important that it leads to some material or tangible benefits.[28] He sets the tangible benefits as beneficial to both the individual and society; therefore, someone cannot be said to be educated when he learns how to steal and cause harm to society in general. To him, education is not the name of a process, but rather 'something of value; manner in which learning and teaching takes place and the outcome'.[29]

[25] Some of the formal institutions created by the society include primary/basic, secondary and tertiary institutions. Formal education is presently the centre of any discussion of the education cycle.

[26] Bowen and Hobson, *Theories of education studies of significant innovation in Western education thoughts*, 1–3.

[27] Bowen and Hobson, *Theories of education studies of significant innovation in Western education thoughts*, 18.

[28] Bowen and Hobson, *Theories of education studies of significant innovation in Western education thoughts*, 348.

[29] Bowen and Hobson, *Theories of education studies of significant innovation in Western education thoughts*, 349–350.

Makarenko sees education as a process where every individual, from the earliest years of life, builds a value for learning and labour, stating that it comes with the reality of a good society emanating from every individual's ability to achieve education.[30] To him, education must enhance the subordination of the individual for the collective common good of the society at large. To achieve this, all institutions of society must be construed as having the potential to educate, as the ultimate goal of an educational process emanates from the ultimate goals of society.[31] The position of Makarenko goes some way towards validating the African style of education that was more people-centred, as opposed to the Western education[32] concept that was more individualistic.

Irrespective of the school of thought, one may align with an underlining premise is the fact that education is a core basis for the realisation of social and economic proficiency of an individual and also a nation's development.

Apart from the various concepts of education advanced above, it is reiterated that certain contents or thresholds must be met for education to achieve the above-mentioned criteria. Issues of quality of education, dignity and elimination of discrimination are all very important concepts that must be core aspects of education. It was in this respect that Nkrumah is quoted as having urged that 'Western education be

[30] Bowen and Hobson, *Theories of education studies of significant innovation in Western education thoughts*, 29.

[31] Bowen and Hobson, *Theories of education studies of significant innovation in Western education thoughts*, 223–224.

[32] It is noted as discussed that Western education has an inherent challenge that reduces the extent of access among other things, however, 'The core challenges facing the western style of education aside its cost implication include the inability of the state to plan and come up with verifiable data that will sustain the implementation of plans. This has been established in the failure of both the UPE and the UBE to take off effectively. While the UPE was marred for poor planning and sudden population growth, the UBE started off on a slow pace with late implementation of the UBE Act'. See generally S. D. Bolaji, "Intent to action: Overcoming barriers to Universal Basic Education policy implementation in Nigeria," unpublished Ph.D. thesis available at http://ro.ecu.edu.au/cgi/viewcontent.cgi?article=2425&context=theses (accessed 31 October 2017); S. Ademola Ajayi, "The development of free primary education scheme in Western Nigeria, 1952–1966: An analysis," www.ajol.info/index.php/og/article/download/52320/4044 (accessed 31 October 2017); Akinjide Aboluwodi, "Political will and strategic planning in the implementation of universal basic education in Nigeria: The Obafemi Awolowo example," *Journal of Education and Research* 5(1) (2015): 41.

embraced by the people of the Gold Coast, but with a *caveat* of ensuring that cultures and personalities are not forgotten'.[33]

If education, as already mentioned, possesses latent transformative potential, then getting education right at the basic level is paramount. This is because, as opined by Socrates, '[s]ince character is formed at an early age, the education of guardians must begin in the earliest years'.[34] The importance attached to the role of basic education, realising this obligation, is hinged on the premise that it is the start-off point in the building block of self-sufficiency, therefore requiring attention and input of all stakeholders to ensure that its quality is well guaranteed. Consequently, when quality is guaranteed at a basic education level, then the socio-economic development of a nation is highly guaranteed.[35]

Also, an important basis for education must be respected for the dignity of the individual. There is a need to advance the importance of education in respecting the worth and dignity of each individual by encouraging freedom of inquiry and expression. It is posited that the style of education in every society determines to a great extent the type of society that is built. According to Ravitch[36]:

> Nations that rule by coercion require citizens who have been educated to accept coercion. A free Society, Committed to popular rule, must provide an education that prepares people to think for themselves and to function as a free citizen.

The outcome of the above attests to the development or otherwise of a society taking into cognisance the style of education that is embraced.

[33]Biny, *The political and social thoughts of Kwame Nkrumah*, 22.

[34]As narrated in GMA Grube, *The Cleitophon of Plato, classical philology* 302 (1931), 3; Bowen and Hobson, *Theories of education studies of significant innovation in Western education thoughts*, 33.

[35]D. A. Olaniyan and E. O. Olabanji, "A critical review of management of primary education in Nigeria," *International Journal of African and African American Studies* VII(1) (2008): 9.

[36]Diane Ravitch, "The democratic-liberal tradition under attack," in S. F. Semel (ed), *Foundations of education: The essential texts* (UK: Routledge, 2010), 101.

2.3 The Theories of Rights: An Overview

The existence of rights has been questioned by authors like Cranstone.[37] Cranstone brings to the fore the challenges confronting the concepts of the rights of man, which is perceived as largely political. This division, to some extent, brings to the fore the various perspectives of rights from the various generations. The first generation of rights are generally perceived as traditional rights which are civil and political rights; the second generation represents the economic, social and cultural rights within which the right to access basic education falls; and the third are the solidarity rights which are also seen as group rights.[38] However, despite this seeming division of rights, human rights are generally today perceived as indivisible and universal. As shown from the concept of education and its impact on development, the purpose and benefit of education span across all societies and thus the concept of rights is viewed from the perspective of interdependence and interwoven.[39]

It is noted that the concept of rights remains an unsettled one. However, it is my assumption that the question of rights implies that an individual is entitled to a particular obligation, which another has a positive responsibility to ensure its realisation.[40] Conceptualising rights is, however, not as simple, as stated above. Its scope and understanding vary from one jurisprudential school of thought to another.

Dembour groups the concepts of rights into four broad categories, namely natural, protest, deliberative and discourse.[41] Each of Dembour's groupings of rights could be aligned with early jurisprudence on the

[37] Maurice Cranstone, "Are there any human rights?" *Daedalus* 4 (1983): 1–17.

[38] See generally Stephen P. Marks, "Emerging human rights: A new generation for the 1980s," *Rutgers Law Review* 435 (1980): 33.

[39] For a detailed discourse on the debate on the interdependence of rights and their indivisibility, see generally James W. Nickel, "Rethinking indivisibility: Towards a theory of supporting relations between human rights," *Human Rights Quarterly* (2008): 984–1001; Lisa J. Laplante, "On the indivisibility of rights: Truth commissions, reparations, and the right to development," *Yale Human Rights and Development Law Journal* 141 (2007): 10.

[40] J. Veit Wilson, "No rights without remedies: Necessary conditions for abolishing child poverty," *European Journal of Social Security* 8 (2006): 317–320; for further commentaries on the various categories and philosophies of rights, see generally W. Leif, "Rights," *The Stanford Encyclopaedia of Philosophy*; E. N. Zalta (ed) (2011), http://plato.stanford.edu/archives/fall2011/entries/rights/ (accessed 31 August 2017).

[41] Marie B. Dembour, "What are human rights? Four schools of thought," *Human Rights Quarterly* 32 (2010): 1–20.

concept of the meaning of law and rights. From early writers, such as Hobbes, Locke and Holmes, the issue of rights has deferred in its meaning.[42] It is necessary to state, albeit briefly, the incline of the schools of thought.

The natural school argues that rights are divine and thus God-given. The natural school places reliance on a supernatural being dictating what should constitute rights and what should not.[43] Austin in his positive approach differs by viewing the source of rights to be that which is codified and from laws made by the powerful.[44] The sociological school sees the concept as the influence of society on practices that have become structured and elevated as guiding norms and principles.[45]

The above concepts of rights do not suppose that Africans did not have an inherent concept or philosophy on what rights entail. As observed by Mbiti[46]:

> One of the difficulties in studying African religions and philosophy is that there are no sacred scriptures. Religion in African societies is written not on paper but in people's hearts, minds, oral history, ritual and religious personages like the priests, rainmakers, officiating elders and kings.

[42]For the various jurisprudential concerns of these writers, see generally the following: Oliver W. Holmes, "Natural law," *Harvard Law Review* 32 (1918), http://teachingamericanhistory.org/library/document/natural-law/ (accessed 21 May 2017); John Locke, *Essays on the law of nature* (1954), http://plato.stanford.edu/entries/locke-moral/ (accessed 31 July 2017); B. Norberto, *Thomas Hobbes and the natural law tradition* (1993); R. P. George, "Natural law," *Harvard Journal of Law and Public Policy* (2007): 31.

[43]Aristotle and Thomas Aquinas remain the early advocates of the natural school of thought. For a generally reading on the natural school of thought, see P. S. Nair, *Human rights in a changing world* (2011); C. A. Stumpf, *The Grotian theology of international law* (2006).

[44]The legacy of John Austin's jurisprudence eds. M. Freeman and P. Mindus (2013); J. Austin, *The province of jurisprudence determined* The Law Book Exchange (2012), first published (1832) Richard Taylor, London.

[45]See generally A. Podgorecki and C. J. Whelan, *Sociological approaches to law* (1981); E. Ehrlich, *Fundamental principles of the sociology of law* (2009).

[46]John S. Mbiti, *African religions and philosophy* (1989), 3.

The import of the above is hinged on the lack of documentary nature of the various philosophies that guided the conduct of affairs in Africa.[47] However, the traditional African society had recognition for rights and punishments, which were seen as emanating from nature or the divine control of the universe.[48]

An example of equality in Africa is captured in some proverbs. For example, among the Igbo and Yoruba tribes in Nigeria, it is said that *Apa kan o ga jukan lo, afi eyi toba g'ori ebe* (all sparrows are of the same height except the one that climbs a heap); *Nwoke tosia, ochelu ibe ya* (a man will grow and wait for others to grow too); *Igwe nile na eje n'uzo*a (all men have the same destination); *Ibi o ju ibi, bi a se bi eru, beeni a se bi omo* (the way a slave was born, so the child was born); *Egbe belle ugo belle,nke si ibe ya ebelle,uku kwa ya* (the eagle perches, also should the kite; any that does not allow the other to perch, may the wings break).

This is a philosophical undertone to represent the rejection of any form of discrimination, while stressing the equality of all humans and, by extended interpretation, rights. Mutual respect and harmony are also enshrined in the philosophy of *Emenyere nwaogugu emenyere nwanosike* (what is done for one must be done for the other).

Whatever position is adopted in the classification of rights, the issue of the supremacy of rights and which right should be respected more remains an unsettled debate.[49] However, it is assumed that it is not right 'to arrange rights in a strict hierarchical order'.[50] The central place of understanding the concept of rights is advanced by Piron, restating the importance of rights in ensuring the realisation of social concepts such as education and development.[51]

[47] For a detailed insight into African literature and the underpinning philosophies, see generally O. Owomoyela, *African literatures: An introduction* (1979).

[48] John S. Mbiti, *African religions and philosophy* (1989), 205.

[49] The issue of dominance of civil and political rights, which are called first generation rights, being superior to economic and social rights, known as second generation rights, still remains. While the two rights are separated on the global level, the African Charter on Human and Peoples' Rights contains the two groups of rights. It is also noted that the two groups of rights depend on each other, and therefore, it is wrong to accord supremacy to any above the other.

[50] W. Bray, *Human rights in education* (2008), 17.

[51] Laurene H. Piron, *Rights-based approaches to social protection* (2004), 3, Overseas Development Institute London, available at http://www.sed.manchester.ac.uk/research/events/conferences/documents/Winners%20and%20Losers%20Papers/Piron.pdf (accessed 21 December 2017).

Furthermore, in his discussion of the theory of rights, Wellman examines rights as having some link with legal duties, legal liberties and legal claims.[52] Thus, in his view, what must be termed as a right must find the basis of its claim under the law. If basic education, therefore, will be deemed as a right, its legal basis must be settled. Also, it must be determined that a duty to protect a legal right exists and, for the purposes of this book, this legal onus is argued to be on the state and also on individual actors or non-state actors in the education industry.

Rights are also seen as 'the rights that human beings have simply because they are human beings and independent of their varying social circumstances and degrees of merit'.[53] Donnelly supports this line of thought when he restates that '[r]ights are seen to be rights and accrue to human beings because one is human...they are held by all human beings, irrespective of any rights or duties one may or may not have as a citizen or member of families'.[54] From the above, education can be construed as a right in the sense that each individual is entitled to be educated about the environment, health and social sphere; thus grounding its link to the development of any society. This is advanced on the premise of education being emancipatory and a path to different ends, as desired by individuals.

Deschowitz, in advancing various definitions of rights, is of the opinion that

> [r]ights are something that is due to a person by just claim, legal guarantee, moral principle... A power, privilege, or immunity secured to a person by law... A legally enforceable claim that another will do or will not do a given act; a recognised and protected interest, the violation of which is a wrong.[55]

The above definition brings to the fore that, while rights could accrue to a person for being human, they also entail some form of protection by

[52] Carl Wellman, *The theory of rights* (Totowa: Rowman & Allanheld Publishers, 1985), 17.

[53] Jerome J. Shestack, "The philosophy foundations of human rights: Concept and language of human rights and related ideas" in Heyns and Stefiszyn above.

[54] Jack Donnelly, *International human rights* (1993), 19.

[55] Alan Deshowitz, *Rights from wrongs: A secular theory of origins* (New York: Basic, 2004), 15.

the law as well as attributing both positive and negative responsibilities. In this regard, providing education for an individual ought to be protected by law.

As already pointed out, despite the African society being described as one that lacks legal regulation in some quarters, it is pertinent to note that the philosophical *cum* religious undertones in Africa had great respect for humanity and attendant repercussions when a breach of human rights occurred.[56]

With the different meanings of the term 'rights' according to the various schools of thought examined above, it is conceded that the concept of rights is one that is unsettled, just as the case is with the social phenomenon. However, the working definition adopted is that:

> [r]ights are those fundamental preferences that experience and history-especially of great injustices-have taught are so essential that the citizenry should be persuaded to entrench them and not make them subject to easy change of majorities.[57]

The definition adopted above is instrumental in the sense that previous experiences of conflict and violence plaguing societies are traceable to issues of tensions occasioned by not upholding various rights.[58] This is important, as most basic rights should include a mixture of traditional negative socio-economic and positive political rights.[59] It is advanced on the premise that rights work in part by taking 'certain powers away from temporary majorities and vesting the capability to constrain these powers in those who lack traditional political influence or who are otherwise

[56] It is underscored that, while the African philosophy and practices may be argued to inherently have respect for rights, some practices were in violation of human rights. For a good argument on some practices that negate human rights, see generally O. Martin Ejidike, "Human rights in the cultural traditions and social practice of the Igbo of South-Eastern Nigeria," *Journal of African Law* 71 (1999): 43.

[57] Alan Deshowitz, *Rights from wrongs: A secular theory of origins*, 81.

[58] Nigeria has been through various phases of social conflict. The majority of the conflicts are traceable to issues of resource control, agitations and requests for certain benefits that are seen as a denial of entitlements (rights). Some of the conflicts have also been ethnic and religious. It is also argued in this thesis that the ethnic and religion-fuelled conflicts are hinged on the failure in education.

[59] Amartya Sen, *Development as freedom* (1999), 152.

subject to discrimination or marginalisation'.[60] This position also fits the underlining principle of the struggle approach, as canvassed by Heyns, when he opines that 'a component of struggle or its potential emanates from the violation of human rights'.[61] In this regard, the move to fashion out specific education for a minority group like the Alternative Basic Education for the Karamoja (ABEK) in Uganda and, recently, the *Almajiri* model schools in Nigeria, is testimony to the position that rights are not just to be upheld for the majority but also positively for the minority.[62]

In addition, upholding basic education as a right is also crucial to development as there is an inevitable relationship between political and socio-economic rights, grounding the need to ensure the justiciability of socio-economic rights, such as the right to education. The line of argument here suggests that for the perfect enjoyment of traditional positive rights, such rights that are today regarded in Nigeria as not having positive obligations must be viewed differently to ensure the realisation of a better society. This speaks to the importance of protecting individual rights even as against group rights, noting the interdependence of both economic and social rights on civil and political rights.[63]

From whatever prism or hierarchy rights are grouped or looked at, the right to education is a pivotal one. This is premised on the fact that no other right could be enjoyed if people do not get access to adequate information on how to maximise such rights. Education, as a basis for the realisation of health, life and civic responsibilities, should be regarded

[60] Alan Deshowitz, *Rights from wrongs: A secular theory of origins*, 160.

[61] Heyns, "A 'struggle approach' to human rights," 15.

[62] Part of the present Nigerian government's initiative to educate minority groups aside the Almajiri Education Programme includes, but is not limited to; the Girl-Child Education Programme and the Special Vocational Programmer for Boy Traders in the South–South and South–East. The classification of the Almajiri's as minority is based on the notion that they form a percentage which refuses to access education based on religious perception and inclination. However, it must also be noted that the Almajiri constitute a large percentage of the Nigerian out-of-school children statistics. Describing the Almajiri practice, it is to be noted that mainly boys are involved in this practice, in which they are loyal to an Islamic scholar teacher who serves as role model to them, teaching them the study of Quran education while they resort to street begging and menial means of survival.

[63] See generally R. Howard, "The full-belly thesis: Should economic rights take priority over civil and political rights? Evidence from sub-Saharan Africa," in Heyns and Stefiszyn (eds), *Human rights, peace and justice in Africa: A reader*, 75.

as a right *stricto* sensu. The right to education, therefore, can be inferred and read into every right. In addition, construing education as a right places a responsibility on the state to ensure its protection, promotion and fulfilling.

2.4 Basic Education and International Human Rights Law

With an understanding of the importance of education, generally, it is important to analyse the meaning of basic education, which is an aspect of the entire concept of education and its relationship with international law.[64] Basic education is best described as education which is delivered to a child from the age of inception to the end of the basic education curriculum.[65] According to Skillbeck:

> Basic education commences at birth and may be achieved through both formal or non-formal means and agencies. Competencies, skills and substantive learning's defined as basic, when provided for in schools and similar institutions, are usually cast in the form of a core curriculum which while it includes and builds on literacy includes numeracy, social and scientific knowledge, physical and health education and the arts and crafts.[66]

[64] For an in-depth discussion of education generally relating to secondary and university education internationally, the work of Beiter will be good reading; Klaus D. Beiter, *The protection of the right to education by international law* (2006).

[65] Underscoring the importance of this phase in the life of a child, the Committee on the Rights of the child has in General Comment 7 (CRC/C/GC/7/Rev.1 20 September 2006 (Implementing children's rights in early childhood) (para 4) opined that 'early childhood varies in different countries and regions, according to local traditions and the organisation of primary school systems. In some countries, the transition from preschool to school occurs soon after 4 years old. In other countries, this transition takes place at around 7 years old. In its consideration of rights in early childhood, the Committee wishes to include all young children: at birth and throughout infancy; during the preschool years; as well as transition to school. Accordingly, the Committee proposes as an appropriate working definition of early childhood the period below the age of 8 years; states parties should review their obligations towards young children in the context of this definition'. It is thus important that Nigeria pays attention to the phase of education development of the child.

[66] Malcom Skillbeck, "Education for all—Global synthesis," 16, http://www.unesco.org/education/wef/en-docs/findings/globsynt.pdf (accessed 21 November 2017).

A conceptualisation of basic education in entails 'the mastering of the skills of reading, writing and development of simple arithmetic skills; in addition, the ability to develop a good basis of conduct and behaviour; ability to appreciate basic skills and work'.[67]

Zukker opines that the right to basic education

> is an unqualified right requiring the priority attention of the state, also in respect of budgetary allocations. The right requires the state to provide quality education to all children irrespective of whatever challenges that they may face.[68]

Beiter underscores the importance of basic education by finding that 'an education system, premised on false educational ideals, constituted a threat'.[69] Beiter further applauds the importance placed on basic education by the Committee on Economic, Social and Cultural Rights (ESCR Committee), when they obliged state parties to ensure that priority is paid to basic education and development of proper skills in reading and numeracy.[70]

In the current structure of Western education that has been embraced by the majority of states, the school is pivotal to the concept of education and, therefore, advancing the argument for a right to basic education cannot be done without arguing for the importance of schools.[71] This is so because schools provide 'organisational mechanisms *cum* structure that an individual requires to meet his goals and life targets' (development).[72] Basic education, when provided, ensures that society enjoys peace and stability to a large extent and, therefore, the availability of schools is paramount in the discourse.[73]

[67] Aliu B. Fafunwa, *History of education in Nigeria* (London: George Allen & Unwin, 1974), 15.

[68] M. A. Zuker, *Education law* (London: Carswel, 2002), 281.

[69] Beiter Right to Education in International Law, 483.

[70] Beiter Right to Education in International Law, 278.

[71] In this regard, the central focal point of school is important in determining the extent to which a state has been able to meet the responsibility of meeting its threshold access, to say the least. It is impossible, therefore, to talk about the right to basic education in the absence of school and the quality of such schools eventually.

[72] M. A. Olivas and G. R. Scheider (eds), *Education law stories* (2008), 1.

[73] W. Bray, *Human rights in education* (2008), 1.

Furthermore, basic education also suggests the pivotal nature of the family. This is because 'the family is the most permanent and immediate educational unit… children learn the first social, economic and cultural skills in the home and then schools'.[74] Considering the idea that basic education takes root in early childhood education, the views of parents must be taken into consideration in determining the style and quality of education the child receives.[75] Consequently, a major premise of ensuring quality control besides government oversight is ensuring the involvement of parents. In this manner, the role of parents is highlighted in ensuring the sustenance of access to quality basic education.

Besides the responsibility of parents and the role they play, another important aspect is the oversight function of the state. There is an obligation on states to ensure that decisions taken to affect children must be done with consideration of the best interests of the child. This can only be achieved by the state, ensuring that an environment fit for this is achieved by the control of quality and curricula of education provided in both the public and private education environment.[76] In this light, one must interrogate the space within which children can determine the content of basic education delivered to them.

While it may be seen as a challenge to determine at what stage in a child's development a child is able to meaningfully contribute to decisions that affect the child, it is set out by law that any person taking such decisions must of necessity do so in the best interests of the child.[77]

[74] R. Aldrich, *An introduction to the history of education* (1982), 9–10.

[75] M. A. Zuker, *Education law* (2002), 284.

[76] M. G. Flekkoy, "A framework for children's participation," in E. Verhellen (ed), *Understanding children's rights* (1996), 224, collected papers presented at the first international interdisciplinary course on children's rights.

[77] Art 12 of the CRC specifically provides for the right of the child to be respected in the forming of opinion on issues that affect the child. In the same manner, both international and regional law instruments also protect the right of the child as a group member. It is therefore based on this reasoning that it is important that the content of basic education that a child receives is channelled after the child's cultural and religious affiliation. It is only in so doing that the level of acceptance of basic education will be on the increase. Wouter suggests that the 'best interests of a child can be looked at from two perspectives, one dealing with the objective of the state to ensure actions to be carried out in the best interests of the state and the other to ensure that nothing is done that will deny the realisation of issues concerning the best interest of the child'. See P. Wouter, "International human rights law and its relation with national law: Monism, dualism and the self-executing character of human rights," in Verhellen (n. 81 below). This will seem to suggest that the state has

Thus, in the provision of basic education, the child's inherent right is important to ensure that the child 'acquires skills and competencies that will prepare them for a wide variety of possible futures'.[78]

In establishing what the content of the right to education entails, what must be taken into consideration is the free choice of education that is accessed.[79] Another important basis for ascertaining the content is also found in the premise of measuring the quality of education itself.[80] Tomasevski advances the obligation on the state to 'regulate education and its gains as an underpinning system on ensuring quality towards ascertaining content'.[81] In this regard, choice and quality speak to the concepts of the fact that basic education must be laden with an acceptable curriculum that is also adaptable to the individual development. Consequently, the provision of a standard infrastructure which must be able to take care of the learning needs of pupils, irrespective of their religion, custom, gender and physical state, are core contents of the right.[82]

In addition, the crucial place of the curriculum as a core component of the content of education cannot be overlooked.[83] In arriving at the need to ensure a proper curriculum base for a nation, it is germane to ensure that[84]

> [c]hildren's participation should be based on the evolving capacities of children, tempered by what is in the best interest of the child and aimed at developing participatory skills in the best possible way.

a responsibility to ensure that the provision of basic education within both the public and private sectors in Nigeria are well regulated. The state must therefore ensure that quality is not compromised, and that the rights in education are also not violated and adequately punished when breached.

[78] M. G. Flekkoy, "A framework for children's participation," in Verhellen above.

[79] Fons Coomans, "Clarifying the core elements of the right to education."

[80] Fons Coomans, "Clarifying the core elements of the right to education."

[81] Katrina Tomasevesk, "The right to education mission to the United Kingdom," in A. Fisher (ed), *The content of the right to education—Theoretical foundations* (2004), 8.

[82] The assumption advanced here is that while education there is need for accessibility and availability of education, the importance of acceptability must also be treated as integral component.

[83] J. W. Meyer and Fransico O. Ramirez, "The World institutionalisation of education," in J. Schriewer (ed), *Discourse formation in comparative education* (Frankfurt: Peter Lang, 2000), 113.

[84] M. G. Flekkoy, "A framework for children's participation," in Verhellen above.

The core content of education must then be viewed from a broad perspective so as to be able to meet the desired human rights standard required. It requires a positive obligation from the state in its actions and policies towards meeting an international standard.[85] Thus, basic education involves not just the 'formal learning sector, but also the informal and non-formal and to meet the threshold of an international standard, basic education must prepare an individual for a better life ahead'.[86]

From the foregoing, it is clear that basic education, to a large extent, requires that a state meets the obligation of protection, promotion and fulfilment of the provision of education by ensuring the availability of schools.[87] The provision is imperative if life must be enjoyed to its fullest in a developed society.

In short, it is the position of this research that 'basic education means education up to a level of functional literacy, in other words, reading, writing, arithmetic and an elementary knowledge or awareness of economics, culture and politics'.[88] In addition, it also entails that the government gives further support to ensure the 'adequacy of schools, proficiency of educators and other incidental support to ensuring and guaranteeing quality'.[89]

With the above overview of the concept of rights, education and an understanding of the core content of basic education, the international legal instruments that provide for the right to basic education are analysed in the following sections. This is done with a view to establishing further that basic education is a right that must be respected, promoted and protected by the state as it has deep and strong influence on the development of both the individual and the state. The section commences with an analysis of global instruments before regional instruments.

[85] Fons Coomans, "Clarifying the core elements of the right to education."

[86] See generally the Jomtien Declaration.

[87] As will be argued later, availability has more to it than the mere physical presence of school buildings.

[88] W. Bray, *Human rights in education* (2008), 83.

[89] W. Bray, *Human rights in education* (2008), 84.

2.4.1 *The Advent of Recognising Education as a Right*

The adoption of the Universal Declaration of Human Rights (UDHR)[90] remains an important landmark in the bid to realising human rights. The Declaration provides for several rights, among which is the right to education. Article 26 states:

> (1) Everyone has the right to education. Education shall be free, at least in the elementary and fundamental stages. Elementary education shall be compulsory. Technical and professional education shall be made generally available and higher education shall be equally accessible to all on the basis of merit.
> (2) Education shall be directed to the full development of the human personality and to the strengthening of respect for human rights and fundamental freedoms. It shall promote understanding, tolerance and friendship among all nations, racial or religious groups, and shall further the activities of the United Nations for the maintenance of peace.
> (3) Parents have a prior right to choose the kind of education that shall be given to their children.

The wording of Article 26 covers three major ambits in its scope. The starting point is to ascertain whether or not the Declaration envisaged basic education as a fundamental right. Although the UDHR does not provide in specific terms for 'basic education', mention of the terms 'elementary' and 'fundamental' stages of education can be construed to encompass the term 'basic education'.[91] Consequently, it is argued that the concept of basic education is well enshrined in the ambit of the UDHR.

The second ambit covers the content of education, which goes beyond the basic level, but also to other tiers of education. In this respect, the content of education curricula must be designed in such a way as to meet the aspirations of the UDHR. For instance, the obligation to ensure that education is not used to create diversity or to foster

[90] 10 December 1948.

[91] Dogulas Hodgson, *The human right to education* (1998), 11; Beiter goes a step further to construe education not just as a human right but a basic need. See generally Beiter above.

inequality is an important aspect. As of necessity, the curriculum of education must promote development, tolerance, respect and the upholding of all other human rights.[92] The third ambit puts forward the role of parents in ensuring that the education given to their children is acceptable and conforms to their cultural and religious inclinations. It is important to note that, despite assuming that a free rein is given to parents in determining the type of education their children will receive, such education must be in conformity with the spirit of the second ambit discussed above.

In understanding the ambit of parental involvement in the education of the child, we rely on the European case of *Jeldsen, Busk Madsen & Pedersen v Denmark*.[93] The case was premised on the introduction of sex education in Denmark. The contention was on the propriety or otherwise of introducing sex education in Denmark. While the government argued that there were many private schools where the curriculum could reflect some individual views and beliefs, as opposed to public schools, were the Minister of Education influenced the curriculum content, the parents argued on the non-availability and insufficiency of private schools.[94] The government of Denmark argued that the underlying reason for starting sex education was the increase of unwanted pregnancies and the large number of applicants seeking help as unmarried singles schools. The applicants, however, argued that this was against their religious belief and therefore in contravention of their duty to protect their children in the ambit of the right to education and parental obligations. It was found by the judges, in an overwhelming decision of six votes to one, that there was no violation. The decision in the above case is instrumental as it underscores the importance of parental responsibility and its

[92] Audrey Osler, "Universal Declaration of Human Rights and education," in J. A. Banks (ed), *Encyclopaedia of diversity in education* (London and Los Angeles, CA: Sage, 2012), 12.

[93] Application 5095/71; 5920/72; 5926/72.

[94] In Nigeria, private schools still have some form of obligation under law to ensure the general education of children. See para 34 which provides that '[a]lthough primary education in private schools must in principle cover all the topics obligatory at state schools (paragraph 18 above), sex education is an exception in this respect. Private schools are free to decide themselves to what extent they wish to align their teaching in this field with the rules applicable to state schools. However, they must include in the biology syllabus a course on the reproduction of man similar to that obligatory in state schools since 1960'.

limits to ensure that children are not indoctrinated when useful information is passed on to them.[95]

The above positions consequently draw a nexus of a horizontal as well as a vertical relationship. The state must ensure the promotion, protection and fulfilment of the right to education, and parents must ensure that it complies with the cultural, religious and other orientation of the family.[96] A contrast can be seen from the position, as reinforced by Beiter when he opines that 'parents' rights over the child's education is an agency right...the moment they fail to act in the best interests of the child, states must in lieu of parents see to it that the child's best interests are promoted'.[97]

The main problem of education, whether basic or otherwise, is enshrined in the fact that the ultimate recipient is still treated as an object and not as a subject.[98] For the full concept of education to be realised, it must be in the best interests of the child leading to the development of the child. While it may be a valid argument that the child at the level of basic education is unable to make sound judgments as a minor, it is reiterated that there exists scientifically proven curriculum content that will protect the child's best interests.[99] Consequently, the parental role in upholding the obligation regarding a child's right to education is not one that is cast in stone, but the need exists to draw the link when there is an apparent encroaching of the various roles as defined by international law.

The UDHR further envisages the importance of access to education, and 'access to education is a precondition for the full realisation of the

[95] The basis of the applicant's case was the alleged violation of art 2 of Protocol 1 of the European Convention for the Protection of Human rights and Fundamental Freedoms. The article provides that '[n]o person shall be denied the right to education. In the exercise of any functions which it assumes in relation to education and to teaching, the state shall respect the right of parents to ensure such education and teaching in conformity with their own religious and philosophical convictions'.

[96] It is important also to note that in parental exercise of functions, such philosophical belief and religious tenants must not be contrary to the general objective of respect for the UN Charter that calls for respect and dignity of the human person. See generally the case of *Case of Campbell & Cosans v The United Kingdom* Application 7511/76; 7743/76.

[97] Beiter above.

[98] See generally Katrina Tomasevski, *Removing obstacles in the way of the right to education*. Primers No. 1 (2001), 44.

[99] Audrey Osler, "Universal Declaration of Human Rights and education."

right to education. Without access, it is not possible to guarantee the right to education'.[100] Closely related to the issue of access is that of quality. In this respect, whatever education is provided must be structured in such a way as to ensure the total emancipation of the child from poverty and to enable the child to take part in community life and to realise all other human rights. Access is relevant to every human being, whether physically challenged or otherwise. Although the UDHR does not explicitly include education of people with learning challenges, this group is covered within the ambit of the right to education.

2.4.2 *Masked or Unmasked: The Central Role of Education Remains*

With the debate around generations of rights, as discussed earlier, the inclusion of education in the two separate documents that enshrine fundamental rights provides another interesting perspective to education as a right. The first discussed is the International Covenant on Civil and Political Rights (ICCPR). Although the right to education is not expressly mentioned in the ICCPR, the rights mentioned in the ICCPR require education to be realised. For instance, the rights to hold an opinion and to freedom of expression are both hinged on the level of literacy, which is a main result of quality basic education.

The first mention of education in the ICCPR is captured in relation to the promotion of religious and moral education. The Covenant provides[101]:

> The States Parties to the present Covenant undertake to have respect for the liberty of parents and, when applicable, legal guardians to ensure the religious and moral education of their children in conformity with their own convictions.

The provision in Article 19, provides for the right to hold an opinion, encompasses the major components of the concept of education.[102] The idea of the right to hold an opinion, to share ideas and to transmit

[100] "Right to education: Human rights education associates," http://www.hrea.org/index.php?doc_id=402 (accessed 21 December 2017).

[101] Art 18(4).

[102] Mieke Verheyde, *A commentary on the United Nations Convention on the Rights of the Child, Article 28—Right to education* (2006), 8. Art 19 provides: '(1) Everyone shall have the right to hold opinions without interference. (2) Everyone shall have the right to freedom of expression; this right shall include freedom to seek, receive and impart information and ideas of all kinds, regardless of frontiers, either orally, in writing or in print, in the form

these is a core aspect of education and thus it is assumed that the right to education is provided for. The right to education is also impliedly valid when taking into consideration the reservation made by the German Democratic Republic (GDR) during the adoption of the Covenant, when it alluded to the fact that the GDR has 'such fundamental human rights … the right to education has been fully implemented in the GDR'.[103]

The additional Protocol to the ICCPR[104] creates a channel through which individuals can bring complaints about the violation of their rights as contained in the Covenant. The use of such channels is hinged on the realisation of education and, as stated above, the role of education as an empowerment right is crucial and a lack thereof will defeat the purpose of the realisation of rights contained in the Covenant. This argument is further supported by the fact that education has 'a double dimension both as a right in itself and an indispensable means of realising other human rights'.[105] Therefore, it is important that the obligation of state parties to the Covenant be respected by striving towards achieving the right to education. The purport of the articles cited above indicates that the right to education is one that must be treated individually as against the other economic, social and cultural rights. In this sense, as an intrinsic right, the majority of other rights are dependent on the right to education to function. An important inference that can be drawn from this is the fact that the provisions in the articles make the right to education justiciable.

of art, or through any other media of his choice. (3) The exercise of the rights provided for in paragraph 2 of this article carries with it special duties and responsibilities. It may therefore be subject to certain restrictions, but these shall only be such as are provided by law and are necessary (a) for respect of the rights or reputations of others; (b) for the protection of national security or of public order (*ordre public*), or of public health or morals'.

[103] http://treaties.un.org/doc/Publication/UNTS/Volume%20999/volume-999-I-14668-English.pdf (accessed 21 November 2017).

[104] Optional Protocol to the International Covenant on Civil and Political Rights, adopted by General Assembly Resolution 2200 (XXI) of 16 December 1966, available at http://www.un-documents.net/iccpr-op.htm (accessed 21 March 2013).

[105] Verheyde (n. 108 below), 7.

2.4.3 Unmasking Basic Education as a Right

The International Covenant on Economic, Social and Cultural Rights (ICESCR)[106] provides for the right to education in two articles.[107] States to the Covenant not only agree to recognise that education is a right which must be made accessible, but goes further to stipulate the end result of education. In this regard, education as a right must be able to ensure that every individual attains full development so as to be able to function and also maintain dignity.[108] Article 13(2)(a) provides that '[p]rimary education shall be compulsory and available free to all' and the realisation of this obligation is to be done with particular reference to the 'liberty of parents, cultural and religious beliefs' in the best interests of the child.[109] The urgency of realising this right is evident from the commitment that is required of every state party to ensure that the right to education is realised within a time frame by ensuring the 'progressive implementation' of policies and legal framework.[110] In most circumstances, reliance on the phrase 'progressive realisation' has formed the basis for the majority of states to decline from the obligation that is expected of them as set out in the ICESCR. However, case law from the African human rights system has set out a clear jurisprudence towards the constructive approach to reliance on progressive realisation.[111]

In its concluding observations, the United Nations (UN) Committee on Economic, Social and Cultural Rights (ESCR Committee) identified challenges to the realisation of the right to education. It found:

> Some groups have limited access to education, ranging from traditional attitudes preventing girls from attending school to the limited availability of schooling, including teachers, in rural areas. A further ground of exclusion represents the limited financial means of persons living in poverty, who frequently may also be members of minority or indigenous communities.[112]

[106] 16 December 1966.

[107] ICESCR, arts 13 & 14.

[108] ICESCR, art 13(1).

[109] ICESCR, art 13(3).

[110] ICESCR, art 14.

[111] *Purohit & Another v The Gambia* (2003), AHRLR 96 (ACHPR 2003).

[112] UNESCO: Inclusive Dimensions of the Right to Education: Normative Bases Concept Paper. Prepared for the Eighth and Ninth Meetings of the Joint Expert Group UNESCO (CR)/ECOSOC (CESCR) on the Monitoring of the Right to Education—2008, 5.

In order to have a better understanding of the provisions of the ICESCR, it is important to peruse General Comment 13, which broadens the scope of understanding education as a right, its application and the extent to which it should be protected.

2.4.4 General Comment 13[113]

In the first paragraph, the importance of education, both as 'a human right and indispensable means of realising other rights', is reiterated. The General Comment (GC) sheds more insight into the interpretation of Article 13 of the ICESCR and reinforces the import of the purpose of UNESCO in ensuring that education is devoid of any form of exploitation and discrimination based on the grounds of religion, culture and other grounds.

In paragraph 6 of the GC, the concepts of availability, acceptability and adaptability are set out as minimum core content of the right to education. The components of access include the elimination of all forms of discrimination, ensuring physical access and also economic access. It is important to reiterate here that the content and quality of education are germane concepts that can be read into acceptability. Efforts made by a state party to ensure that the education accessed is of quality influences to a large extent the level of acceptability of such educational curriculum.

In the same vein, the adaptability of education to the cultural, religious and moral beliefs of people must seriously be taken into consideration to ensure that the education curriculum is in line with the lifestyle of people. As major agents in realising the right to education, the welfare of teachers is not overlooked. The GC recommends good conditions of service for teachers and a dedicated and consistent development of both institutions and infrastructures in the realisation of the right to education.[114] The question of progressively realising the right to education imposes certain obligations on a state party which the GC identifies, the

[113]ESCR Committee General Comment 13: The Right to Education (Art 13), Adopted at the 21st Session of the Committee on Economic, Social and Cultural Rights, on 8 December 1999 (Contained in Document E/C.12/1999/10).

[114]General Comment, paras 25–27. For some insight into the obligation envisaged by the GC, see, generally, Grace Mbajiorgu and Thinavhudzulo Mafumo, *Striving for quality education: The right to education as a socio-economic right* (2014), 303, http://www.mcser.org/journal/index.php/mjss/article/download/2560/2528 (accessed 15 January 2018).

obligation to guarantee as the first major task. It is, therefore, only when the guarantee is in place that the state is expected to pursue progressive realisation, which must show 'deliberate, concrete and targeted' steps towards the full realisation of the right to education.[115] To avoid misrepresentation of the concept of progressive realisation, the GC opines that[116]:

> The realisation of the right to education over time, that is 'progressively', should not be interpreted as depriving States parties' obligations of all meaningful content. Progressive realisation means that States parties have a specific and continuing obligation 'to move as expeditiously and effectively as possible' towards the full realisation of article 13.

As stated above, albeit briefly, the GC sets forth the concept of the 4A's in an attempt to give further meaning to the content and scope of the right to education as provided for in the ICESCR. The starting point for the 4A's concept of education understands the importance of ensuring the realisation of the right to education. Tomasevski advances the crucial importance in her works, highlighting the need to ensure that education meets the threshold in all states. The Special Rapporteur notes that the 'simple 4A scheme structures governmental human rights obligations to making education available, accessible, acceptable and adaptable... captures both horizontal and vertical division of competence in education'.[117] Major obstacles to the full realisation are identified to be the role of several institutions, such as the World Bank, whose policies have at some point made access to basic education out of the reach of children from developing nations.[118] The pivotal role of the concept is also well reiterated by Wolman and Fleisch.[119] Below is a detailed discussion of the 4A's concept of education.

[115] General Comment para 43.

[116] General Comment para 44.

[117] Katrina Tomasevski, "The right to education report submitted in accordance with Commission resolution 2002/2023, mission to Indonesia," 1–7 July 2002. E/CN.4/2003/9/Add.1 4 November 2002.

[118] Katrina Tomasevski, "Six reasons why the World Bank should be debarred from education," 1, http://www.brettonwoodsproject.org/2006/09/art-542516/ (accessed 21 May 2017).

[119] S. Woolman and B. Fleisch, "On the right to an 'adequate' basic education," in Woolman and Fleisch (ed), *The constitution in the classroom: Law and education in South Africa*, 109–164.

i. Availability

Availability of basic education speaks to the sufficiency of infrastructures.[120] It is paramount to take cognisance of the fact that there are basic acceptable standards of infrastructure that must be in place, especially as it relates to ensuring that the sanitation and health situation of girls are well taken care of. It is noted that an educational infrastructure that does not provide separate toilet facilities for girls is discriminatory and also contributes to the growing level of out of school children and dropout rates.

Availability is also viewed from the act of denying basic education as a right which, in the words of Tomasevski, 'is hidden behind quantitative targets and evasive vocabularies used by global educational bureaucracies'.[121] The meaning of this proposition by Tomasevski speaks to the ill-framed policies that eventually make educational institutions unavailable to pupils.[122] Consequently, it is important to ensure that the policies put in place to govern the administration of education are formulated with the specific needs of people. For education to be available, it must meet the lifestyle and natural inclinations of people, adapting to their cultural way of life and not creating any form of strife as to their religious beliefs. This explains the basis on which special education policies for indigenous peoples' or minorities are fashioned to ensure that their way of life is not disrupted.

With the above in mind, it is also important to take cognisance of the fact that available education which is not accessible is ultimately unavailable. This concept is already described in Chapter 1 as threshold and actual access to basic education.

[120] The meaning of this as conceptualised by General Comment 13 on education opines that '[f]unctioning education institutions must be available so as to ensure that its programmes are sufficient to cater for the need of peoples'.

[121] Tomasevski above. See also the Commonwealth Secretariat, Business Guide to the General Agreement on Trade in Services that recognises education as a right, but goes further to restate the need to pay for its access.

[122] Tomasevski advances this concept in her top-down approach of financial policies by the World Bank that ensured the low value of public education and enhanced private education. See generally K. Tomasevski, "Globalising what: Education as a human right or as a traded service?" *Indiana Journal of Global Legal Studies* 12(1) (2005): 30.

ii. Accessibility

Accessibility of available educational institutions is another important aspect of the content of basic education. Importantly, threshold access must be distinguished from real access.[123] This is important, as enrolment speaks only to the threshold, and completion rate to real access. A child who enrols in school and is unable to continue through the basic education cycle cannot be deemed to have access. Certain factors affect access. These include, but are not limited to, poverty, discrimination and poor curriculum content.[124]

Basic education must be free and non-fee demanding.[125] Tomasevski suggests that this is not the case; she decries this situation by stating[126]:

> The oldest international human rights law mandated free and compulsory education for all children up to the minimum age of employment. Thenceforth it specified safeguards for labour rights and trade union

[123] J. K. Enaohwo, "Access, cost and quality in Nigeria education," Keynote address to the 23rd Annual Congress of the Nigerian Academy of Education.

[124] For further insight into factors that inhibit access beyond basic education in Nigeria, see generally O. Aluede, P. O. Idogho, and J. S. Imonikhe, "Increasing access to university education in Nigeria: Present challenges and suggestions for the future," *The African Symposium* 12(1) (2012). The enumerated challenges are not peculiar to basic education in Nigeria. Tertiary education also faces the same challenges. For a general insight into the effect on tertiary education, see, generally, C. K. Ayo, J. A. Odukoya, and A. Azeta, "A review of open and distance education and human development in Nigeria," *iJET* (2014).

[125] In South Africa, the argument on whether Sec 29(1)(a) grants an unqualified right to education has raised some concerns. Some scholars have attempted to align the case of basic education with the decision of the Constitutional Court in the *Soobramoney* case. See generally S. Liebenberg, "The interpretation of socio-economic rights," in S. Woolman, T. Roux and M. Bishop (eds), *Constitutional law of South Africa* (2004); S. Woolman & B. Fleisch, "On the right to an 'adequate' basic education," in Woolman and Fleisch (n. 124 above), 122. Tomasevski argues that the 'willingness of governments to provide education must be channelled towards the show of the will and ability to raise revenue and devote maximum available resources to human rights, especially the right to education'. See generally K. Tomasevski, "Globalising what: Education as a human right or as a traded service?" *Indiana Journal of Global Legal Studies* 12(1) (2005): 30; Enaohwo describes issue of cost in accessing basic education as an iron triangle, where cost is the base on which effective access must be hinged. See generally J. K. Enaohwo, "Access, cost and quality in Nigeria education," Keynote address to the 23rd Annual Congress of the Nigerian Academy of Education.

[126] K. Tomasevski, "Six reasons why the World Bank should be debarred from education," 1, http://www.brettonwoodsproject.org/2006/09/art-542516/ (accessed 21 May 2017).

> freedoms. This provides worldwide protection for the rights of children and their teachers, but has been excluded from the World Bank's model. Financial responsibility for education has been transferred from governmental to family budgets, dooming poor children to grow up without the qualification and socialisation which education should provide.

In a report, Tomasevski further denounces the role of international financial institutions that have reinforced the non-accessibility of education by making underlined financial requirements that end up locking out several children from accessing basic education, by stating[127]:

> The core of human rights is jeopardised by transposing the language of rights to the sale and purchase of education. Human rights are entitlements inherent in human beings and are regulated by public rather than private law. Blurred vocabulary camouflages this legal duality, with a risk of obfuscating the boundaries between trade law and human rightslaw. Both domestically and internationally, concerns about the future of education as a free public service have heightened the need to reaffirm and reinforce education as a human right.[128]

The language of rights expressed above could be interpreted as the absence of explicit legal guarantees in the majority of constitutions, including that of Nigeria, where the constitutional provision is interpreted as 'guidance for government policy rather than specific obligations'.[129] Consequently, the negligence of public schools with regard to funding and administrative control has put the private school on a pedestal, namely that it provides better quality education in and, thus, reinforcing the assumption that public schools are for lowly placed children in society.[130] The effect hereof is that there is a tendency to discriminate both in the social

[127]E/CN.4/2001/52 of 11 January 2001, paras 55–59. The Structural Adjustment Programme (SAP) introduced stringent financial burdens on Nigeria during the military rule of General Babangida. This resulted in a large number of children not being able to access any form of education.

[128]K. Tomasevski, "The right to education report, mission to United States of America," 24 September–10 October 2001E/CN.4/2002/60/Add.1 17 January 2002.

[129]K. Tomasevski, "Globalising what: Education as a human right or as a traded service?" *Indiana Journal of Global Legal Studies* 12(1) (2005): 30.

[130]Tomasevski reiterates that '[a]ccess to school may be secured for all children but this does not mean that schools are good, and those schools that are good may not be affordable. Opting out of public schools is possible for those parents who can afford private and/

sphere and in the labour market. Ultimately, it reduces the threshold access to quality basic education, as the majority of children fall in the poverty range with parents who are unable to fund private education.[131]

Thus, to ensure that basic education is free and compulsory, it has been advanced that this may not be attainable because 'to compel somebody to attend a school he cannot afford, does not make sense'.[132] In support of this position, state parties are encouraged to devote the 'maximum amount of resources available towards the realisation of right to education'.[133] The importance of basic education been free of all forms of fees is further supported by Obidike and Onwuka when they find that[134]:

> Apart from developing in the entire citizenry a strong consciousness and strong commitment to the promotion of education, Universal Basic Education in Nigeria is meant to be free and compulsory for every Nigerian Child of school age.

Furthermore, the restriction of access to basic education on the basis of financial challenges in Nigeria was highlighted in the National Education Data Survey (NEDS) report, which stated[135]:

or religious education. Parental choice amongst public schools is determined by their ability to afford living in a neighbourhood where schools are good. The varying quality of schools is exemplified by advertisements for the sale of family houses, which include testing scores of neighbourhood schools as an important marketing item. This process of economic exclusion flouts the common school ideal'.

[131] This is treated as an assumption because in several circumstances children from the public-funded schools perform better than their counterparts in the private sphere. It is therefore paramount that if the public-funded schools are empowered appropriately, then the level of educational quality will be increased.

[132] Beiter Right to Education in International Law 97.

[133] See arts 28(1) & 4 of the CRC and art 10 of the African Women's Protocol on the need to dedicate sufficient funds to the realisation of education. Particular attention is directed to the plight of the girl child and also the disabled. It is important that the concept of making education for the most vulnerable groups free must entail all aspects, including the elimination of distance and cost alongside other obstacles that negate the realisation of the right to basic education.

[134] N. D. Obidike and L. N. Onwuka, "Enhancing the implementation of Universal Basic Education in Nigeria," *Research Journal in Organizational Psychology & Educational Studies* 2(4) (2013): 185–190, 185.

[135] National Population Commission (Nigeria) and RTI International, 2011 Nigeria Demographic and Health Survey (DHS) EdData Profile 1990, 2003 and 2008: Education Data for Decision-Making 2011 Washington, DC, USA: National Population

> Nearly all pupils' households spent money on books and supplies, and nine in ten (92 percent) spent money on handworks, and school uniforms and clothing. Six in ten pupils' households spent money on PTA fees, and one in two pupils household spent money on food. About one-quarter of pupils' households spent money on extra lessons, a third on the school development levy, and on tuition.

The GC on education highlights the importance of access by stating that education must be devoid of discrimination, physical accessibility and financial ability of pupils to be exposed to facilities in a sufficient manner. Discrimination addresses the content of education curriculum, stereotypes and attitudes of both teachers and government administrators. It also guarantees the freedom component of education, which ensures that no one must be denied access to education in a discriminatory manner.[136]

The question of physical accessibility is enunciated by the fact that students must be able to access available educational institutions within a determined distance. Physical access by people with disabilities is an ongoing challenge in Nigeria. Regarding physical access, inclusive education of persons living with some form of disability is also crucial to the matter of threshold of access as conceptualised by the GC.

The position of the GC is further supported by the Standard Rules on the Equalisation of Opportunities for Persons with Disabilities, which calls for the following[137]:

> General educational authorities are responsible for the education of persons with disabilities in integrated settings. Education for persons with disabilities should form an integral part of national educational planning, curriculum development and school organisation.

Commission and RTI International 25 available at https://www.google.co.za/url?sa=t&rct=j&q=&esrc=s&source=web&cd=1&cad=rja&uact=8&ved=0CBwQFjAA&url=https%3A%2F%2Fwww.eddataglobal.org%2Fdocuments%2Findex.cfm%2FTechR_NEDS_Nigeria_EdData_Survey_2010(lgrpt).pdf%3Ffuseaction%3Dthrowpub%26ID%3D329&ei=NoCbVe6jOcPfU7WAk6gL&usg=AFQjCNG7CauKZDPvJWgFqJ2JmpLuKKkQcg&sig2=2wo0ZQjRlofxwYtgJzkxJA&bvm=bv.96952980,d.ZGU (accessed 7 July 2017).

[136] Beiter Right to Education in International, 101.

[137] Rule 6 of the Standard Rules on the Equalisation of Opportunities for Persons with Disabilities, adopted by the United Nations General Assembly, 48th session, Resolution 48/96, annex, 20 December 1993 (my emphasis). This is to underscore the importance of access in line with the best interests of children suffering from disability.

> Education in mainstream schools presupposes the provision of interpreter and other appropriate support services. *Adequate accessibility and support services*, designed to meet the needs of persons with different disabilities, should be provided.

Buttressing this challenge within the Nigerian education framework, it was captured in the NEDS report:

> As expected, children in rural areas face longer distances and walking times to the nearest primary and secondary schools than children in urban areas. Children living far from school may be likely to start attending school over-age or not to attend school at all. Among over-age children, those in rural areas are more likely than those in urban areas to have started school over age because of the distance to the nearest school. In addition, the distance to school in part explains why young school-age children do not attend school, since it may be difficult or unsafe for children to walk long distances to school …

The position of Tomasevski is therefore reiterated, that any form of education for which fees are charged is a violation of the right of the child to access basic education. The claims of availability without the necessary accessibility still amounts to a violation of the right and negligence on the part of the governments with regard to its obligation to promote access to basic education.

iii. Acceptability

As shown in the conceptualisation of the meaning of education, all early scholars seem to agree on one basic aspect of education: that education must be central and acceptable to the individual. However, the position of determining the curriculum content of basic education based on the intellectual ability of pupils is an unacceptable premise and violates the acceptability test. The best interests of the child therefore remain the nucleus of fashioning any style of education that is offered to a child.

Another important aspect of acceptability is hinged on compliance of education curricula with the cultural and religious inclinations of people. A perusal of global and regional human rights instruments highlights the importance of taking into consideration the culture and religious beliefs of people. In addition, the language of communication is another aspect of the acceptability framework.

Furthermore, the main problem of acceptability within the Nigerian context, and especially in Northern Nigeria, is hinged on the parochial approach of the colonial powers. Omotoso opines that[138]

> [t]he colonisation of Africa by the Europeans which lasted about a century has come and gone but its impacts linger on many decades after. While some of these impacts are good and desirable, some are in conflict with the African culture and are not desirable.

This proposition, it is argued, is one of several reasons for the rejection of Western education in the northern part of the country, as the early missionaries had an agenda to convert the existing beliefs in the region to the beliefs of the colonial powers.[139] Another offshoot of the above proposition is captured by Azikiwe when he states:

> ... forces which, hitherto, had encouraged the brain-washing of Nigerians to lose faith in their innate genius and to doubt their capacity to stand by themselves are now ...converted to believe in education as an investment which should yield rich dividends in the future.[140]

Another factor that affected acceptability is advanced by Fajana who, in restating the difference between the African traditional style of education and that of colonialism, reiterates the pivotal role of both moral learning

[138] S. A. Omotoso, "Education and emancipation: An African philosophical perspective," *The Journal of Pan-African Studies* 3(9) (2010): 223. The theory adopted for the interpretation of acceptability defers slightly from the concept of acceptability that might be linked to quality in education. While it is taken into consideration that for education to be acceptable it must include basic amenities as further discussed in Chapter 3, it is important to note the need to ensure that every education curriculum must also be acceptable in terms of not seeking to erode dignity and beliefs of a people.

[139] Omotoso argues that '[w]hen the colonialists came to Nigeria in the nineteenth century, together with Christian missionaries, they discovered that Islam had firmly established itself in most parts of the North and in some parts of the West of the country. Apparently, they would have preferred to replace Islam with their own religion. The educational system was virtually in the hands of the missionaries who ensured that the learning process in schools encouraged and in some cases demand the conversion of beneficiaries of the system into Christianity. Although they did not quite succeed in converting everybody who went through the system into their own religion, the effect of their attempt left a lasting impact on the mentality of the Muslims' at 52.

[140] Foreword as written by N. Azikiwe in O. Ikejiani (ed), *Education in Nigeria* (1965), xiii.

and other forms of education, as opposed to the Western style, which concentrated only on the form and in addition mind training.[141] This view also finds support in the views of Omotoso, who claims that Islamic education was preferred in some quarters of Nigeria because it was more all-encompassing than Western education.[142] It is, therefore, important that for education to be acceptable, it must embrace a large perspective of people and seek an all-encompassing approach to building an educational philosophy. Finally, it is emphasised that acceptability is linked to an educational policy accommodating cultural differences of people. Where a policy is put in place and the culture of the people is not properly captured, such a policy will not be acceptable and be tantamount to a denial.

iv. Adaptability

Woolman and Fleisch advance that adaptability speaks to 'curriculum and school environment able to adapt and accommodate persons with different capabilities'.[143] The GC conceptualises adaptability to include the consideration of 'diverse social and cultural inclination'. Consequently, it can be inferred that the educational curriculum must fulfil this threshold in order to be able to meet this standard.

Ikejiani argues that colonial policies (education included) favoured the maintenance of colonial territories and not with intent to adapt to the colonised people.[144] To ensure adaptability, the community must be engaged so as to appreciate the 'common good' which they are to benefit from.[145]

Thus, for education to meet the core content of adaptability, it must take into consideration the general culture, religion and way of life of people. Furthermore, it must also ensure that conditions that could make a certain group feel discriminated against and unable to adapt to

[141] A. Fajana, *Education in Nigeria 1842–1939 (A Historical Analysis)*, (1978), 30–31.

[142] A. O. Omotosho, "The impact of colonial education and culture on the Muslims of Nigeria," *Journal of Arabic and Islamic Studies* (1998): 52–61.

[143] Woolman and Fleisch, *The constitution in the classroom: Law and education in South Africa*, 135.

[144] O. Ikejiani, "Background to the problems of Nigerian education," in O. Ikejiani (ed), *Education in Nigeria* (1965), 3.

[145] E. Unterhalter, "Ensuring a fair chance for girls, global campaign for education," in S. Aikman and E. Unterhalter (eds), *Beyond access transforming policy and practice for gender equality in education* (2005), 51.

a particular schooling schedule, such as physical and geographical limitations, are taken into account when designing an educational model.

2.4.5 *Inextricable Link Between Education and Development*

Where basic education is devoid of quality, the recipient is unable to have the full benefit of education.[146] The link between the right to education and other rights, such as the right to development and particularly of health, is described by Lundy as a 'perfect example of the indivisibility and interdependence of human rights obligations, restating that the right to education and the right to health are inextricably linked'.[147] This argument is advanced in the light of the fact that education provides an insight into healthy living and a way of handling challenges.

Article 28 of the Convention on the Rights of the Child (CRC) provides for the core basis of the realisation of the right to education. Enshrined in the article is the three-layered responsibility of the state to ensure the realisation of the right to education. The first area covers the responsibility to recognise[148]; the second is a protective, ensuring compliance[149]; and the third is that of promotion and seeking international co-operation.[150] A joint reading of the three arms of Article 28 shows a 'new dimension that is put in existing education rights, by broadening the arsenal of binding international provisions on the right to education'.[151] Notwithstanding the fact that the wording of Article 28 suggests the progressive realisation of the right, it has been canvassed that it is important to entrench an effective means of holding the government to account to ensure that they comply with the responsibility regarding the right to education.[152]

[146] L. Lundy, "School children and health: 'The role of international human rights law'," in N. Harris and P. Meredith (eds), *Children, education and health: International perspectives on law and policy* (2005), 4.

[147] As above. Apart from health, education is linked to other aspects of human rights; see, generally, D. C. Hodgson, "The role and purposes of public schools and religious fundamentalism: An international human rights law perspective," http://files.eric.ed.gov/fulltext/EJ979441.pdf (accessed 7 July 2017).

[148] CRC, art 28(1).

[149] CRC, art 28(2).

[150] CRC, art 28(3).

[151] Verheyde, *A commentary on the United Nations Convention on the Rights of the Child, Article 28—Right to education*, 9.

[152] K. Tomasevski, "Globalising what: Education as a human right or as a traded service?" *Indiana Journal of Global Legal Studies* 12(1) (2005): 30.

Another important significance of the provisions of Article 28 is that of the protection of the right to education. Jjuuko and Kabonesa debate the importance of the realisation of the right in education, insisting that its elimination is a sure way of enhancing access beyond the threshold point.[153] Among indigenous groups, for instance, a lack of respect for their status and consequently their rights in education results in the eroding of their self-dignity and liberty.[154] Examples of rights in education are any acts that are tantamount to inhuman and degrading treatment, which manifests in terms of verbal abuse, corporal punishment and discrimination.[155]

Another core content of the protection of the right to education is with respect to the right of persons living with disabilities. In this regard, reliance on Article 23 of the CRC is important to ensure that basic education is not denied to children who are suffering from disabilities. Lundy argues that this will ensure that a child is able to 'achieve the fullest possible integration and individual development'[156] when the right to basic education is effectively interpreted.

The reading of this provision in line with Article 24 of the Convention on the Rights of Persons with Disability (CRPD) further reinforces the need to adapt the inclusive education model to ensure that the right to education is realised. The importance of ensuring an integrated approach to education is further advanced by the fact that

> [p]ersons with disabilities live a more degraded life which is dependent of the educational system that excludes them from the society. Consequently, if these problems must be solved, then it must be taken into cognisance that education lightens the burden of various forms of social disadvantages and opens the door to better living conditions.[157]

[153] F. Jjuuko & C. Kabonesa, *Universal primary education (UPE) in contemporary Uganda: Right or privilege?* (Working Paper 8) (2007), 6 HURIPEC.

[154] Among the Batwa group in Uganda, discrimination which results in the violation of the right to education is a major factor that has affected the right to education of the Mutwa child. See, generally, A. C. Onuora-Oguno, "Assessing the right of the indigenous child to education: Case study of the Batwa," available at http://repository.up.ac.za/bitstream/handle/2263/8005/azubike.pdf?sequence=1 (accessed 21 May 2017).

[155] Verheyde, *A commentary on the United Nations Convention on the Rights of the Child, Article 28—Right to education*, 60.

[156] Lundy, "School children and health: 'The role of international human rights law'," 11.

[157] Monitoring the implementation of the Standard Rules on the Equalisation of Opportunities for Persons with Disabilities [A/52/56—Report on First Mandate of the Special Rapporteur]—part 2 available at http://www.un.org/disabilities/default.asp?id=59

2.4.6 Education Abhors Discrimination

The UNESCO Convention against Discrimination in Education[158] recognises the right to education as a core component of its aims and terms.[159] To achieve this, the Convention[160] seeks to protect the individual against all forms of discrimination that may exist in the pursuit of the right to education. The challenges recognised by UNESCO do not, however, preclude the three-layered obligation on a state to ensure the promotion, protection and fulfilment of ensuring 'full and equal opportunities for education for all'.[161]

In addition, UNESCO is alive to the importance of the effective implementation of the obligation that is placed on a state. This can be achieved by reliance on both legal and policy frameworks that must be implemented in line with the international guidelines set. An integral part of the UNESCO oversight function is grounded in the fact that UNESCO member states have the constitutional obligation to report to the organisation on measures taken for implementing UNESCO Conventions and recommendations.[162]

Furthermore, UNESCO, in realising the right to education, set up the Education for All (EFA) campaign, which aimed at ensuring the realisation of the basic aim of UNESCO.[163]Another programme initiative in this regard is the Dakar Framework for Action.[164]

The UNESCO Convention has 19 articles that seek to protect the right to education. It describes discrimination as

(accessed 22 May 2017). See Lundy 11 for further discussions on the import of rule 6 of the Standard Rules on the Equalisation of Opportunities for Disabled People.

[158] Convention entered into force on 22 May 1962.

[159] UNESCO, *The right to education*.

[160] 14 December 1960.

[161] Preamble of UNESCO Constitution.

[162] C. L. McNeely, "Prescribing national education policies: The role of international organisations," *Comparative education review* 39(4) (1995): 483–507.

[163] UNESCO: *Inclusive Dimensions of the Right to Education: Normative Bases Concept Paper* prepared for the 8th and 9th Meetings of the Joint Expert Group UNESCO (CR)/ ECOSOC (CESCR) on the Monitoring of the Right to Education (2008), 4.

[164] 2000. The Dakar Framework was adopted during the World Forum on Education. Part of the target set during the forum was a reaffirmation of the importance of education and the urgent need to realise it. In addition, 2015 was set as a target for achieving equal education for the child (boy and girl inclusive). Aside the issue of the child, adult literacy levels were also set as targets.

> distinction, exclusion, limitation or preference which, being based on race, colour, sex, language, religion, political or other opinion, national or social origin, economic condition or birth, has the purpose or effect of nullifying or impairing equality of treatment in education…[165]

The significance of this provision restates the importance of ensuring that no state policy violates the religious or cultural beliefs of people.[166] This speaks to the extent of the acceptability of basic education and its curriculum content. The strong wording of the Convention and the Constitution of UNESCO stresses the role of states, ensuring that the right to education of every child is protected. Thus, education is referred to as 'all types and levels of education, and includes access to education, the standard and quality of education, and the conditions under which it is given'.[167]

The importance of the UNESCO Convention is further reinforced by its reference to the UDHR and other global and regional human rights law that provides for the right to education. According to Daudet and Eisemann:

> The preamble to the Convention against Discrimination in Education is an extension of the Universal Declaration of Human Rights, which, as the preamble states, 'asserts the principle of non-discrimination and proclaims that every person has the right to education' … the Constitution of UNESCO affirms…that 'the States Parties to this Constitution believe in full and equal opportunities for education for all, in the unrestricted pursuit of objective truth, and in the free exchange of ideas and knowledge'.[168]

Based on the above, it is clear that discrimination in any form is not acceptable within the ambit of the human right approach to access to basic education. Discrimination against persons with disabilities has further received legal protection in international law and is discussed below.

[165] UNESCO, Convention against Discrimination in Education, art 1.

[166] UNESCO, Convention against Discrimination in Education, art 4.

[167] UNESCO, Convention, art 2.

[168] Y. Daudet and P. M. Eisemann, *Right to education: Commentary* (2005), 9–12 UNESCO.

2.4.7 *Eliminating Discrimination Against Persons with Disabilities Within the Space of Basic Education*

The need to specifically protect persons with disabilities informed the putting into place of the Convention on the Rights of People with Disabilities (CPRD).[169] While the Convention deals with several rights of people living with disabilities, Article 24 provides specifically for the right to education. Unlike the wording of other international instruments providing for the right to education, the CRPD mentions in specific terms states' obligation to recognise the 'right of persons with disabilities to education'.[170] It further restates the wording of the UNESCO Convention to ensure that the right is devoid of any form of discrimination. A model of inclusive education is enshrined in Article 24, stating that 'persons with disabilities are not excluded from the general education system on the basis of disability'.[171] For education to be inclusive, it must entail an extra effort by the state to ensure support as far as infrastructure is concerned and personnel with skills to ensure effective and quality access to education at all levels.[172] This further entails taking into account that every child, apart from having a fundamental right to education, must be 'given an opportunity to have an acceptable level of learning and ensuring that each child's unique interest, abilities and learning needs are protected'.[173]

2.4.8 *Right to Basic Education in African Regional Human Rights Law*

Discussing education under the African human rights system requires a brief restatement of the concept of education in Africa. This is important as it goes a long way towards effecting the level of acceptability

[169] http://www.un.org/disabilities/documents/convention/convoptprot-e.pdf (accessed 29 October 2017).

[170] CRPD, art 1.

[171] CRPD, art 24(2)(a).

[172] Serge D. Kamga, "The right to education of persons with disability," lecture delivered during the Advanced Human Rights Courses, Centre for Human Rights, University of Pretoria, March 2013.

[173] The Salamanca Statement and Framework for Action on Special Needs Education adopted by the World Conference on Special Needs Education: Access and Quality Salamanca, Spain, 7–10 June 1994 Principle 2. See also generally General Comment 9 of the CRC.

and adaptability as envisaged in the ICESCR. The fact that Africa had a style of education that was peculiar to it has been reiterated in several literatures.[174] Relying on Nduka[175] and Nwonwu,[176] the importance of education and its meaning in Africa is reiterated, as allowing for African indigenous knowledge and the transmission of culture from one generation to another.[177] The following section details the provisions of the right to education in several regional human rights instruments within Africa.

2.4.9 *Africa Respects Education*

The African Charter on Human and Peoples' Rights (ACHPR),[178] in enshrining the protection of the right to education, provides in unqualified terms that 'every individual shall have the right to education'.[179] Although not expressly stated, it can be implied that the ACHPR reiterates the importance of ensuring that education as a right must be realised within the ambit of cultural, traditional and religious beliefs.[180] It is certain that this is in line with the provisions of the ICESCR and the GC in ensuring that education is acceptable and adaptable. Thus, basic education curricula, policy frameworks and implementation should respect the provisions of Article 17 of the ACHPR.

[174] See e.g. the works of Aliu B. Fafunwa, *History of education in Nigeria* (1974); W. T. Kalus, "Indigenous education in pre-colonial Africa," in H. T. Msango et al. (eds), *Selected topics in philosophy and education* (2000), 24–23.

[175] O. Nduka, Western education and the Nigeria cultural background (1964), 12.

[176] Francis O. C. Nwonwu, *Indigenous knowledge systems in Igbo traditional agriculture* (2011), 11.

[177] Hansungule and Onuora-Oguno, "African perspective of education: A catalyst for the desired Africa of tomorrow?"

[178] Adopted 26 June 1981, entered into force on 21 October 1986. The African Charter is the first instrument that sets out obligations from both state parties and individuals. In addition, it does not distinguish between rights in any particular hierarchy in terms of dividing rights into civil and political or economic and social rights.

[179] Art 17(1) of the African Charter provides that '[e]very individual shall have the right to education'.

[180] Arts 17(2) & (3) African Charter.

2.5 Education Is Culture in Africa

The African Cultural Charter[181] brings to the fore the pivotal role education plays in the cultural life of African society. The system of African education promotes communalism depicted in the concept of *ubuntu*.[182] To this effect, the realisation of education is set out in the principles of the Cultural Charter, with 'African states solemnly subscribing to ensure access of all citizens to education and culture'.[183] The Charter further enshrines the 'transcription, teaching and development of national languages and the adaptation of educational curricula to development needs'.[184] The scope of these provisions speaks to the importance of ensuring that education must be acceptable and adaptable to the existence of a group and should not in any form derogate from its cultural existence.[185]

This is further referred to when the Charter in its *modus operandi* for realising education specifically encourages the introduction of African culture, language and the establishment of appropriate institutions.[186] The role of teachers is further emphasised by providing that states must invest in the training of competent staff.[187]

The appropriateness of education is also enshrined in the Charter,[188] thus addressing the core aspect of the obligation on the state to realise the right to basic education.

[181] Adopted at the 13th ordinary session of the OAU 1976, available at http://au.int/en/sites/default/files/CULTURAL_CHARTER_AFRICA.pdf (accessed 29 May 2013).

[182] Hansungule & Onuora-Oguno African Concept of Education.

[183] African Cultural Charter, art 2.

[184] African Cultural Charter, Priority 1(a) & (c).

[185] African Cultural Charter, art 10 provides that 'African states shall endeavour to raise continually the cultural awareness of young people through the introduction of African cultural values into education and through the organisation of national and Pan-African festivals, conferences, seminars and training and refresher courses'.

[186] African Cultural, Priority 2(a)–(c).

[187] African Cultural Charter, Priority 2(d).

[188] African Cultural Charter, art 16: 'African governments should take steps to organise continuous training in a rational way and to establish an appropriate system of education which satisfied the specific needs of their people'.

2.5.1 Education and the African Child

The African Charter on the Rights and Welfare of a Child (African Children's Charter)[189] focuses specifically on the protection of the rights of the African child. It may be seen as a version of the UN CRC, but is unique in the sense that it places obligations on the child. The African Children's Charter provides a further elaboration on the rights that can accrue to a child. Considering that the emphasis in this thesis is on basic education, the period covered will mostly fall under the scope of the definition of a child. It is imperative that the provisions of the African Children's Charter as regards the right to education be considered. A starting point is reiterating the basis that, whatever decisions are taken by the government or the parents of a child, they must be in the best interests of the child.[190] The best interest of the child must therefore be seen from the holistic development of mental, physical and economic well-being of a child.

The first mention of the right to education in the African Children's Charter is couched in the same terms as in the ACHPR, restating the compulsory nature of the right of every child to an education.[191] It further addresses the importance and outcomes of the education received by a child, that it must assist the child and the community. As put forward by Mandela, the general import of education is to emancipate, as education is the greatest engine of personal development. Mandela further reiterates that '[i]t is through education that the daughter of a peasant can become a doctor; that a son of a mine worker can become the head of the mine'.[192]

The African Children's Charter lends support to a style of education that must promote the child's personality,[193] promote respect of human rights,[194] that it should ensure the protection of the cultural heritage, and sustain mutual respect for individuals and the state.[195] Furthermore,

[189] http://acerwc.org/acrwc-charter-full-text/ (accessed 30 June 2017).

[190] African Children's Charter, art 2.

[191] African Children's Charter, art 11.

[192] Nelson Mandela Quotes http://www.education.gov.za/LinkClick.aspx?fileticket=8d-6cPhef%2FL8%3D&tabid=656&mid=1849 (accessed 29 May 2017).

[193] African Children's Charter, art 11(2)(a).

[194] African Children's Charter, art 11(2)(b).

[195] African Children's Charter, arts 11(2)(c)–(e).

the obligation of the state to protect the right to education follows the spirit of the wording of the ICESCR.[196]

However, an interesting provision of the African Children's Charter seeks to safeguard the place of the girl child. It provides:

> States Parties to the present Charter shall have all appropriate measures to ensure that children who become pregnant before completing their education shall have an opportunity to continue with their education on the basis of their individual ability.[197]

The interests of children with disabilities are also established by a call on state parties to ensure that 'special measures are taken to promote self-reliance and participation in the community'.[198] The use of the phrase 'subject to available resources' in Article 13(2) of the Charter does not suggest a leeway for states to fail in their obligation. It is assumed, therefore, that an application of the recommendations of the GC will suffice here. Indeed, the judicial use of available resources to ensure the integrative inclusion of children with disabilities can be construed to mean disapproval of the menace of corruption.[199] It is argued that, if the obligation placed on the child is realisable, quality basic education in African countries, and Nigeria in particular, is not a negotiable option, since education has been accepted as a basis for the realisation of other rights.[200]

[196] While it recognises the liberty of private individuals to provide education, art 11(7) of the Charter provides that '[e]ducation given in such institutions shall conform to such minimum standards as may be laid down by the states'. In the state's responsibility to ensure that the content of education curriculum in non-public schools are regulated to meet a minimum core is established.

[197] African Children's Charter, para 6.

[198] African Children's Charter, art 13(1).

[199] African Children's Charter, art 13(3). It is argued here that the call to use available resources to progressively realise the right to education of children with learning challenges precludes the wanton corruption that has eaten deep into the quest for the realisation of the right to education. As will be shown later in the session of the challenges confronting the realisation of the right to basic education in Nigeria, corruption remains a monster that must be subdued if the question of basic education will not remain political rhetoric.

[200] African Children's Charter, art 31.

2.6 Conclusion

A preliminary conclusion of this chapter begins by reiterating the indispensability of the right of access to basic education as a fulcrum for the realisation of other human rights.[201] 'Human rights are universal legal guarantees protecting individuals and groups against actions and omissions that interfere with fundamental freedom, entitlements and human dignity'.[202] In these circumstances, the realisation of the right to basic education places an onus on government to ensure the promotion, fulfilment and protection of fundamental rights. It is also concluded that Africa has a unique perspective of education and the concept of rights, with the sole aim of enabling individuals to contribute meaningfully to society and its development.

Individuals are also expected to ensure that the guaranteed rights to education are not violated. Consequently, 'education as a fundamental human right is key to sustainable development, peace and stability among countries'.[203] It is also trite to conclude that the right to education 'imposes an obligation on states to ensure that all citizens have opportunities to meet their basic learning needs'.[204] All the instruments discussed clearly envisage the intention of state parties to implement them and also to adopt guidelines when provided.[205]

The next chapter analyses the various obstacles and challenges inhibiting access to basic education. It will also bring to the fore the impact of identified challenges on the education system, particularly on the Nigerian society.

[201] World Education Forum (2000).

[202] Frequently asked questions on a human rights-based approach to development Co-operation Geneva 8, 2006.

[203] UNESCO Round Table on Constitutional and Legal Bases of the Right to Education as a Fundamental Human Right, 5 December 2002, 12, para 9.

[204] As above.

[205] UNESCO (n. 211 below), para 13.

CHAPTER 3

Obstacles Affecting Access to Basic Education

3.1 Introduction

The state of access to basic education remains at its lowest ebb in majority of African countries, with Nigeria having the highest percentage of the out of school children.[1] The challenge does not only lie in the realisation of the right to access basic education, but also with the education received being a quality one. I shall rely strongly though on the challenges inherent in Nigeria with the presumption that most if not all of the challenges are also tenable in majority of African states.

3.2 Quality Basic Education—A Brief Overview

According to the World Education Forum, giving quality content to education is very important.[2] To achieve this, it is stated that education must not only be accessible, but that the accessed education must

[1] Nigeria is rated to be one of the 10 nations in the world with the highest number of adult illiterates. This figure is presently put at about 46 million adults ranging from ages 15 and above. The World Bank has already expressed concerns over this worrying statistic and is trying to collaborate with the Federal Ministry of Education in trying to see how this percentage can be reduced. However, it is the author's conviction that if the challenges that will be discussed in this chapter are not tackled properly, the projects may yield limited results. For more news on the World Bank planned project, see *The Sun Newspaper*, 21 October 2013.

[2] Ulf Fredriksson, "Quality education: The teachers' key role," Workshop 4, 1, *Education International*, available at www.ibe.unesco.org (accessed 4 December 2017).

A. C. Onuora-Oguno, *Development and the Right to Education in Africa*,
https://doi.org/10.1007/978-3-319-90335-4_3

'improve all aspects of the quality of education to achieve recognised and measurable learning outcomes for all-especially in literacy, numeracy and essential life skills'.[3] These indices are prerequisite for the sustainable development of any society. As aptly captured by Fredriksson, the importance of quality education and the role teachers must play are both central to ensuring enhanced access to basic education. Fredriksson notes that[4]:

> As gleaned from various international instruments, the quality of education must be in place to ensure that the life of the child is empowered to the point that the child is able to make an impact on the community and personally. The background on the Dakar action point reiterates further the importance of quality education.

A quality basic education system must provide all children and young people with a comprehensive education and with appropriate preparation for working life, life in society and private life. This should be achieved without distinction of any kind, such as that based on the parent's income, colour, gender, language, religion, political or other opinion, national or social origin. This is important particularly if we take into cognisance that developmental issues should cut across the society and be beneficial to all and not just a few. Education as an agent of development must be general and not to a privileged few.

Ajayi and Adeyemi, relying on the reports of the World Bank, observe that, although the situation of poor access to quality education is not

[3]Dakar Framework for Action Article 7, World Education Forum, 2000. It is important to note that the concept of quality may be seen or approached from two perspectives. While the one deals with questions of infrastructure the other deals with outcome. It is arguable that the later may have some inclination on capabilities of the individual child, but is noted that the impact of the former may greatly affect outcome. For detailed insight into the linkages between inputs and outcomes in assessment of quality in education, see generally UNESCO, "Understanding education quality," (2005), EFA Global Monitoring Report; National Basement of Education Series developed by the World Bank, available at http://web.worldbank.org/WBSITE/EXTERNAL/TOPICS/EXTEDUCATION/0,,contentMDK:22301663~menuPK:5495844~pagePK:148956~piPK:216618~theSitePK:282386~isCURL:Y,00.html (accessed 14 October 2017); Y. Cheong Cheng and T. Wai Ming, "Multi-models of quality in education," *Quality Assurance in Education* 5(1) (1997): 22; A. Case and A. Deaton "School inputs and educational outcomes in South Africa," *Quarterly Journal of Economics* (1999): 1047.

[4]See generally Fredriksson, "Quality education: The teachers' key role."

peculiar to Nigeria, the situation in Nigeria is highly deplorable as basic education in Nigeria today 'suffer[s] from very poor conditions of learning in dilapidated or half-completed buildings, insufficient desks, overcrowded classrooms, inadequate learning materials, poorly educated and motivated teachers'.[5] Abbass notes that 'public schools in Nigeria have degenerated beyond limits in terms of physical structures, infrastructure, and the commitment or quality of teachers as well as the concern of authorities in ensuring standard and achievement of objectives'.[6]

Issues surrounding basic education and other levels of education have become greatly politicised. The political class, rather than treat the provision of quality education as a right, approaches it as a mere obligation seeking to score political points by attempting to shift blame and responsibilities.[7] In the Nigerian situation, apart from the political tone of the Nigerian nation on and the rhetoric of achieving the right to basic education, another interesting issue is the apparent rejection of education based on religious and cultural philosophies. Notably, the events that led to the seeming rejection of education as hinged on culture and religion were premised on the intent of the colonial powers in attempting to erode the mind of Africans. Ngugui clearly paints the picture of post-independent Africa and its reliance on colonial thought as follows[8]:

> Berlin of 1884 was affected through the sword and the bullet but the night of the sword and the bullet was followed by the morning of the chalk and the black board. The physical violence of the battlefield was

[5] Kayode Ajayi and Muyiwa Adeyemi, "Universal Basic Education (UBE) policy implementation in facilities provisions: Ogun State as a case study," *International Journal on New Trends in Education and Their Implications* 3 (2011): 35; Teboho Moja, "Nigeria education sector analysis: An analytical synthesis of performance and main issues," 10, report produced for the World Bank (2000), available at http://siteresources.worldbank.org/NIGERIAEXTN/Resources/ed_sec_analysis.pdf (accessed 24 September 2017).

[6] I. M. Abbass, "Community participation in education: Challenges and prospects in Nigeria's democracy," *European Scientific Journal* 8 (2012): 3.

[7] Various political parties in Nigeria in the build-up to 2015 have been organising various forum on governance, education and infrastructural development. It is my opinion that the majority of the discussions are laden more with political and vote-canvassing techniques as opposed to resolve to foster a sustainable education initiative.

[8] Wa Thiongo Ngugi, *Decolonising the mind: The politics of language in African literature* (Nairobi: East African Publishers, 1981), 9.

> followed by the psychological violence of the classroom. Where the former was visibly brutal the later was visibly gentle.

The gentility spoken about was that of a gradual erosion of identities which graced the education landscape of African nations. The impact of colonial education came with its objectives of redirecting the perception of the African personality. It is consequently important that a re-conceptualisation or renaissance must be achieved about the true nature of Africa if education must be accepted and embraced, enhancing access and eliminating various forms of culture-religious philosophies inhibiting it must be achieved. The shock of the cultural diversity which greeted Africans at the advent of the colonial education is succinctly put thus[9]:

> The language, through images and symbols, gave us a view of the world, but it had a beauty of its own. The home and the field were then our pre-primary school but what is important… the language of our evening teach-ins, and the language of our immediate and wider community, and the language of our work in the fields were one. And when I went to school, a colonial school, the harmony was broken. The language of my education was no longer the language of my culture.

Consequently, quality education encompasses sufficient availability of infrastructure and value laden respect and preservation of human dignity that ultimately drives societal development.

3.3 Challenges to Accessing Basic Education

3.3.1 Failure of the Executive Arm of Government

The executive has the responsibility of ensuring the implementation of laws and adhering to the state obligations. As signatory to several international law instruments that recognise access to basic education as a right, some African states are yet to put in place appropriate institutional mechanisms to ensure the realisation of the state obligation to basic education. With the exception of South Africa and Ghana, Nigeria still leads the several African nations that are yet to recognise education as a fundamental right. The inability or reluctance to curb the menace of corruption, which is rife in all arms of the executive, also presents another

[9] Ngugi, *Decolonising the mind: The politics of language in African literature*, 9.

challenge. The need, therefore, exists for the executive arm of government to drive a targeted and concerted effort of ensuring that the right to access basic education is protected, promoted and fulfilled.[10]

3.3.2 *Legislative Challenges*

Having identified and discussed the place of education under international law and states' obligations to the laws that should influence legislative attitude towards the basic education sector and ensure that it meets the standards of the Education for All or the UNESCO framework and aspirations, it is important to underscore the fact that legislative regulation of basic education still remains a challenge. For instance, the inconsistencies relating to the implementation of educational policies in Nigeria have, instead of creating stability in the uniform implementation of policies, created disparity and inequality. This is evidenced by the existence of several standards relied on by both government-funded institutions and privately funded ones.

Speaking of the failure of the UPE in its debut in Nigeria, Abbass notes[11]:

> When the Universal Primary Education (UPE) was launched in 1976, for example, there was no adequate plan to achieve the enshrined objectives in all respects and at all levels. These include the projected number of pupils/students, number of schools/classrooms needed, the number and quality of teachers required and other infrastructures and instructional materials.

Stability in policy formulation and implementation is hinged on policy consistency pertaining to the realisation of access to education with basic education at the foundation.[12] Basic education in itself is a tool

[10]For a detailed responsibility placed on the executive arm of government of Nigeria in ensuring that education is provided, promoted and fulfilled, see generally the Federal Ministry of Education's Status Report, available at http://planipolis.iiep.unesco.org/upload/Nigeria/Nigeria%20Ed%20Sector%20Status%20May%202003.pdf (accessed 17 April 2017).

[11]Abbass, "Community participation in education: Challenges and prospects in Nigeria's democracy," 3.

[12]It is noted here that several other policies as it affects the access to secondary and tertiary education also exist. While the tertiary education in Nigeria is currently confronted with huge challenges and strikes hinged on the non-implementation of policies, it does not fall with the scope of the education discussed in this thesis.

that ensures that the individual is functionally literate.[13] This is further underscored by the fact that it lays the groundwork for further education and development. This culminates in ensuring that all possible challenges capable of derailing its realisation are limited to a large extent by ensuring proper formulation and implementation of policies and laws.[14]

The changing faces of several policies during the various governments in Nigeria, especially with the advent of the military junta regimes, remain a core example of the negative effect of inconsistencies in the implementation of national education policies. Kazeem and Ige, for instance, pinpoint the inconsistencies as a major clog in Nigeria's basic education sector and inversely her development. During the Alhaji Sheu Shagari-led government, to boost access to university education, which was alternatively meant to ensure the production of quality teachers and other needed skills to fill the gap created by the lack of qualified professionals in Nigeria, the National Open University of Nigeria was established.[15] With the takeover of government by the General Buhari military regime, the initiative was abolished. The end of food for school policy also represents an era in which educational policy was discarded with no regard for its positive effect.[16] The aftermath of these inconsistencies meant that 'Nigerian education descended into a further dismal situation, resulting in the total dislocation of indigent students, who constitute more than 90% of the student population'.[17]

Decrying the very strong effect on inconsistent policy, Atoyebi, echoing Umezurike, reiterates the situation in Nigeria thus: 'If there is

[13] For further reading on adult functional literacy in Nigeria, see generally Joseph B. Ayodele and Mary O. Adedokun, "Towards achieving functional adult literacy in Nigeria," *European Scientific Journal* 8 (2012): 209–235.

[14] David A. Olaniyan and Olabanki E. Obadara, "A critical review of management of primary education in Nigeria," *International Journal of African and African American Studies* VII(1) (2008): 10.

[15] National Open University of Nigeria (NOUN) was initially established on 22 July 1983 and subsequently closed on 25 April 1984. For a detailed history and challenges to NOUN, see T. N. Ambe-Uva "National Open University of Nigeria (NOUN): A historical perspective and challenges," *Turkish Online Journal of Distance Education-TOJDE* 8(1) (2007): 1302.

[16] K. Kazeem and O. Ige, "Redressing the growing concern of the education sector in Nigeria," *Edo Journal of Counselling* 3(1) (2010): 42.

[17] Kazeem and Ige, "Redressing the growing concern of the education sector in Nigeria," 42.

anything in which we have become experts in this country, it is our propensity to bungle the implementation of policies'.[18]

The policy inconsistencies discussed above also manifest in inconsistent education curricula in the various basic education outfits in Nigeria. 'Curriculum is the heart of any educational programme without which such programme will be in jeopardy; and curriculum is also a structured plan of action that guides the process of education'.[19] Curricula and teaching plans are not consistent in Nigeria, ranging from individually managed schools to mission-based and government institutions; educational resources used for teaching vary. Unfortunately, despite the fact that the 'UBE necessitated a curriculum change and innovation as a result of the desire for the improvement and transformation of the educational system'[20]; many schools do not adopt the curriculum.[21] In Danmole's observation, the failure to adopt the UBE curriculum pattern is attributed to the incompetency on the part of the teachers who are invariably not learned in the envisaged style of teaching. Danmole observes that the UBE curriculum is a 'spiral curriculum which requires child-centred and activity-oriented teaching and learning processes' but which is still not fully adhered to by teachers.[22]

This has obvious implications for the level of quality in education being churned out. The first implication affects equality in education,

[18] J. A. Atoyebi, "A critique of the five main objectives of the philosophy of Nigerian education in the contemporary socio-economic and political trends in the country," available at http://www.unilorin.edu.ng/publications/atoyebi/J.A.%20ATOYEBI.htm (accessed 23 September 2017). See generally A. Adegbite, "Languages and the challenges of education in Nigeria," *Journal of the Nigerian English Studies Association (JNESA)* 14(1) (2010): 14, where Adegbite describes policy formulation in Nigeria in these words: 'In Nigeria, several policies have been formulated and programmes initiated and embarked upon, albeit sporadically and haphazardly in many areas'.

[19] B. T. Danmole, "Emerging issues on the Universal Basic Education curriculum in Nigeria: Implications for the science and technology component," *Pakistan Journal of Social Sciences* 8(1) (2011): 62.

[20] Danmole, "Emerging issues on the Universal Basic Education curriculum in Nigeria: Implications for the science and technology component," 62.

[21] Some of the factors responsible for this range from the fact that some schools, especially the private-owned schools, because of better availability of funds, employ more skilled teachers who invariably are supposed to have better skills. Subsequently, many disparities on educational facilities available to them exist from one school to another.

[22] Danmole, "Emerging issues on the Universal Basic Education curriculum in Nigeria: Implications for the science and technology component," 62.

as children from less economically empowered homes tend to attend schools where the curriculum is argued to be of poorer quality than others. This invariably affects the level of competence that a child can imbibe in enabling the child meet the target of education in the home and community as a whole. This factor I argue is contributory to the imbalance that is evident the spread of development in African cities.

While taking into cognisance the challenges that curriculum development constitutes, it is important to underscore the fact that the education curriculum as of a necessity must be developed with the best interests of the child in mind and not the child trying to adapt to the curriculum.[23] Beiter is of the opinion that[24]:

> Education must be flexible so that it can adapt to the special situation of working children, if it is not possible to bring child to where education is given, education must be adapted so that it can be brought to where children are.

Thus, in developing education curricula, it is very central that various classes of children must be taken into consideration. In this regard, the development of curricula for children with disabilities, working children and far to reach children must all be taken into consideration. Talking about the development of curriculum for children with disabilities, it must be noted that an inclusive approach is advanced as opposed to the present situation of special education. The impact of a relevant curriculum is generally underscored by the fact that it enhances and discourages non-attendance.[25]

3.3.3 *Judicial Challenges*

The judiciary represents the third estate in the realm of governance. Its major responsibility is to ensure the interpretation of laws and, by extension, protect the rights of individuals. While the judiciary is primed in the implementation of economic and social responsibilities, the role it

[23] Katrina Tomasevski, *Removing obstacles in the way of the right to education.* Primers No. 1 (2001), 12.

[24] Klaus D. Beiter, "The protection of the right to education by international law," *International Studies in Human Rights* 82 (2006): 509.

[25] Beiter, "The protection of the right to education by international law," 512.

can play in ensuring strict adherence of the executive to its obligation is settled. The Nigerian judiciary's inability to play this role in the sphere of accessing basic education is worrisome and presents a huge challenge.

The entrenchment of corruption in the executive arm of government and Nigeria's lack of respect for its obligations under international law further exhibits the failure of the Nigerian judiciary in aiding the realisation of access to basic education.[26] This suggests why litigation is taken to the ECOWAS Community Court of Justice (ECCJ) for issues that inhibit the actualisation of realisation of access to basic education.

Despite the assumption in most states that education is a non-justiciable right, it is suggested that African judiciaries can rely on judicial activism like in India to contribute a positive jurisprudence for the enhancement of the realisation of the right to education. South Africa is noted to be a very good standard for majority of African states to emulate.

3.3.4 Access to Basic Education of Persons with Disabilities

The CPRD is the first treaty that specially protects the rights of persons living with disabilities. The first challenge that must be noted in inclusive education is that put forward by McClain-Nhlapo, who reiterates[27]:

> In Africa, exclusion, prejudice and discrimination remain common experiences for millions of people with disabilities. Poverty, malnutrition, *low school enrolment rates for children with disabilities*...as do negative cultural beliefs about disabilities and attitudes towards persons with disabilities remain real and well entrenched.

Realising that ab initio persons living with disabilities (PLWD) are disadvantaged, it brings to the fore the further disadvantage suffered by children in accessing basic education. It is important to underscore the fact that disability in some quarters has been construed to be evil omens in

[26] Nigeria corruption busters, available at https://www.unodc.org/unodc/en/frontpage/nigerias-corruption-busters.html (accessed 15 October 2017); G. Okojie, "Nigeria judiciary frustrating war against corruption," available at http://allafrica.com/stories/201507220125.html (accessed 15 October 2017).

[27] I. Grobbelaar-Du Plessis and T. Van Reenen, *Aspects of disability law in Africa*, forward by C. McClain-Nhlapo (Pretoria: Pretoria University Law Press, 2012), VII (my emphasis).

some cultural and religious philosophies, leading to severe negative social concepts of PLWDs.[28]

In attempting to conceptualise the meaning of disability, the following definitions are agreeable for the purposes of this book. 'A disability may be generally defined as a condition which may restrict a person's mental, sensory, or mobility functions to undertake or perform a task in the same way as a person who does not have a disability'.[29] Disability can also be viewed as 'any continuing condition that restricts everyday activities'.[30] According to the World Health Organisation[31]:

> Disabilities are an umbrella term, covering impairments, activity limitations, and participation restrictions. Impairment is a problem in body function or structure; an activity limitation is a difficulty encountered by an individual in executing a task or action; while a participation restriction is a problem experienced by an individual in involvement in life situations. *Disability is thus not just a health problem. It is a complex phenomenon, reflecting the interaction between features of a person's body and features of the society in which he or she lives.* Overcoming the difficulties faced by people with disabilities requires interventions to remove environmental and social barriers.

The above definitions bring to the fore the underpinning fact that disabilities are not just medical in nature but can also be social.[32] Another important inference from the definition is that disabilities are the complete handicapping of PWLD. Consequently, with the requisite support, access to basic education of PLWD can be enhanced. Also gleaned from the definitions is the fact that PLWDs have the capacity to engage and interact with others within the society with some form of support provided. The provision of the Convention on the Rights of People with Disability (CRPD) in Article 24 calls for inclusive education is important. Inclusive education seeks to ensure substantive equality among all persons. The dichotomy between special and inclusive education is, however,

[28] Plessis and Van Reenen, *Introduction to aspects of disability law in Africa*, XV.

[29] http://www.dwa.org.au/whatisadisability.htm (accessed 23 October 2017).

[30] http://www.disability.wa.gov.au/understanding-disability1/understanding-disability/what-is-disability/ (accessed 23 October 2017).

[31] http://www.who.int/topics/disabilities/en/ (accessed 23 October 2017) (my emphasis).

[32] For a detailed discussion on the medical and social models of disability, see Grobbelaar-Du Plessis and Van Reenen, XXIII–XXVII.

viewed as not a paramount issue to be dwelt on in Nigeria at this time. It is advanced that the realisation of quality education is of greater importance to the nomenclature of special or inclusive education.[33]

The core challenge arising from educating people with disabilities in Nigeria is embedded in the lack of resources (human and capital).[34] Teachers at the basic education level lack any form of acquisition of skills and expertise to take responsibility for PLWD. The challenge of accessing education facilities by PLWD is still at very low ebb.[35] In Nigeria, for instance, there exist some special schools meant to educate PLWD but the availability of the institutions is insufficient.[36]

[33]I have discussed this concept in a separate chapter premised on a research I titled "Special education or inclusive education: Bridging the gap of access to quality education," (paper presented at the Global Alliance for Justice Education, 10–14 December 2013).

[34]Kathryn E. Hill and G. M. C. H. Gindiri, "Problems encountered by visually-handicapped Nigerian candidates in schools and public examinations and some strategies to overcome them," available at http://www.icevi.org/publications/educator/winter_99/nigeria.htm (accessed 23 October 2017).

[35]See generally D. Awanbor, "Ten years of the national policy on education in Nigeria: An assessment of policy on special education," *International Journal of Disability, Development and Education* (1995): 42. Awanbor underscores the point of proper implementation of the education for PLWD and suggests that a robust legal framework is a major basis for the realisation of the aspiration of the national policy on education. It therefore seems that with the current plans by the Nigerian Senate to enact an Act that will deal specifically with the need of PLWD is a welcome development in this regard. However, other challenges that are attendant, such as skill acquisition by teachers who are expected to be responsible for the education of the child at this level, still loom large.

[36]Notable among the list of special schools in Nigeria includes, but is not limited to, the Special Education Centre, Orji River, Anambra State; the Special Education Centre, Ogbunike, Anambra State; St Francis School for the Handicapped Vandekiya, Benue State: School for the Handicapped, Tudun Maliki, Kano State; Community School for the Handicapped, Ogbomosho, Oyo State; Special Education Unit, Ayegbaju, Ile Ife, Osun State; Handicapped School, Iwo, Osun State; Special Education Unit, St Philips Anglican School, Ilaro, Ife, Osun State; School for Handicapped Children, Ibereodo, Ogun State; Special Education Centre, Orlu, Imo State; Special School Ikoyi, Osun State; HILA Special Education, Agodi, Ibadan, Oyo State; Special School for the Handicapped, Ilesa, Ogun State, Lagelu; Special Education Unit, Lalupon, Oyo State; Omoyemi Special Unit, Ibadan, Oyo State; Special Education Centre, Jada; School for Handicapped Children, Benin City, Edo State; School for the Handicapped, Roni, Kano, CMML; Special School Iyale; St Louis Centre, Ifohu, Ikot Ekpene, Akwa Ibom State; The Children Special School Ikot Ekpene; Sokoto State School of Handicapped Sokoto; School for the Handicapped, Bauchi; Good Shepherd Special Education Centre, Ogojo, Cross River State; All Saint Special School, Osogbo, Osun State; School for Handicapped Children, Ilaro, Ogun State; School for Handicapped Children, Shagamu Remu, Ogun State; and Modupe Cole Centre, Akoka Lagos State.

However, the main aim of ensuring inclusive education is based on the fact that the need to ensure equal access to education of PLWD is important. In addition, the non-provision of educational opportunities beyond the basic education level is also another challenge coupled with the discrimination that PLWD face in the school environment.[37]

Furthermore, the right of education of PLWD is further enunciated by the ESCR Committee when it reiterated that[38]:

> States should ensure that teachers are trained to educate children with disabilities within regular schools and that the necessary equipment and support are available to bring persons with disabilities up to the same level of education as their non-disabled peers. In the case of deaf children, for example, sign language should be recognised as a separate language to which the children should have access and whose importance should be acknowledged in their overall social environment.

In the jurisprudence of the German Court in the *Integrated Schooling* case,[39] it was found that the inability of the government to provide an integrated secondary school for a girl was not entirely a violation of the right to education of the child. However, in the analysis of the case by Beiter, he reiterates that 'a referral to a special school could result to discrimination if such referral excludes the child from opportunities which are generally available because of lack of support'.[40] Beiter further opines that it is needful for schools to 'take substantial measures to adapt to the needs and abilities of disabled pupils'.[41] Quality assurance resonates in

[37] It is the author's personal experience of having classmates at the University and the Nigeria Law School that did not get any form of support from the institution; this remains a challenge that is worth noting. As was the case, the individuals had to rely on their friends and incurred huge financial responsibilities before they could realise their academic objectives. If special schools must therefore continue to exist in Nigeria, there is a need to ensure that there is continued support for PLWD to attain their educational aspirations. The need for equal access is further captured in the case of a blind student. See generally B. Obi, "Equalising education opportunities for the Nigerian–Ghanaian blind girl-child," available at http://wecando.wordpress.com/2007/11/11/paper-equalizing-educational-opportunity-for-the-nigerian-ghanaian-blind-girl-child/ (accessed 23 October 2017).

[38] ESCR Committee General Comment 5, para 35.

[39] Decision of 8 October 1997.

[40] Beiter, *The protection of the right to education by international law*, 303.

[41] Beiter, *The protection of the right to education by international law*, 508–509.

the case as a basis of referral if it must be recommended. This challenge is further deepened by the lack of statistics and protection of the access to basic education of children that are described as children with Special Education Needs (SEN). Akyeampong et al. find that[42]:

> There is little research on disability, Special Educational Needs (SEN) and access to education in Nigeria. Indeed, there is little statistical data on prevalence rates or access for children with SEN, each state government funds a special school for students with disabilities. However, there is no special provision within the UBE policy to mainstream disabled students into the mainstream schools.

Thus, it is advocated that more efforts are required in the provision of education for PLWD.

3.4 Infrastructural and Institutional Challenges

To achieve a strong educational foundation, the education system needs adequate facilities such as blocks of classrooms, furniture, teachers, instructional materials, libraries and other school equipment. The pivotal role of adequate infrastructures is expected to provide for effective teaching and learning to take place: adequate classroom population; effective classroom climate; and standard pupil–teacher classroom ratio and pupils' academic achievement to be attained, among others.[43]

The importance of effective design and management of learning environments is identified as a major source of determining the quality of education at the basic level.[44] It is paramount that the planning of the basic education landscape is a must to engage all the required institutional support to ensure that learning is advanced in a safe and healthy environment. In achieving this target, recourse must of necessity be had to

[42] K. Akyeampong, R. Sabates, F. Hunt, and J. Anthony, "Review of research on basic education provision in Nigeria," available at http://www.academia.edu/257936/Review_of_Research_on_Basic_Education_Provision_in_Nigeria (accessed 7 May 2017).

[43] K. Ajayi and M. Adeyemi, "Universal Basic Education (UBE) policy implementation in facilities provisions: Ogun State as a case study," *International Journal on New Trends in Education and Their Implications* (2011): 35.

[44] G. O. Udo and A. P. Chuks, "Effect of design, layout and management of primary school facilities on performance of pupils," available at http://www.aibuma.org/archive/proceedings/.../Chukwu,%20Nigeria.doc (accessed 24 September 2017).

adequate capacity and planning ranging from the physical infrastructure and institutional surveys for an effective education system.[45] It was found by the Department for International Development (DFID) that[46]:

> A school environment that may be acceptable to boys may be hostile to girls. The physical and sexual violence against women that is common in many societies is reflected in the school environment in a number of countries. Physical abuse and abduction are not only a major violation of girls' basic human rights; they also present a major practical constraint in getting to school. Parents feel a duty to protect their daughters and may decide to keep them at home if they feel the school is too far away. Violence against girls and women has been identified as a key barrier to girls' education.

It is argued that there exists a direct link between the quality of teachers and the quality of education.[47]

Apart from the poor quality in the teachers' education process, the recruitment procedure presents huge challenges. It is not encouraging that people that do not have any form of teacher education are currently preferred to teach in basic education institutions. The effect of this is that, although graduates of universities, non-professional teachers without the requisite skills to impact knowledge and guide learners are saddled with teaching responsibilities with little or no effort aimed at inculcating these skills in them. Bad as this may seem, the recruitment process continues to present huge challenges. This challenge is presented by Kazeem and Ige when they opine that[48]:

> The problem of quality of teachers in the system can also be traced to teachers' recruitment practice… The practice is doing more harm than good to Nigerian education. The situation is worse in Colleges of Education and Polytechnics, where the Ministries direct Provosts and Rectors to 'admit bearer'.

[45] T. Moja, "Nigeria education sector analysis: An analytical synthesis of performance and main issues," 10, produced for the World Bank (2000), available at http://siteresources.worldbank.org/NIGERIAEXTN/Resources/ed_sec_analysis.pdf (accessed 24 September 2017).

[46] "Girls' education: Towards a better future for all," 9, published by the Department for International Development (2005), available at http://www2.ohchr.org/english/issues/development/docs/girlseducation.pdf (accessed 14 October 2017).

[47] See generally U. Fredriksson, "Quality education: The teachers' key role," Workshop 4, 1, *Education International*, available at www.ibe.unesco.org (accessed 4 December 2017).

[48] K. Kazeem and O. Ige, "Redressing the growing concern of the education sector in Nigeria," *Edo Journal of Counselling* 3(1) (2010): 45.

It is therefore suggested that, while it is not completely wrong that some individuals without experience and skills from fields other than education be saddled with teaching responsibilities, the responsible authorities should as a matter of policy insist on the acquisition of educational experiences from recognised teacher certification and training institutions for such individuals.[49]

Closely related to the challenge posed by poor teacher training and recruitment process is that of teacher welfare. As pointed earlier, General Comment 13 advocates the importance of teachers' welfare and remuneration. While international human rights law does not set standards for what must be the minimum amount paid to teachers, it is argued that it must be able to enable teachers live above the $1 per day benchmark.

Employers, especially at the privately managed basic school, in lieu of limiting costs, employ unqualified personnel, while in the government-owned school salaries are poor and not consistent.[50] In some circumstances, teachers turn their classrooms into mini markets and valuable time designed for teaching and researching is used for selling commodities.[51] In the same light, the 'job context, job content and reward systems' have been described as core factors that affect the productivity of teachers.[52]

[49] The assumption here is that students of education are better equipped to impact knowledge, by virtue of the training and exposure as teachers. The process of learning various teaching pedagogy cannot be overemphasised and there needs to be some level of adherence. It is also assumed that this will further enhance the professional status of the teaching profession.

[50] Primary schools in Anambra State did not operate for one calendar year in 2001 because teachers were owed salaries and the NUT was on strike. The effect was that children whose parents could not afford to travel to other states in the federation lost one academic year and could not proceed with their studies. For information on the number of strike actions by primary schools teachers in Nigeria, see the following links: "Primary school teachers end strike in Edo," available at http://www.vanguardngr.com/2013/07/primary-school-teachers-end-strike-in-edo/ (accessed 31 October 2017); "No going back on primary school teachers strike in Kogi—NUT," available at http://www.vanguardngr.com/2013/07/no-going-back-on-primary-school-teachers-strike-in-kogi-nut/ (accessed 31 October 2017); "The silence of government of the Cross River State of Nigeria on the current teachers strike is worrisome," available at http://www.elombah.com/index.php/articles-mainmenu/17884-the-silence-of-government-of-the-cross-river-state-of-nigeria-on-the-current-teachers-strike-is-worrisome (accessed 31 October 2017).

[51] Kazeem and Ige, "Redressing the growing concern of the education sector in Nigeria," 45.

[52] M. A. Adelabu, "Teacher motivation and incentives in Nigeria," (2005), available at http://www.eldis.org/vfile/upload/1/document/0709/Teacher_motivation_Nigeria.pdf (accessed 31 October 2017).

3.5 Cultural and Religious Challenges

Another important challenge to the realisation of the right to access basic education is culture and religion. In Northern Nigeria, the rejection of the concept of Western education can to a very great extent be hinged on the fact that the introduction of Western education in the north brought with it an apparent erosion and aspiration to replace the Islamic way of thinking with the Christian way of thought. The continued attacks on educational facilities in the north of Nigeria provide a serious challenge to access. Besides the activities of *Boko Haram*, the practice of early child marriage of girls and the *almajiri* practice are other core cultural and religious practices that hinder access to basic education.

For education to meet the threshold of properly being so called, it must be acceptable and act as a tool for bolstering the religious and cultural belief of the beneficiaries. The seeming conflict between formal education as introduced by the colonial masters and the informal structures that existed in the majority of African societies is described as a world of two realities. Ngugi opines that 'African realities as they are affected by the great struggle between the two mutually opposed forces in Africa, an imperialist tradition and resistance tradition'.[53] This addresses the continued friction between embracing formal education in some cultural and religious domains in Nigeria. The viability of the African way of thinking that was discredited in the case of Nigeria by the British colonialists remains an issue to be discouraged. The experience, as already noted, resonates across the continent, leading to Ngugi reiterating the fact thus: 'Indeed contrary to opinions, indigenous African language meant more than words, as they had very strong suggestive powers that were able to crystallise'.[54] This elucidates the strength and viability of the thought process that was suddenly rejected by the colonialists, leading to inevitable friction witnessed today in the northern part of Nigeria.

Consequently, based on the above proposition, the roles that communities play in ensuring the provision and management of education as well as teaching, learning and enforcement processes are an enormous one.[55] According to Hansungule, although enforcing the right to

[53] Ngugi, *Decolonising the mind: The politics of language in African literature*, 2.

[54] Ngugi, *Decolonising the mind: The politics of language in African literature*, 10.

[55] Abbass, "Community participation in education: Challenges and prospects in Nigeria's democracy," 3.

education remains the sole responsibility of government, Africans must grow to the point of individuals and corporate organisations committing their resources to the advancement of education.[56] This also underscores the possibility of communities assisting in the maintenance of educational facilities already provided by government,[57] ensuring that they contribute in curriculum development in line with the standard set by policy and the general purpose of education, ensuring stability and safety of education providers and even pupils who access schools.[58]

Underscoring the importance of community participation further, it is noted that the failure to find support from the community would inevitably lead to project failures and the creation of new problems. This challenge finds further expression in recent killings in Nigeria by the members of the *Boko Haram* sect of teachers and students in Northern Nigeria.[59] Presently, there looms an unprecedented reluctance by individuals who are meant to be engaged in the National Youth Service Commission (NYSC) scheme that sends fresh graduates to teach in several rural communities as part of their compulsory service in Nigeria. This is occasioned by several killings of these corps members by some hostile host communities.[60] The resultant effect is the continuous increase in the already poor supply of human resources in the education sphere of the affected areas.

The hostility of some communities reinforces the failure and tragedy of the fact that government efforts are undermined by host

[56] During an interaction with Michelo Hansungule in the office during the process of writing this thesis, Hansungule hinges his argument on the fact that the African Charter places obligations on individuals, that wealthy African individuals must take a cue from their counterparts in the USA and Europe by committing substantial amounts of money towards education support and research.

[57] This argument is advanced with the *caveat* that the government must not envisage it as a leeway of abdicating its obligations under international law. It is noted that no matter the participation of individuals and communities, the provision of adequate quality education is the core responsibility of the government.

[58] Abbass, "Community participation in education: Challenges and prospects in Nigeria's democracy," 3.

[59] Boko Haram has continued in the north-eastern states of Nigeria since 2010, see generally http://www.aljazeera.com/topics/organisations/boko-haram.html (accessed 22 January 2018).

[60] M. I. Tsiga, "Killing of NYSC members: My worst moment," available at http://leadership.ng/news/111013/killing-nysc-members-my-worst-moment-tsiga (accessed 31 October 2017).

communities. It is therefore germane that community involvement is canvassed and encouraged.[61]

Abbass succinctly captures the importance of community support for education thus[62]:

> School-community connections must be vigorously pursued and developed in order to significantly improve the schools as well as strengthen the community that also ensures that other elements in the participatory approaches and democratic development strategy are all combined together for the enhancement of education through community participation. Since direct community participation in education builds integral and sustainable linkages.

3.5.1 *The Challenge of Language in Access to Basic Education in Nigeria*

The place of language in achieving enhanced access to basic education is germane as 'the ability to read and write in a language, whether it is exogenous or indigenous, constitutes an integral part of defining a literate individual'.[63] In support of the fulcrum of mother tongue in enhancing literacy, UNESCO[64] supports learning in native languages.[65] It has been argued by several scholars that basic education achieves the best impact if undertaken in the native language of the child. Fafunwa championed the use of local languages in basic education in Nigeria. Fafunwa insisted that the colonial legacy of education needed to be reviewed in

[61] Tsiga, "Killing of NYSC members: My worst moment."

[62] Abbass, "Community participation in education: Challenges and prospects in Nigeria's democracy," 9.

[63] C. I. Ofulue, "Literacy at a distance in multilingual contexts: Issues and challenges," *International Review of Open and Distance Learning* (2011): 84.

[64] United Nations General Assembly Resolution A/RES/61/266, February 21 is declared as International Mother Language Day. According to UNESCO 'the date represents the day in 1952 when students demonstrating for recognition of their language, Bangla, as one of the two national languages of the then Pakistan, were shot and killed by police in Dhaka, the capital of what is now Bangladesh'. See http://www.un.org/en/events/motherlanguageday/ (accessed 24 October 2017).

[65] The EFA report of 2005 states the importance of language in enhancing literacy when it opines clearly that learning in one's mother tongue naturally improves the ability to learn other languages and also improves literacy and educational development.

several ways to enable Nigerians to benefit from education. Speaking on the erosion of cultural dignity of Nigeria, Fafunwa posited[66]:

> In its colonial and non-colonial stages, Nigeria's education has impacted negatively on the people and society in terms of cultural alienation and the erosion of positive traditional, spiritual and moral values of self- realisation, job orientation, social responsibility and collective participation.

The philosophy of educating in local languages as advanced by Fafunwa nevertheless received much criticism as it was pinpointed to have retarded the educational advancement of several children. Part of the criticism was because there was no thought-out progressive policy that would ensure the smooth transition from basic education to other levels of education.

Adegbite attempts to proffer a solution to the challenge of language in ensuring the realisation of basic education by advancing the focal nature of the right to education as an integral aspect of a nation's cooperative existence. He lays out the following as to how education must be elevated for it to achieve its goals by reliance on use of languages[67]:

> … a recognition of the primary roles of language as an instrument of thought, cognition and emotions, a means of social communication and cohesion and a medium of earning, use and broadcasting of knowledge and information; a recognition that no policy in any of the areas mentioned above can be effectively implemented without language considerations; a recognition that … are interconnected and has to be integrated in the formulation of policy(ies) on any area of experience; for example, we can talk of a lingual-cultural policy of education.

This argument is advanced on the premise of the link between language and education which is argued to represent the major driving basis for any sustainable development.[68] Adegbite further argues that the seeming disparity in development of not just Nigeria but black Africa compared

[66] A. B. Fafunwa, "An integrated primary school curriculum scheme in Nigeria: A six year project," in A. Afolayan (ed), *Yoruba language and literature* (1982), 15. http://fafunwa-foundation.tripod.com/fafunwafoundation/id9.html (accessed 24 December 2017).

[67] Adegbite, "Languages and the challenges of education in Nigeria," 21–22.

[68] Adegbite, "Languages and the challenges of education in Nigeria," 13.

to other parts of the world is traceable to the neglect of indigenous languages. In his position, he reiterates that[69]:

> Developmental paradigms elsewhere outside Black Africa did not ignore language because this uniquely human possession plays an extremely important role as a facilitator in thought, description, analysis, and argumentation that are so crucial in development and which are so often taken for granted.

Along this paradigm, it is agreeable that the importance of language in achieving effective education is one that cannot be overemphasised. Nigeria is currently one of the poorest in educational output and literacy levels. However, in Nigeria, the large population and prevalence of several ethnic languages possess some challenges on its own. While English remains the *lingua franca*, it is still a case for the argument that the majority of the Nigerian population are not literate in the English language and are also unable to access basic education in their own language.[70]

The question of an individual having a right to be educated in his own language needs also to be settled. In international law, the place of language in education is well captured, but it remains unsettled as to the extent that an individual's right is guaranteed under international law. According to De Varennes, such a right does not exist, but it is paramount to take into consideration the population of a particular language speaking group in advising on the propriety of the state having a responsibility to provide learning in their mother tongue.[71] This suggests that,

[69] Adegbite, "Languages and the challenges of education in Nigeria," 14. See generally Ngugi, *Decolonising the mind: The politics of language in African literature.*

[70] For further insight into the multilingual situation in Nigeria, see generally Efurosibina E. Adegbija, *Multilingualism: A Nigerian case study* (Abeokuta: African Word Press, 2003); L. Aronin and D. Singleton, *Multilingualism: Impact studies in language and society* (The Netherlands: John Benjamin, 2012), particularly chapter 5 where multilingual and personal development is discussed. It is underscored in chapter 79 that the link between language and identity is strong as it goes to the extent of defining the identity and personality of an individual. It follows, therefore, that the role of languages in basic education is crucial as it is a means of preserving the identity of a child as the child grows up in society.

[71] F. de Varennes, "International and comparative perspectives in the use of official languages models and approaches for South Africa," (2012), Centre for Human Rights, University. During the presentation of this report, the author was opportune to interact with De Varennes on the crucial role of language in education, especially with the difficulty it presents. It is De Varennes's opinion that the place of language must be sustained by the government, whatever the economic implications. This, he advanced largely on the relationship between dignity and language and the fact that language was a major source of ethnic violence.

while an individual may not make a claim to learn in a particular language, the population of a particular language speaking group within a location can warrant the teaching in that particular language.

In his opinion, Beiter finds that 'it remains conceivable that the state's denial of education in a certain language may violate the right to education'.[72] He further posits that '[e]ducation rights cannot be separated from language issues noting that in certain circumstances, the failure to provide education in the mother tongue, in fact, violates the right to education'.[73] This circumstance, as envisaged by Beiter, seems to the author to be in line with the position advanced by De Varennes, considering the population of a particular linguistic group being a basis for advancing the use of local language.

An examination of some judicial jurisprudence is central to the understanding of the position in international law, namely, from the jurisprudence of the European Court of Human Rights. In the Belgian linguistic case,[74] some individuals who spoke French in an area occupied majorly by Flemish-speaking people in Belgium sought to access schools in their chosen language as their Dutch-speaking counterparts. Reliance was placed on the legal provisions of Section 4 of the Belgian Act pertaining to the use of language in education. It was argued by the applicant that this constituted a violation of Articles 8 and 14 of the European Convention of Human Rights (ECHR) and also of Article 1 of the additional protocol to the ECHR. While the case was centred on the issues of language and discrimination, the decision on language was to the effect that the state had no obligation to ensure the provision of schools in languages demanded by each individual citizen of the state. This is especially as in situations where such individuals have the option of attending private institutions.

Considering the diversity that is peculiar to Africa, and Nigeria in particular, it is suggested that the decision of the ECHR might not have been the same in Nigeria. As already advanced, the multiethnic diversity in Nigeria presents a unique situation. It is, however, maintained that the only way to make a path is to keep walking thereon; consequently,

[72]K. D. Beiter, "The protection of the right to education by international law," *International Studies in Human Rights* (2006): 425.

[73]Beiter, "The protection of the right to education by international law," 427.

[74](No 1) (1967), Series A, No 5 (1979–1980) 1 EHRR 241 (No 2) (1968), Series A, No 6 (1979–1980) 1 EHRR 252.

building a strong and viable language policy for basic education in Nigeria can only be sustained by usage and development over time.

However, when confronted with the question of a sustained policy of providing language education, as earlier described in Nigerian policy implemented by Fafunwa, the European Court of Human Rights found that a 'state's failure to provide sustainable education in a language after providing same at the primary level could be assumed to be a violation of the right to education obligation held by a state'. The position was taken in the case of *Cyprus v Turkey*,[75] where it was found[76]:

> As to the provision of primary-school education in the Greek language, the Commission considered that the right to education of the population concerned had not been disregarded by the Turkish-Cypriot authorities and that any problems arising out of the vacancy for teaching posts had been resolved.

The ECHR further found[77]:

> However, in the Court's opinion, the option available to Greek-Cypriot parents to continue their children's education in the north is unrealistic in view of the fact that the children in question have already received their primary education in a Greek-Cypriot school there. The authorities must no doubt be aware that it is the wish of Greek-Cypriot parents that the schooling of their children be completed through the medium of the Greek language. Having assumed responsibility for the provision of Greek-language primary schooling, the failure of the 'TRNC' authorities to make *continuing provision for it at the secondary-school level must be considered in effect to be a denial of the substance of the right at issue.*

From the two cases above, it is gleaned that the need to be consistent in policy implementation is important, the failure of which is a violation of the right to education.

[75] Application 25781/94.

[76] See para 276, http://hudoc.echr.coe.int/sites/eng/pages/search.aspx?i=001-59454#{'itemid':['001-59454 (accessed 31 October 2017).

[77] See para 278, http://hudoc.echr.coe.int/sites/eng/pages/search.aspx?i=001-59454#{'itemid':['001-59454 (accessed 31 October 2017) (my emphasis).

3.6 The Challenges of Cultural and Religious Perceptions of the Child and Impact on Access to Education

The practice of child marriage of girls and the *almajiri* practice are two crucial factors that inhibit access to basic education. However, considering that the girl child is more vulnerable than the boy child, this section discusses the girl child in further detail. Thus, the perception on the non-importance of the education of the girl child remains a challenge hinged on cultural practice and belief.

It should be reiterated that '[e]ducation has a profound effect on girls' and women's ability to claim other rights and achieve status in society, such as economic independence and political representation… having an education can make an enormous difference to a woman's chances of finding well-paid work, raising a healthy family and preventing the spread of diseases such as HIV and AIDS'.[78] Despite the general acceptance of the importance of education to the child, it is estimated that close to 58 million girls and about 45 million boys are unable to access education systems across the world.[79] Nigeria records for 10.5 million of the statistics.[80]

Cultural practices contribute to the hampering of access to education for particularly the girl child. It must be noted here that, while the ACHPR supports the protection of African culture, it supports only positive cultures. Article 29(7) of the ACHPR provides:

> The individual shall have the duty to preserve and strengthen positive African cultural values in his relations with other members of the society,

[78] "Girls' education: Towards a better future for all," (2005), 4, published by the Department for International Development. The DFID report further enumerates other important factors regarding the education of the girl child by an ability to avoid poverty by women with basic education, better employment and healthy living of both the woman and the children.

[79] "Girls' education: Towards a better future for all," (2005), 2, published by the Department for International Development.

[80] These statistics have received some criticism by people in Nigeria. Governor Fashola of Lagos State in his comments during the governors' forum, monitored on television channels, questions the basis of the statistics. In a bid to ascertain the actual number of out of school children, Nigeria plans to have a census of children in school. See generally http://www.premiumtimesng.com/news/139547-nigeria-plans-census-of-out-of-school-children.html (accessed 26 May 2014).

in the spirit of tolerance, dialogue and consultation and in general, to contribute to the promotion of the moral well-being of society.

Culture continues to hamper the access of the girl child to access education, and the implication of this as found by Ofoha is based on the effect of gender stereotype as fuelled by the cultural bias towards the girl child in Africa.[81]

On the religious challenge to access to basic education, the impact of violence perpetrated on the basis of religion remains the most recent disturbing situation.[82] For access to education to be stable in a country, it is important that peace and security are in place.[83] Security of life guarantees free movement and ease of mind. The absence of same will in several ways limit the extent to which people are willing to access public places while also hampering development.[84] In recent times, the decline of access to basic education in Nigeria can be blamed on the different shades of violence. Violence, though not alien to Nigeria, is assuming a different dimension in recent times. It is noted that several forms of violence have in the past thwarted peace in the country, but the recent spate of attacks on educational facilities is more alarming now than ever.[85]

[81] D. Ofoha, "Gender stereotypes and girl-child education in Nigeria," available at http://pcfpapers.colfinder.org/bitstream/handle/5678/11/Paper%2019%20%20(Supplementary%20File).pdf?sequence=1 (accessed 15 October 2017).

[82] For the impact of religion and activities of the Boko Haram group see generally O. Abdulrasheed, A. Onuselogu, and G. O. Uzoechina, "Effects of insurgency on Universal Basic Education in Borno State of Nigeria," *American Journal of Educational Research* 3(4) (2015): 490.

[83] For the impact of violence on educational development in a country, see generally B. Barakat and H. Urdal, "Breaking the waves? Does education mediate the relationship between youth bulges and political violence?" (2009), available at https://elibrary.worldbank.org/doi/abs/10.1596/1813-9450-5114 (accessed 21 October 2017).

[84] J. O. Arowosegbe, "Violence and national development in Nigeria: The political economy of youth restiveness in the Niger delta," *African Political Economy* 36(122) (2009): 575. While Arowosegbe comments more on the impact of violence on economic life of Nigeria with particular respect, he notes that the influence of violence on other spheres of the nation's development also abounds.

[85] The effects of religious, domestic and electoral violence have at different times had a serious impact on the existence and enjoyment of social services like education in Nigeria. For instance, in domestic violence, the girl child has suffered severely by not being allowed access to school or being subjected to domestic help. During electoral violence, unassuming pupils are engaged by politicians to engage in several forms of violence. In some instances, the already insufficient educational facilities are destroyed in the process of

In particular, in the north-eastern part of Nigeria, statistics remain very high of the poor level of access to and completion of basic education. Violence has been employed to ensure that this negative statistic continues to swell. While violence has distorted access to basic social services in Nigeria over the years, a new conundrum is the rise of the *Boko Haram*, a supposed Islamist group which in 2012 alone 'burnt down 14 schools in Maiduguri, the capital of Nigeria's Borno state, forcing over 7000 children out of formal education and pushing down enrolment rates in an already ill-educated region'.[86] This has led to a reduction in access to basic education in the region and the closure of schools.[87]

In 2013, several students lost their lives in coordinated attacks on educational institutions in Nigeria. Various news reports have highlighted the sad incidences that have continued to ensure that access to education remains at a low. For instance, it was reported[88]:

> Thousands of students and teachers across northern Nigeria have been forced to abandon their schools due to increasingly brazen attacks by radical Islamist group Boko Haram (BH). In the latest school attack, on 29 September, BH gunmen on four-wheel-drive vehicles and motorbikes stormed student dormitories at a college of Agriculture in the town of Gujba, in the northern Yobe State, opening fire on sleeping students and killing 40.

According to Amnesty International (AI), the attacks are not just violent attacks, but violence and attacks on the right to education. In a report,

violence. For further insight into the different forms of violence underscored, see generally O. N. Aihie, "Prevalence of domestic violence in Nigeria: Implications for counselling," *Edo Journal of Counselling* 2(1) (2009): 1; N. O. Obakhedo, "Curbing electoral violence in Nigeria: The imperative of political education," *International Multidisciplinary Journal, Ethiopia* 5(5), Serial 22 (2011): 99.

[86] http://www.protectingeducation.org/news/nigeria-school-attendance-down-after-boko-haram-attacks (accessed 13 November 2017).

[87] A state-by-state literacy status compiled by the Commission covering 2008–2010 shows that very few states have done well. Most of the states in the north-east and north-west zones have not done well at literacy level. Borno State has only 14.5% of literate population; Gombe has 39%; Jigawa has 24%; while Katsina has 21%. Those doing well are Lagos with 92%; Anambra has 75.1%, Abia has 72.5% while Ekiti has 74.7%. FCT has 61.4%. See http://nigerianpilot.com/index.php/-other-section/-features/4085-the-challenges-of-mass-illiteracy-in-nigeria (accessed 13 November 2017).

[88] http://www.irinnews.org/report/98878/boko-haram-violence-takes-toll-on-education (accessed 21 October 2017).

AI, in calling attention to the dangers of an attack on the right to education in Nigeria, restated that[89]:

> At least 70 teachers and over 100 students have been killed or wounded in Northern Nigeria. Educational facilities have been burned, thousands of children forced out of schools and teachers made to flee for safety.
>
> In July 2013, purported leader of Boko Haram Abubakarr Shekau, in a video statement, said Boko Haram were attacking schools because they are 'un-Islamic'. He also called for more teachers to be killed. In it he said: 'teachers who teach Western education, we will kill them. We will kill them. We would burn down the schools, if they are not Islamic schools. We don't touch small children. Our religion does not allow that, but we'll burn down the schools'.[90]

Consequently, religious and cultural activities impact to a great extent on the limitation of access to basic education in Nigeria.[91] According to Ekanem and Ekefre[92]:

> A cursory look at all these factors reveals religious intolerance, fundamentalism and extremism. Indeed, this tripod is what carried the pot of religious conflicts in Nigeria. This tripod is however fuelled by lack of education that is on a sound philosophic foundation.

[89] "Nigeria: 'Keep away from schools or we'll kill you': Right to education under attack in Nigeria," http://www.amnesty.org/en/library/info/AFR44/019/2013/en (accessed 21 October 2017).

[90] For the video clip, see http://www.youtube.com/watch?v=bS-5v-QhWug (accessed 21 October 2017).

[91] There exists the need therefore for the government agencies responsible for the development of basic education curriculum to ensure that communities, parents and all other relevant institutions are effectively engaged towards building a robust model of basic education that will be accessible and adaptable. This concern is treated in detail in section 6.7 of the thesis.

[92] S. A. Ekanem and E. N. Ekefre, "Education and religious intolerance in Nigeria: The need for essencism as a philosophy," *Journal of Educational and Social Research* 3(2) (2013): 303–310, 305. Yusuf recommends that a change in curriculum and implementation has some potentials in limiting the challenges fronted by religion, see H. O. Yusuf, "Promoting peaceful co-existence and religious tolerance through supplementary readers and reading comprehension passages in basic education curriculum," *International Journal of Humanities and Social Science* 3(8) (2013): 224.

3.7 The Challenges of Corruption and Ethics

It is to be noted that, while some lapses exist in the institutional and policy frameworks in the implementation of basic education, a major challenge is the ethical approach of individuals saddled with the responsibility of implementing policies. A major cankerworm in this respect, apart from attitude to work and responsibility, is that of corruption. As a developing country, Nigeria faces several challenges, one of the three of such challenges identified by Sen, that have a direct impact on education is corruption.[93]

Corruption has been described as an 'endemic monster that has eaten deep into the fabric of the operational existence of the country'.[94] For instance, Ajayi and Adeyemi underscore this fact when they posited[95]:

> The inadequacy in the provision of the UBE facilities to primary schools in the State as pointed out in the findings of this study shows that a lot has need to be done not only in the area of fund commitment to the programme *but also ensuring that such are utilised for the purpose they are meant for and not diverted for other uses as widely reported of State Governments in the country.*

It may not be safe to argue that Nigerian governments over the years have failed to commit some amount of money into the education industry, especially as seen in the UBE scheme. However, the menace of corruption is one of the major conduits that ensure that such funds committed are not utilised. The role of education as an emancipator cannot be overemphasised, but 'the paradox accompanying this belief is that, despite the huge investment in education, there exists no strong evidence of growth-promoting externalities of education in Nigeria'.[96]

[93]Y. Sen, "Challenges and prospects of Nigeria's development at 50," Golden Jubilee Symposium Paper at Carleton University, Ottawa, Canada, available at https://carleton.ca/africanstudies/wp-content/uploads/yima-sen-lecture.pdf (accessed 10 January 2018).

[94]K. Ajayi and M. Adeyemi, "Universal Basic Education (UBE) policy implementation in facilities provisions: Ogun State as a case study," *International Journal on New Trends in Education and Their Implications*, April–June 2(2) (2011): 43.

[95]Ajayi and Adeyemi, "Universal Basic Education (UBE) policy implementation in facilities provisions: Ogun State as a case study" (my emphasis).

[96]N. A. Ndiyo, "A dynamic analysis of education and economic growth in Nigeria," *The Journal of Developing Areas* 41(1) (2007): 3. Ndiyo further asserts that in Nigeria 'education has utilised large amounts of the country's resources because of the perception that education is important to the unity of the country'. See n. 4.

It is claimed that there is a possible loss of about US $500 billion of Nigeria's wealth due to corruption annually.[97] Corruption emanates from the Greek word *corruptus*, translating to some kind of aberration or a misnomer; corruption can also be described as 'abuse of power for private gain'.[98]

Waziri, describing the various facets of corruption in the corporate existence of Nigeria, describes it in the following words[99]:

> award of contracts by public office holders to cronies and personally held companies, bribery, fraud, political corruption e.g. nepotism or favouritism, ethnicity, rigging of elections, misappropriation and conversion of public funds for personal gains, bureaucratic corruption, extortion, manipulation of procurement processes e.g. by over-inflation of contracts, leaking tender information to friends and relations etc., corporate corruption e.g. diversion and misappropriation of funds through manipulation or falsification of financial records.

Corruption, therefore, could be argued to have ensured that 'the educational system apart from being a poor social service in Nigeria lacks quality, proper orientation and quantity'.[100] Considering the enormity of the corruption menace, the tendency to assume that corruption is an innate way of life for not just Nigerians, but Africans in general, exists. However, this position, as argued by Odinkalu, is erroneous and lacks any basis.[101]

This notwithstanding, Nigeria is not the only country that suffers from corruption and its huge retarding of the benefits of development, especially in the realisation of the right to basic education. For instance, in South Africa, corruption is said to be manifested by the number of accumulated riches in the 'absence of visible means of accumulation of such riches'.[102] Aptly put, Madonsela captures the effect of corruption in the case of South Africa thus[103]:

[97] Sen, "Challenges and prospects of Nigeria's development at 50," 12.

[98] The United Nations Global Programme Against Corruption (GPAC).

[99] F. Waziri, "Chairman's opening remarks," CLEEN Foundation Monograph Series No 7 (2010): 1.

[100] Sen, "Challenges and prospects of Nigeria's development at 50," 10.

[101] C. A. Odinkalu, "Corruption and governance in Africa: How do we break the cycle in Nigeria?" CLEEN Foundation Monograph Series No 7 (2010): 16.

[102] T. N. Madonsela, "Corruption and governance challenges: The South African experience," CLEEN Foundation Monograph Series No 7 (2010): 45.

[103] Madonsela, "Corruption and governance challenges: The South African experience."

> We cannot deny that corruption is behind a lot of the underdevelopment in our countries and continent. It causes, among others, poor quality goods and services, lack of efficiency, excessive costs, and ineffective public programmes. Corruption basically destabilises societies. In many instances corruption also endangers the security of our states.

The above assertion brings to the fore the impact of corrupt acts on the provision of state responsibilities *vis-à-vis* the provision of the right to access basic education and the quality component.[104] While it is accepted that corruption is indeed a challenge to the realisation of the right to access basic education in Nigeria, it is important to reiterate the fact that it is not, in itself, the biggest challenge.[105]

Corruption, as argued by Ribadu, is unable to strive without the presence of impunity: 'The challenge of impunity remains the main reason behind the continued survival of corrupt acts'.[106] Particularly in the education industry, money voted for the provision of textbooks and provisions of other learning materials to enhance access to quality of basic education in Nigeria has mysteriously found its way to individual pockets. Despite the obvious abnormality, there does not seem to be any mechanism put in place to curb this menace. It is argued that if institutions that are saddled with the responsibility of ensuring that educational policies and funds are managed effectively, the progressive elimination of structural challenges and welfare issues will be within reach.

While there are several institutions that have been set up by government to stem the continued decimation occasioned by corruption, it is assumed that 'in the effort to enhance governance and combat

[104] India is not absolved from the menace of corruption in education. The recent cases of serious examination malpractice raise issues of concern on the level of corruption in India. See generally J. A. Ogunji, "Examination management and examination malpractice: The nexus," *Journal of International Education Research* (2011): 53; First class exam malpractice in Bihar India, available at http://cynthiasbay.blogspot.com/2015/03/first-class-exam-malpractice-in-bihar.html (accessed 17 April 2017).

[105] N. Ribadu, "Obstacles to effective prosecution of corrupt practices and financial crime cases in Nigeria," available at http://www.nigerianlawguru.com/articles/criminal%20law%20and%20procedure/OBSTACLES%20TO%20EFFECTIVE%20PROSECUTION%20OF%20CORRUPT%20%20PRACTICES%20&%20FINANCIAL%20CRIMES%20IN%20NIGERIA.pdf (accessed 26 May 2017).

[106] Odinkalu, "Corruption and governance in Africa: How do we break the cycle in Nigeria?"; G. O. Adeleke, "Prosecuting corruption and the application of plea bargaining in Nigeria: A critique," *International Journal of Advanced Legal Studies and Governance* 3 (2012): 53.

corruption, public agencies suffer a crisis of credibility—they can no longer be taken seriously'.[107] Odinkalu further states[108]:

> The institutional architecture for accountability begins with the political process, which, as demonstrated here, has been fundamentally compromised to the point of denying choice to the citizens. It includes the public finance and accounting systems supervised jointly by the Finance Minister, the Head of Service and the Auditor-General, all appointed by an unaccountable President. Of particular significance is the infrastructure of documented transactions, which has increasingly been rendered irrelevant of redundant.

According to Mkpa[109]:

> The managers of primary, secondary and tertiary institutions in Nigeria are in consensus that these institutions are grossly under-funded. Evidence exists on the degree of dilapidation that characterises the primary and secondary school buildings in parts of the country; the non-payment of teachers' salaries and allowances as a result of which strikes are the order of the day; the lack of necessary teaching and learning materials at all levels of the educational system; poor working conditions of all teachers in the country, among other indices. It has also been argued that financial mismanagement and lack of accountability by officials led to diverting substantial resources[110] from the educational institutions to other ends. Two issues are relevant: need for enough funds and the need for responsible and proper management of the funds.

The challenge, therefore, lies more in the ethical management of funds that the government has in the recent past devoted to education. It is still canvassed that the menace of corruption and the attendant lack of political will, cum impunity to check the acts, deepen the poor quality of access to basic education. The direct impact of corruption in education is

[107] Odinkalu, "Corruption and governance in Africa: How do we break the cycle in Nigeria?" 31.

[108] Odinkalu, "Corruption and governance in Africa: How do we break the cycle in Nigeria?" 35.

[109] M. A. Mkpa, "Overview of educational development: Pre-colonial to present," available at http://www.onlinenigeria.com/education/?blurb=534 (accessed 23 October 2017).

[110] The budgetary commitment of the federal government on education management at primary level will be discussed in further detail in the next chapter.

felt by the poor. Like in any other sector of the society, it is the poor who are unable to access quality amenities like education.

Consequently, it is the poor child from a poor home that is vulnerable to the denial of access to basic education, not to mention access to a quality basic education.[111] As evidenced by the alarming statistics of the number of out of school children in Nigeria, corruption has been identified judicially as the main basis for the violations. The jurisprudence on the impact of corruption on education, unfortunately, has not emanated from a national court but rather from a sub-regional court.

In the case of *The Registered Trustee of the Socio-Economic Rights and Accountability Project (SERAP) V The Federal Republic of Nigeria and Universal Basic Education Commission (UBEC)*,[112] the effect of corruption on basic education in Nigeria was the crux of the matter before the court. The case was brought before the Economic Community of West African States (ECOWAS) Court and hinged on the violation of several provisions of the ACHPR.[113] Particularly, Article 17 provides:

1. Every individual shall have the right to education.
2. Every individual may freely take part in the cultural life of his community.
3. The promotion and protection of morals and traditional values recognised by the community shall be the duty of the state.

The facts of the case were based on alleged corrupt acts that were perpetrated in UBEC which accounted for loss of millions of naira that the Independent Corrupt Practices Commission (ICPC) had as yet been unable to recover. It also raised the level of impunity on the part of the federal government in investigating and prosecuting erring officials. The defence of the defendants was solely based on procedural issues as they contested the jurisdiction of the court, among other technicalities.

The Court, after considering the pleas of both parties, found among other reliefs that:

[111] Chinua Achebe, *The trouble with Nigeria* (Enugu: Fourth Dimension Publishers, 1983). In this work, Achebe captures the paucity of the Nigerian nation and blames corruption for the decline of both human and social capital of a nation he describes as possessing great potential.

[112] Suit ECW/CCJ/APP/12/07; Judgment ECW/CCJ/JUD/07/10.

[113] Arts 1, 2, 17, 21 & 22.

> The right to education though claimed not to be justiciable under the Nigerian law is justiciable under the ACHPR.[114]
>
> In addition the act of corruption alleged by the applicant is sufficient and will ground a 'negative impact' on basic education and thus requires the government to take extra measures to fill in the gap created by corruption pending its prosecution and recovery of looted funds.[115]

In the wording of the Court, this is important[116]

> to ensure a smooth implementation of the education programme, lest a section of the people should be denied a right to education.

It is, however, important to reiterate the fact that the Court declined making a finding on the arrest of the individuals that the applicants alleged were guilty of the embezzlement of funds. This decision was reached based on the fact that they were not parties before the Court. The Court, however, provided a possible avenue to be further explored by NGOs and CSOs involved in public interest litigation in the expansion of the judicial jurisprudence on the realisation of the right to basic education.[117]

3.8 Conclusion

A safe conclusion of this chapter can be drawn from the findings of Abbass when he reiterated that[118]:

> For communities to effectively participate in education, a feasibility study should be conducted amongst relevant communities in order to understand how their common and diverse interests can strengthen partnership in education for the general good. This also goes on to determine the nature and perspectives of learning or educational activities in the communities, support services and the nature of involvement.

[114] Suit ECW/CCJ/APP/12/07; Judgment ECW/CCJ/JUD/07/10, Relief 1.

[115] Suit ECW/CCJ/APP/12/07; Judgment ECW/CCJ/JUD/07/10, Relief 3.

[116] Suit ECW/CCJ/APP/12/07; Judgment ECW/CCJ/JUD/07/10, Relief 3, para 28.

[117] Suit ECW/CCJ/APP/12/07; Judgment ECW/CCJ/JUD/07/10, Relief 2, para 27.

[118] Abbass, "Community participation in education: Challenges and prospects in Nigeria's democracy," 3.

The realisation of the importance of the community can only be reached with the establishment of a good relationship among the various stakeholders in a particular community.

The continued struggle of realising the right to basic education must adopt a means of creating awareness to all of the importance of education which must be reconceptualised to elevate the dignity of various indigenous groups. Realising this will ensure that, as put forth by Ngugui, will mean, among several options re-establishing the importance of local languages in education. Ngugui noted this importance when she stated[119]:

> The choice of language and the use to which language is put is central to a people's definition of themselves in relation to their natural and social environment...

Invariably, the challenges that inhibit access to basic education in Nigeria are hydra-headed. From inefficiency on the part of the executive, failure on the part of the legislature and the non-adventurous posture of the judiciary to poor infrastructure, unstable policies and corruption, the need for strengthened institutions is crucial towards realisation of the right to education and development.

[119] See generally Ngugi, *Decolonising the mind: The politics of language in African literature.*

CHAPTER 4

Beyond Nomenclature: Special Education or Inclusive Education—Advocating Quality Basic Education

4.1 Introduction

The realisation of economic, social and cultural rights remains a daunting task especially for developing countries. The progressive approach is often adopted as several needs compete for developing states' limited resources. However, the realisation of basic education as a social right is expected not to fall within the threshold of a progressive realisation. This position is buttressed by Beiter when stating[1]:

> the requirement of free education is not as strict where secondary and higher education are concerned...it is submitted that the implementation of elementary (basic) education is subject to the notion of progressiveness to a far lesser extent...

The reason behind this is that education is seen as an intrinsic right and should be realised without budgetary or economic constraints if the aims of

[1] Klaus D. Beiter, "The protection of the right to education by international law," *International Studies in Human Rights* 82 (2006): 92, Martinus Nijhoff, the Netherlands. This position is also supported by A. Skelton in her analysis of Section 29 (a) of the South Africa Constitution stating that the right to basic education demands immediate realisation and not subject to the progressive argument. See generally Ann Skelton, "The role of the courts in ensuring the right to a basic education in a democratic South Africa: a critical evaluation of recent education case law," *Southern African Public Law Journal* 27: 398–408.

A. C. Onuora-Oguno, *Development and the Right to Education in Africa*,
https://doi.org/10.1007/978-3-319-90335-4_4

education are to be realised.[2] The importance of education is captured by the Universal Declaration of Human Rights (UDHR) underscoring the need to ensure that every individual is educated.[3] The core aim of education, as advocated, is to ensure the respect for human dignity, human rights, individual empowerment and the maintenance of peace and security in the world.[4]

Every nation, over the years, has evolved a philosophy of education which is either enshrined in the laws or in the various policy documents that govern the administration of education. However, the quest to ensure access to basic education by the world population remains a daunting task informing the institution of several projects like the Education For All (EFA) and a host of other initiatives by UNESCO.[5] This desire led to the Millennium Development Goals (MDGs) with its Goal 2 as the realisation of compulsory primary education. As the 2015 deadline set by the comity of nations on the MDGs draws near, the realisation of the aspiration remains obviously a task yet unachieved.

Aside the poor state of education the world over, the child in sub-Saharan Africa is statistically the most vulnerable in the quest to attaining basic education. The poor statistics on access to basic education is occasioned by numerous factors. Most children in Africa face either the dangers of forceful conscription into armed hostilities; child trafficking and slavery; child prostitution and denial of basic needs occasioned by poverty; thus affecting either their access or completion rate in schools. The importance of education is so intrinsic that it has been advanced by Nelson Mandela that[6]:

> Education is the great engine of personal development. It is through education that the daughter of a peasant can become a doctor, that a son of a mineworker can become the head of the mine that a child of farm workers can become the president of a nation.

[2] Fons Coomans, "Clarifying the core elements of the right to education."

[3] *Universal Declaration of Human Rights UDHR*, Article 26.

[4] *United Nations Charter*, Article 1.

[5] See, for instance, UNESCO Global Education Initiative, "Education consistently ranks at the top of business, government and civil society agendas as one of the most crucial issues to prepare the next generation of citizens in today's increasingly interconnected world." http://www.unesco.org/education/GEI_brochure.pdf (accessed 28 February 2017); see also UNESCO Education for All Flagship programme, available at http://www.unesco.org/education/efa/know_sharing/flagship_initiatives/ (accessed 28 February 2017).

[6] Nelson Mandela quotes http://www.searchquotes.com/quotation/Education_is_the_great_engine_of_personal_development._It_is_through_education_that_the_daughter_of_/15875/ (accessed 29 May 2017).

Aside the general challenges that face the child in access ing basic education, a Child With Disability (CWD) is further relegated to the background occasioned by the conditions of learning with some form of disabilities.[7] Children who are differently abled or as popularly referred to as disabled children find themselves at the lower rung of the discrimination and denial already suffered by children.[8] In Nigeria, for instance, provision of basic education for hearing impaired children leaves nothing to be desired as there is paucity of teachers who are skilled in the sign language of the deaf. This is more so the case as the unfriendly school environment subjects students to sexual violence in the case of the female child and other forms of societal harassment.[9]

The emergence of special education globally was conceived to enable every child realise the importance of education. In the bid to ensure that CWD is also educated most African countries—like Nigeria—adopted the concept of special education.[10] However, several apparent deficits are synonymous with special education system not just in developing countries but also in developed ones with the core of these challenges being that of ensuring equality in education and elimination of all forms of discrimination and violation of rights in education.[11]

[7] Okey Abosi, "Educating children with learning disabilities in Africa learning disabilities," *Research & Practice* (2007): 196.

[8] According to Peters, this challenge continues to be a 'dominant problem in the disability field ... the lack of access to education for both children and adults with disabilities'. Peters Susan J., "Inclusive education: An EFA strategy for all children," *World Bank* 31195 (2004): 1.

[9] Vivian Ihuoma Okpala, "Excluded and forgotten: Education of the hearing impaired child in Anambra State of Nigeria" (paper presented at the conference on Disability, University of Pretoria 4–6 November 2013).

[10] Louis Mbibeh, "Implementing inclusive education in Cameroun, evidence from Camoerounian Baptist convention health board," *International Journal of Education* (2013): 1.

[11] Rights in education have been argued to be different from the right to education. Right to equality, discrimination and dignity are components of the rights in education. For discussions on this see generally Azubike Onuora-Oguno, Assessing the Right to Education of Indigenous People: A Case Study of the Batwa people of Uganda (2008) VDM Verlag Dr. Müller; *Frederick Juuko & Constance Kabonesa*, "Universal Primary Education (U.P.E) in contemporary Uganda: Right or privilege?" HURIPEC working paper No 8, 2007, available at http://huripec.mak.ac.ug/pdfs/working_paper_8.pdf (accessed 28 February 2017).

The post-2015 propositions of MDGs advocate no longer for mere access to education but quality education.[12] A human rights perspective to quality includes: the availability of education; access; adaptability; and affordability.

In the views of Tomasevski, education as a right must be made available to every child and any obstacles to its realisation must be eliminated.[13] With this core concept guaranteeing quality lacking in the present circumstances in education in majority of African States, it is advanced that the recent debate on the abolition of special education for inclusive education portends some attendant dangers. This is so considering that the present structure of special education and mainstream education have both failed in ensuring enhanced access and improved quality. The assumption here is based on the poor statistics of out of school children in Nigeria and other sub-Saharan African countries.[14]

It is therefore premised on the crucial place of quality in basic education that I advance the need to move beyond the question of nomenclature of special or inclusive education occupying countries in Africa presently. I advocate that states should strive towards the realisation of quality basic education and not dwell on the nomenclature. I note that 'given the confusion and uncertainties that exist, advancing towards the implementation of inclusive education is far from easy and evidence of progress is limited in most countries'.[15]

[12] In a round-table discuss with NGO's held at the Legal Resource Centre Johannesburg office in October 2013, the UN Special Rapporteur on the right to education Kishore Singh expressed the need to match access with quality in the post-millennium aspirations on the realization of the right to basic education.

[13] For a detailed discussion on the 4A approach to realization of the right to education see generally Katrina Tomasevski, *Removing obstacles in the way of the right to education*. Primers No. 1 (2001); Mieke Verheyde, "A commentary on the United Nations convention on the rights of the child, Article 28—Right to education," *Nijhoff* (2006); Chikezie Anyanwu and A. C. Onuora-Oguno, "Ten years of the AU protocol on the rights of women in Africa: An overview of the girl child access to basic education in Africa," available at www.equalitynow.org/sites/.../MaputoProtocol_JourneytoEquality.pdf (accessed 15 January 2018).

[14] UNESCO, "Nearly 30 million African children out of school," available at http://www.unesco.org/new/en/dakar/aboutthisoffice/singleview/news/nearly_30_million_african_children_out_of_school/#.UxCWpuOSy2U (accessed 23 December 2017).

[15] Mel Ainscow and Cesar, "Inclusive education ten years after Salamanca: Setting the agenda," *European Journal of Psychology of Education* (2006): 235.

Consequently, I argue that to enhance the rights of the African child especially CWD with particular focus on basic education, there is need to move beyond the nomenclature of special or inclusive education but rather guarantee quality in basic education for the African child. I discuss the concepts of special and inclusive education; the place of the Convention on the Rights of Persons with Disabilities (CRPD) and other global and regional human rights instruments.

4.2 Conceptual Framework: Unpacking Special and Inclusive Education

4.2.1 Special Education

The need for special education was conceived as CWD was perceived to have need for greater attention to ensure that they are able to benefit from school activities. In this respect, 'special education policies were articulated in terms of concern for the individual and the challenge of ensuring that individual needs are identified and met'.[16] Special education was therefore anticipated to be a deviation from the universal or general style of education a child who is assumed not to have any form of peculiarities would need. The emergence presumes the need that was existent in filling the gap of ensuring that CWD also accessed education. Thus, special education could be seen as 'special classes with a goal of avoiding conflict in universal education.'[17] The session of conflict envisaged here could be interpreted as the challenges of education in the mainstream sector with the obvious lack of expertise to provide dedicated support for CWD.

In Aristotle's choice of the children that deserved education, CWD was not included as it was seen as a waste of the resources of the state. Aristotle advanced that only those children who meet a certain intelligent quotient standard should be selected and educated to become guardians of the state.[18] Thus, the emergence of special education could be seen

[16] Seamus Hegarty, "International perspectives on special education reform," *European Journal of Special Needs Education* 13(1) (2006): 113.

[17] Kenneth A. Kavale and Steven R. Forness, *History, rhetoric, and reality analysis of the inclusive debate* (London: Sage, 2000): 280.

[18] James Bowen and Peter R. Hobson, *Theories of education studies of significant innovation in Western education thoughts* (Australia: Watson Ferhuson & Co., 1974), 8.

as a positive development in ensuring that education was not an exclusive preserve of the privileged in the society. The assumed achievement of special education is 'grounded on the achievements of people like Jeane-March Gaspard Itard and Anne Sullivan Macy',[19] the process of teaching children with some form of disability in isolation from other children led to the tag special education. It is therefore argued that the need to ensure that CWD was not excluded from accessing education informed the need to provide education to this category of persons in a special way.[20]

Accordingly, governments were compelled to facilitate the establishment of special schools with the responsibility of educating CWD among this category includes but not limited to hearing impaired, speech impaired, sight impaired and other forms of conditions affecting the conditionalities of learning.[21]

The history of special education encompasses some major trends: instructional and environmental paradigms.[22] As restated by Peters, the instructional paradigm speaks to the use of specialised instruments and devices in ensuring that education achieves its target to the child. The environmental paradigm is about the place in which education takes place. More often than not, special education takes place in an isolated school environment. The combination of the above elicits some form of criticisms. For instance, it is stated that some of the criticism has been justified, some unjustified[23]:

> Some criticisms brought to light ineffective practices, such as the inefficacy and inhumanity of relegating all persons with disabilities to institutions. Other criticisms were distractions with disastrous repercussions, such as

[19] See generally Michelle Theriault Messemer "General education teacher perceptions regarding inclusion of students with autism spectrum disorder," at http://udini.proquest.com/view/general-education-teacher-goid:520326624/ (accessed 19 February 2017).

[20] Devery R. Mock, Jennifer J. Jakubecy, and James M. Kauffman, "Special education—Current trends, preparation of teachers," available at http://education.stateuniversity.com/pages/2438/Special-Education.html (accessed 18 February 2017).

[21] See Article 3 of the Salamanca statement and framework for action on special needs education adopted by the world conference on special needs education: Access and quality, available at http://www.unesco.org/education/pdf/SALAMA_E.PDF (accessed 11 October 2017).

[22] Peters, 5–6.

[23] Osler Audrey and Starkey Hugh, *Changing citizenship: Democracy and inclusion in education* (London: Sage, 2005), 283.

> the singular focus on the importance of place while ignoring other inappropriate practices. The beginning of the twenty-first century found new criticisms being launched at special education. Some argue that the use of diagnostic labels is potentially stigmatizing to students, others that minority students are overrepresented in some disability categories, and still others that education of students with disabilities in special classes and schools, even pulling students out for instruction in resource classes, is akin to race-based segregation.

Challenges of discrimination and inequality are core issues that are discernible attributes of special education; in addition to this criticism is the fact that special education is further motivated by the social and medical perspectives. While the former focuses on the environmental challenges the latter is occupied with 'individual who needs fixing-either by therapy, medicine, surgery or special treatment'.[24] These approaches are perceived to encourage stigma, labelling and ultimately discrimination.

4.2.2 *Inclusive Education*

Inclusive education basically interpreted involves the 'movement seeking to create schools that meet the needs of all students by establishing learning communities for students with and without disabilities'.[25] The quest to move from special education to inclusive education was highlighted by UNESCO in 1994 in Salamanca when it stated that[26]:

> Special needs education is an issue of equal concern to countries…it has to form part of an overall education strategy and indeed of new social and economic policies. It calls for major reform of the ordinary school.

In Article 2, it reinforces the importance of embracing inclusive education when it provides that:

[24] Peters, "Inclusive education: An EFA strategy for all children," 8

[25] Kavale and Forness, *History, rhetoric, and reality analysis of the inclusive debate*, 279.

[26] "Salamanca statement and framework for action on special needs education," adopted by the world conference on special needs education: access and quality, available at http://www.unesco.org/education/pdf/SALAMA_E.PDF (accessed 11 October 2017).

We believe and proclaim that[27]:

- Every child has a fundamental right to education, and must be given the opportunity to achieve and maintain an acceptable level of learning;
- Every child has unique characteristics, interests, abilities and learning needs;
- Education systems should be designed and educational programmes implemented to take into account the wide diversity of these characteristics and needs;
- Those with special educational needs must have access to regular schools which should accommodate them within a child-centred pedagogy capable of meeting these needs;
- Regular schools with this inclusive orientation are the most effective means of combating discriminatory attitudes, creating welcoming communities, building an inclusive society and achieving education for all; moreover, they provide an effective education to the majority of children and improve efficiency and ultimately the cost-effectiveness of the entire education system.

The first impression that would be assumed from the above provision will be the abolishment of special schools. However, it is my opinion that there is need to have a conceptual understanding of the need for an inclusive education style and not just on the question of nomenclature.[28]

It is also equally important to underscore the point that inclusive education must not be seen as a mere integration of CWD in mainstream schools but rather the forming of a major philosophy of education for the child.[29] The philosophy of education as advocated is as it pertains to the quality in the content of education that the child receives in the school setting. The question of quality is to determine whether the education given either in a special or inclusive setting enhances the numeracy and literal abilities of the child empowering the child to be able to move towards self-empowerment and actualisation.

[27] *Salamanca statement and framework for action on special needs education* adopted by the world conference on special needs education: Access and quality, http://www.unesco.org/education/pdf/SALAMA_E.PDF (accessed 11 October 2017) emphasis supplied.

[28] See generally Lise Vislie, "From integration to inclusion: Focusing global trends and changes in the Western European Societies," *European Journal of Special Needs Education*, 18 (2003): 1. Vislie asks 'The main question is, of course, whether the new terminology means only a linguistic shift or a new agenda'. Importantly, this paper argues that the question is not that of nomenclature but towards and agenda of quality in basic education for African children especially CWD.

[29] Peters, "Inclusive education: An EFA strategy for all children," 9.

Consequently, inclusion as adapted and advanced is as conceptualised by Vislie[30]:
Inclusion *is not*:

- focusing on an individual or small group of pupils for whom the curriculum is adapted, different work is devised or support assistants are provided;
- about how to assimilate individual pupils with identified special educational needs into existing forms of schooling.

Inclusion *is*:

- a process (rather than a state), by which a school attempts to respond to all pupils as individuals;
- regards inclusion and exclusion as connected processes; schools developing more inclusive practices may need to consider both;
- emphasises the reconstructing of curricular provision in order to reach out to all pupils as individuals;
- emphasises overall school effectiveness;
- is of relevance to all phases and types of schools, possibly including special schools, since within any educational provision teachers face groups of students with diverse needs and are required to respond to this diversity.

This position, as advocated by Vislie, is very germane in that the components that are advocated in the inclusive setting can be attained within a mainstream setting or special setting. Thus, inclusive education must be rightly perceived to mean the pattern of ensuring that steps are taking to ensure that education of a child is achieved even in situations in which special support is required.

An important quality component advanced for inclusive education entails the capacity building of teachers to ensure that all forms of discriminatory or degrading attitudes are eliminated in relating to CWD.[31] In addition, it is important to enhance the role of teachers in delivery of

[30]Vislie, "From integration to inclusion: Focusing global trends and changes in the Western European Societies," 21.

[31]See generally Rose Richard, "Primary school teacher perceptions of the conditions required to include pupils with special educational needs," *Educational Review* 53(2) (2001): 147.

quality education devoid of any form of violations of the right in education of CWD. Invariably, the adoption of whatever nomenclature—inclusion or special education—should eclipse any negative attitudes not enhance stigma especially from the attitudes that teachers in the school setting adopt in their teaching approach of CWD.[32]

4.3 Legal and Policy Regime of Inclusive Education Applicable to Nigeria

The Nigerian Constitution of 1999 (as amended) provides for education in section 18. Education is advanced as mere fundamental objective of state principles and in some quarters is perceived as not demanding a positive responsibility from the state in ensuring the realisation of education. The Universal Basic Education Act of 2004 remains the major document that regulates the basis for the quest for the realisation of access to basic education in Nigeria. Presently, the National Policy of Education of 2013 is the policy document that stipulates in further details the aspiration of the nation's philosophy of education. Before further discussion of the challenges inherent in the above-mentioned legal and policy documents, it is important to reiterate briefly the importance of education especially as it pertains to the child.

With the provision of the right to education generally in the UDHR,[33] the International Covenant on Economic Social and Cultural Rights (ICESCR)[34] and the African Charter on Human and Peoples' Rights,[35] the need to ensure specific protection of child's rights led to the adoption of two important treaties globally and regionally for Africa. The Convention on the rights of the Child (CRC)[36] was adopted by the United Nations. Africa followed suite by adopting the African Charter on the Rights and Welfare of the Child (ACHRWC).[37] Aside the above instruments, UNESCO have also put in place several programmes and aspirations that will drive the realisation of the rights of the child generally and the right to basic education specifically.

[32] Jenny Corbett, "Inclusive education and school culture," *International Journal of Inclusive Education* 3(1) (1999): 53.

[33] *UDHR*, Article 26.

[34] *Covenant on Economic Social and Cultural Rights (CESCR)*, Articles 13 and 14.

[35] *African Charter on Human and Peoples Rights (ACHPR)*, Article 17.

[36] *Convention on the Rights of the Child (CRC)*, Article 28.

[37] *African Charter on Human Rights on the Welfare of the Child (ACHRWC)*, Article 11.

Notwithstanding the various provisions of the above-mentioned treaties, the need to protect the specific interest of persons suffering from disability became a front burner in the discus of international human rights law. The Convention on the Rights of People with Disability (CRPD) was adopted as a response and aptly so.[38] The CRPD strives to ensure equality among all individuals irrespective of the circumstances of their birth or physical conditions while advancing for inclusive rather than special education. The CRPD advocates for inclusive education in the realisation of the right to education of persons living with disabilities.[39] The rationale advanced for inclusive education is premised on the fact that CWD would not grow to live in a special world.

It is, however, argued that it can be gleaned from the General Comment No. 13, albeit in a broad sense that the quest of the CRPD is envisaged in the explanation of the committee. The GC provides that education must be accessible to every individual notwithstanding any form of challenge facing the individual. A broad interpretation of these provisions includes individuals living with disabilities or otherwise. However, the challenge that this portends is that the adoption of special education models by states in itself represents the desire towards the actualisation of the interpretation of the GC.

Stemming from the main challenge of discrimination faced by persons with disabilities and particularly CWD the provision of Article 24 became paramount thereby fuelling the current debate of inclusive or special education models in developing countries like Nigeria. Article 24 of the CRPD reads[40]:

2. In realising this right, States Parties shall ensure that:

a. Persons with disabilities are not excluded from the general education system on the basis of disability, and that children with disabilities are not excluded from free and compulsory primary education, or from secondary education, on the basis of disability;
b. Persons with disabilities can access an inclusive, quality and free primary education and secondary education on an equal basis with others in the communities in which they live;

[38] http://www.un.org/disabilities/convention/signature.shtml (last accessed 21 November 2017).

[39] *Convention on the Rights of People with Disability (CRPD)*, Article 24.

[40] *CRPD*, Article 2.

c. Reasonable accommodation of the individual's requirements is provided;
d. Persons with disabilities receive the support required, within the general education system, to facilitate their effective education;
e. Effective individualised support measures are provided in environments that maximise academic and social development, consistent with the goal of full inclusion.

The above provisions seek to ensure that basic education is provided firstly on the basis that it does not exclude any individual based on their physical or mental inability. Consequently, it is based on this provision that the call for the abolition of special education models which is the norm in most African societies and a call for an inclusive model is hinged.

Nigeria is a state party to the above-mentioned treaties and therefore has obligation in ensuring that the realisation of basic education for every child is attainable. However, as already stated, Nigeria remains at the lower wrung of the ladder of poor statistics in the number of out of school children and poor completion rates. These statistics in my opinion most likely does not include CWD.

However, the question of quality remains elusive with challenges of access, availability, adaptability and well-trained teachers. The question therefore is 'Should Nigeria embrace the concept of inclusive education or thrive towards the realisation of quality in the present special education setup?' The process of embracing inclusive education literally will imply that all special schools are shut down or at least pass through the phase of integration. Also, the enactment of policy document to abolish the existence of special schools and viewing them as inclusive schools is another possible process. A third process is that of the merging of the already existing mainstream schools and admitting CWD into the fold in other to view them as special. It is, however, argued that none of the possible processes above have the potentials of guaranteeing quality within context especially as pertains to the challenges of adaptability and quality of human resources in terms of teachers to provide specific support for CWD.

The obvious reason for the inability of the processes above to drive quality is occasioned by virtue of the paucity of legal or policy framework on the needs of CWD in the education sphere. The UBE Act provides generally for the realisation of education for each individual and does not take into cognisance the needs of persons living with disabilities. Beyond the basic education level, secondary and higher education are fraught with scores of persons living with disabilities that lack any form of support that will lead to the realisation of the aims of education in their individual situations.

On the policy front, the NPE of Nigeria[41] does not make specific mention of the education of persons with disabilities or inclusive education but advances the urgency of ensuring that 'education is to be qualitative, comprehensive, functional and relevant to the needs of the society.'[42] An inference from the above provisions could encompass the inclusive education model as it concerns the issue of comprehensiveness and functionality. In this wise, it is advocated that basic education whether in a special or inclusive model must achieve the ultimate goal of being individual focused and quality laden for the overall good of the state.

The NPE in section 7 provides for special needs education and defines same as 'customised educational programme, designed to meet the unique needs of persons with special needs that the general education programme cannot carter for'. This provision is, however, contradicted when it further provides that 'the aims of special needs education are to provide access to education for all persons, in an inclusive setting…'.[43] The failure of the provisions of the NPE in enhancing the realisation of the right to basic education in Nigeria is blamed on the lack of legal basis for such realisation of the right to basic education of CWD.[44] According to Eleweke, 'educational and other services for individuals with disabilities in Nigeria are in shambles and in some places had collapsed altogether'.[45]

It is therefore my concern that the focus should not be wholly on the legislative impact of specific legislation on issues concerning people with disability but generally on the impact of the legislature on enhancing the realisation of quality basic education. In aspiring towards the

[41] Yaba Lagos; Nigerian Educational Research and Development Council (NERDC) Press, 6th edition, 2013.

[42] *Nigeria Policy on education NPE*, Article 3 (e).

[43] *NPE*, Article 119.

[44] Eleweke C. Jonah, "The need for mandatory legislations to enhance services to people with disabilities in Nigeria," *Disability & Society* 14(2) (1999): 229.

[45] Eleweke, "The need for mandatory legislations to enhance services to people with disabilities in Nigeria," 229.

achievement of quality in the education sector, several factors must play combined roles. Infrastructural and institutional roles are key components of quality.

An important factor to consider in the question of the realisation of education of CWD is to ensure that access, availability and adaptability are enhanced.[46] In the first instance, whether in special or inclusive school system, access must be ensured. This deals with the provision of support for children either physically challenged or otherwise.

The availability concept must ensure that opportunity and sufficiency of school must take care of the need of CWD.[47]

The question of ability of teachers who are not trained and lack skills to assist CWD looms large and raises issues of economic urgency for states.[48] The challenge therefore places some obligation on developed countries to provide both technical and financial support to African states towards ensuring that education is inclusive.[49] The effect of this is that a consensus on the extent of inclusion remains a major task as to the ambit to which it should be implemented[50] in terms of the provision of Article 24 of CRPD.

[46] According to Ajuwon 'Often, it is gratifying that where school and community environments can be made physically and programmatically accessible, children and youth with physical disabilities can function more effectively than would otherwise be the case. It is also apparent that such modifications to the environment often enable others who do not have disabilities to access their environment even more readily'. See generally Paul M. Ajuwon, "Inclusive education for students with disabilities in Nigeria: Benefits, challenges and policy implications," *International Journal of Special Education* 23(3) (2008): 11.

[47] For a brief discuss on the issues of access to education generally and inclusive education, see generally, Lipsky Dorothy Kerzner, "Are we there yet?" *Learning Disability Quarterly* (2005): 2.

[48] Kavale and Forness, *History, rhetoric, and reality analysis of the inclusive debate*, 279.

[49] Vislie, "From integration to inclusion: Focusing global trends and changes in the Western European Societies," 21. This on its own portends some challenges as the challenge of embracing further educational systems not fashioned in line with African philosophies is challenging. For arguments on this see generally Michello Hansungule and Azubike C. Onuora-Oguno, "African perspective of education: A catalyst for the desired Africa of tomorrow?" Presented at the Thabo Mbeki Advanced Leadership Institute August 2013.

[50] Ainscow and Cesar, "Inclusive education ten years after Salamanca: Setting the agenda," 231.

4.4 The Quality Challenge in Education Special and Mainstream

The challenges facing education are enormous.[51] However, in terms of quality inadequate preparation, poor and non-adaptable infrastructure and lack of qualified teachers are of major concerns.[52] It is my view that CWD faces greater challenges because of their more vulnerable position in the society and also because of the societal discriminatory stance and lack of facilities to accommodate them.[53]

In addition, the inability of teachers to effectively provide support for the CWD in the special education institutions continues to loom large.[54] The absence of teachers skilled in the sign language, use of brails and lack of audio-visual supports for children in this category remain un-tackled challenges. According to Eleri, 'general education teachers did not always recognize these disabilities, and even if they did, they might not have had the tools to effectively help the students in the general classroom setting'.[55] In the mainstream education, the issue of poor remuneration of teachers continues to elicit incessant strike actions from teachers causing pupils to be out of school for very long periods in an academic calendar.[56]

[51]The greatest challenge facing education in Nigeria presently is the issue of lack of security and guarantee of lives of students because of the attacks of the *Boko Haram* sect in Nigeria. Thousands of lives have been lost and infrastructure burnt down in the continued and sustained rejection of what the sect has termed Western education. The impact of this is that parents are reluctant to send their children to schools anymore and even teachers scared to access schools as they remain targets.

[52]Supo Jegede and Perpetua I. Ememe, "The inclusiveness of the Universal Basic Education (UBE) Scheme," *Nigeria Journal of Education, Health and Technology Research (NJEHETR)* 1(2) (2011): 128.

[53]Shavaun Wall, Filip Loncke, and Nancy Smith, "Collaborative training for special education and rehabilitation services in the developing world," 2–4, http://faculty.cua.edu/smithd/asdeg/journalarticle.pdf (accessed 3 March 2017).

[54]The author has had the opportunity to visit some special schools in Nigeria like the School for the Disabled in Ozubulu, Anambra State, observations show that most teachers are not skilled in providing efficient support for the pupils under their care.

[55]N. O. E. Eleri, "Teaching effectiveness in elements of special education in NCE awarding institutions in Nigeria: Influence of teacher qualification and experience," *IOSR Journal of Research and Method in Education* 2(2) (2013): 7.

[56]In Anambra State, during the era of Dr. Mbadinuju Primary schools were shut down for 11 months. This ensured that there was no academic activity in the state for a whole session. In late 2013, primary school teachers in Benue State of Nigeria were on strike affecting academic activities. For more insight into the challenge of strike in Nigeria basic education sector see generally "Nigerian education in crisis," available at

Another core challenge facing the education of CWD is that of labelling and discrimination as previously examined. It is reiterated that it is not only CWD that are discriminated against but also children from minority groups and mean backgrounds.[57]

4.5 Inclusive or Special: Moving Beyond Nomenclature Embracing Quality

The huge criticism of special education is grounded on the 'us and them' nomenclature that is argued to create room for definite discrimination and unequal treatment.[58] 'Special' is seen as connoting the treatment of CWD because of the peculiar circumstance, which is seen as ultimately discriminatory and derogatory. It must, however, be appreciated that the historical emergence of the concept of special education was to ensure that every individual has access to education.

The conflict between special and inclusive education stems from the perception that the question of inclusion will alter the basis of education generally. However, it is my opinion that this is necessarily not the case. This is because inclusive education remains a highly contested concept despite the fact that beyond the question of nomenclature it is a realisable agenda. It is underscored that[59]:

> Inclusive education is a highly visible yet contentious notion in contemporary education reform because of conceptual, historical, and pragmatic reasons. From a conceptual perspective, the definition of inclusion is still debated, ranging from physical placement in general education classrooms to the <u>transformation of entire educational systems</u>.[60]

http://educationincrisis.net/country-profiles/africa/item/558-nigeria (accessed 3 March 2017); Nigeria: Teachers' strike: House orders Mbadinuju to pay teachers, available at http://allafrica.com/stories/200202110616.html (accessed 3 March 2017); Teachers' strike: Govt/Labour relations in Federalism, available at http://www.thenationonlineng.net/archive2/tblnews_Detail.php?id=54695 (accessed 3 March 2017).

[57] Olayi James Eburikure, "Overcoming the challenges of inclusive education in Nigeria: a focus on South-South geopolitical zone," *Journal of Exceptional People* 2(3) (2013):10.

[58] Kavale and Forness, *History, rhetoric, and reality analysis of the inclusive debate*, 3.

[59] Alfredo J. Artiles, Elizabeth B. Kozleski, et al., "Learning in inclusive education research: Re-mediating theory and methods with a transformative agenda," *Review of Research in Education 30 Special Issue on Rethinking Learning: What Counts as Learning and What Learning Counts* (2006): 65.

[60] Emphasis provided, this is to provide the understanding that rather than dwell on nomenclature, the need for a transformation towards quality is imperative.

Furthermore, in understanding inclusion, it is advanced that the perspective of educating CWD in mainstream education only in itself advances the challenge of concentrating on the particular disability suffered.[61] Thus, capturing a wider scope of inclusive education, it must be reiterated that inclusions goes beyond education of just persons with disabilities but also ensuring the elimination of all forms of clogs that may deter any individual from realising access to basic education in terms of minorities, languages and even cultures.[62]

In view of a broader interpretation of the notion of inclusive, it is opined that special education itself can provide a basis for quality if a progressive model of ensuring that the school system is empowered to eliminate all forms of inequalities are pursued vigorously.[63]

This approach is canvassed in line with the Education For All (EFA). The EFA seeks to ensure that each individual is not the denied the benefit of accessing quality basic education; the EFA[64]:

> represents an international commitment to ensure that every child and adult receives basic education of good quality. This commitment is based both on a human rights perspective and on the generally held belief that education is central to individual well-being and national development.

Importantly, it must be noted that, whether inclusion or special, there is an important need to ensure that the program design and curriculum content must reflect the need of the child to which it is meant to educate.[65] An impact on the style of education adopted is seen from the attitude of the teacher who is meant to disseminate information and educate

[61] Ainscow and Cesar, "Inclusive education ten years after Salamanca: Setting the agenda," 233.

[62] See generally Singh Kishore and Moumne Rolla, "Inclusive dimension to the right to education: Normative basis" (2008) prepared by the Eighth and Ninth Meetings of the Joint Expert group UNESCO (CR)/ECOSOC (CESCR) on the monitoring of the right to education.

[63] Alvaro Marchesi, "International perspectives on special education reform," *European Journal of Special Needs Education* 13(1) (1998): 119.

[64] Susie Miles and Nidhi Singal, "The education for all and inclusive education debate: conflict, contradiction or opportunity?" *International Journal of Inclusive Education* (2010): 3. The emphasis supplied goes to underscore the point that beyond the nomenclature that could be adopted in education a CWD quality is paramount.

[65] Kavale and Forness, *History, rhetoric, and reality analysis of the inclusive debate*, 283.

the child. It is essential that teacher training curriculum must include human rights education especially in the light of regard for dignity and equality. This way, any form of discrimination that is attendant to special education will be eliminated.[66]

The underlying factor in inclusive education must commence on the basis that 'classroom teachers have basic knowledge and understanding about the needs of different learners; teaching techniques'[67] and 'curriculum strategies'.[68] Aside the role of the teachers and pupils, there is a need to also inculcate an inclusive mentality in the society so as to encourage and build a healthy learning environment described as 'a society open and accessible to all'.[69]

The argument that CWD requires special attention has been found in some circumstance not to be true as CWD with support in mainstream school settings showed traces of greater performance.[70] Thus, the argument of preservationists[71] in ensuring the retention of the special education nomenclature is advocated in this paper to be mere advancement of academic agenda as quality in the school space should be paramount.

It is therefore important to ensure that negative attitudes towards CWD must be eliminated by continued advocacy by all stakeholders involved in ensuring the realisation of the right to basic education.[72]

[66] Kavale and Forness, *History, rhetoric, and reality analysis of the inclusive debate*, 283.

[67] For an insight into the attitude of teachers to education of CWD see generally Olufemi Aremu, O. A. Fakolade, et al., "Attitude of teachers towards the inclusion of special needs children in general education classroom: the case of teachers in some selected schools in Nigeria," *International Electronic Journal of Elementary Education* (2009).

[68] "Teacher education for inclusion International Literature Review European Agency for development in special needs," available at http://www.european-agency.org/sites/default/files/te4i-international-literature-review_TE4I-Literature-Review.pdf (accessed 19 February 2017).

[69] Sarah D. Phillips, "EU disability policy and implications of EU accession for disability rights in education and employment in Bulgaria, Romania, Croatia, and the Former Yugoslav Republic of Macedonia," *Journal of Disability Policy Studies* (2011), http://dps.sagepub.com/content/22/4/208 (accessed 11 October 2017).

[70] Artiles and Kozleski, "Learning in inclusive education research: Re-mediating theory and methods with a transformative agenda," 65.

[71] Artiles and Kozleski, "Learning in inclusive education research: Re-mediating theory and methods with a transformative agenda," 73.

[72] Hegarty, "International perspectives on special education reform," 114.

4.6 Conclusions

The first point as gleaned from the above discussion is the fact that an obvious 'benefits to the inclusive education paradigm, is that children are more likely to learn social skills in an environment that approximates to normal conditions of growth and development'.[73]

It has also been argued that the concept of inclusion does not necessary mean inclusive, advancing this notion it is opined that there is the need to reconceptualise the definition of the inclusive notion. This argument conforms to my position that the process of inclusion must be followed with caution as it is not one that can be embraced in a hurry. It is therefore one that must be followed with a gradual guarantee of quality in the educational structure that is presently in place.[74]

An identified merit of special education system is seen from the fact that the chances of CWD suffering discriminatory language in the school space are limited as opposed to the chances in the inclusive education set-up. A way around this challenge will therefore mean that as with teachers; pupils will of necessity be reoriented to accommodate CWD.[75]

It is also noted that special education entails some key features, among which were the responsibility placed on publicly funded schools to ensure it had facilities to care for children with disabilities; the right to learn and the identification of a defined process for the learning to take place.[76] However, with the provision of Article 24 of the CRPD, inclusive education is currently advocated. Importantly, ensuring that the education delivered meets the quality threshold as should be the preoccupation of human rights law is paramount.

[73] Ajuwon, "Inclusive education for students with disabilities in Nigeria: Benefits, challenges and policy implications," 11.

[74] Mel Ainscow, Peter Farrell, et al., "Effective practice in inclusion and in special and mainstream schools working together," Department for Education Research Brief No. 91, Centre for Educational Needs, University of Manchester 4 (1999).

[75] Kavale and Forness, *History, rhetoric, and reality analysis of the inclusive debate*, 284.

[76] Marvin A. Zuker, *Education Law* (Ontario: Carswell, 2002): 281.

Finally, it is concluded that to achieve quality, rights in education must be pursued vigorously. Education must therefore be treated not just as a mere objective but a fundamental right. The numerous challenges that confront realisation of education also loom large and must thus be eliminated especially as it affects the education of CWD.[77]

[77] For an Insight into the Challenges of the Realization of Special Education in Nigeria see Festus E. Obiakor, "Special education reform in Nigeria: Prospects and challenges," *European Journal of Special Needs Education* (2008): 51.

CHAPTER 5

African Perspective of Education: A Catalyst for the Desired Africa of Tomorrow?

5.1 Introduction

Education as I have already posited is a process that prepares an individual to be able to interact with his society positively so as to achieve both individual and communal goals. Education can be viewed in three broad ways; it is either formal, non-formal or informal. The formal education style refers largely to the organised education system which takes place within the ambit of educational institutions and structures, while the informal is that style of education that makes learning possible outside of an organised system, occurring in families, religious groups and peer groups.[1] The importance to rethink the concept of education based on an African paradigm is 'founded on the perception that the overall character of much of educational theory and practice in Africa is overwhelmingly either European or Eurocentric'.[2]

It has been argued in some quarters that the African education system lacked authenticity and even non-existent. This is further advanced on the perception that 'to the Europeans there was no education in

[1] Kisanji Jospeh, "'Culture and disability': An analysis of inclusive education based on African folklore," Paper presented at the International Expert Meeting and Symposium on Local Concepts and Beliefs of Disability in Different Cultures, Bonn, Germany, 21–24 May 1998.

[2] P. Higgs, "African philosophy and the transformation of educational discourse in South Africa," *Journal of Education* 30 (2003): 5–22.

A. C. Onuora-Oguno, *Development and the Right to Education in Africa*,
https://doi.org/10.1007/978-3-319-90335-4_5

Africa, as they claimed that African education was a restatement of her primitive culture that was incapable of yielding a tangible framework of theories and philosophies'.[3] The above position is grossly untrue as several African scholars have re-echoed the existence and thriving of African educational system long before the advent of the European through their colonial conquest.[4]

Adeyemi recounts that 'the type of education prevalent in Africa before the coming of Western civilisation was generally known as African traditional education or indigenous education of the various communities'.[5] In addition to Adeyemi's view, the concept of education in the traditional African society was beyond the Western concept of classroom education. The claim that education and its philosophy are alien to African because they depended on an unwritten culture can also be refuted as even Socrates did not write majority of his philosophies.[6]

Authors like Rodney have advanced reasons on how Europe underdeveloped Africa[7]; however, the search for a true solution for African woes needs to be found in the re-conceptualisation of various theories that have been accorded to colonial thoughts. Consequently, if education is a vehicle through which an individual receives holistic training to serve the society as well as individual needs towards development, then it becomes paramount to examine education from an African paradigm. With the above in mind, I examine education from an African concept with a view of determining whether it is a possible catalyst for the desired Africa of tomorrow?

[3] Amimo C. Adhiambo, "The characteristics and impact of African traditional education," last modified 4 April 2014, http://www.articlesbase.com/childhood-education-articles/.

[4] Babs Fafunwa, *History of education in Nigeria* (London: George Allen and Unwin, 1974); Walima T. Kalusa, "Indigenous education in pre-colonial Africa," in H. T. Msango, E. C. Mumba, and A. L. Sikwibele (eds), *Selected topics in philosophy and education* (Lusaka: University of Zambia), 24–31 as cited in https://researchspace.ukzn.ac.za/bitstream/handle/10413/13878/Akpan_Okon_%20Louis_2015.pdf?sequence=1&isAllowed=y (accessed 27 December 2017).

[5] M. B. Adeyemi, "Social studies in Nigeria," in M. B. Adeyemi (ed), *Social studies in African education* (Gaborone: Pyramid Publishing, 2000), 247–266.

[6] H. Odera Oruka (eds), *Sage philosophy: Indigenous thinkers and modern debate on African philosophy* (Leiden: J Brill, 1990).

[7] Rodney Walter, *How Europe underdeveloped Africa* (London: Bogle- L'ouverture, 2000).

5.2 Education an African Concept?

As already restated in the introduction, Africans had a style of education that was peculiar to it. Education according to Nduka is the means through which Africans transmitted their culture from generation to generation.[8] Nwonwu describes education as the entrenchment of the African indigenous knowledge that was exemplified in all spheres of the existence ranging from medicine, agriculture and even economics.[9] The import of the above assertions is that pre-colonial Africa had the informal, non-formal and formal systems of education in existence.

The teaching of life long skills and techniques was the preoccupation of the various systems. For instance, prior to marriage the girl child was sent to a formal learning set-up where she was taught the act of home-making. The same would also be said of the boy child who learnt several handicrafts and skills through mentorship. The informal learning was grounded in observation in the various activities and folklore systems in Africa. These represented the informal set-up where morals and humanness were thought as lifelong virtues.

However, the advent of the colonial masters discredited the education system known to Africa by presenting a style of education which was largely orchestrated towards ensuring the perpetration of colonial administration.[10] For instance in Nigeria, the British set up two styles of education for the Northern Province and the Colonies of Lagos and Southern Nigeria.[11] The difference in the perception of education from the colonial lenses and that of African leads to a conclusion that education in the African context was not the precursor of a few but a union of the home and the community. Serequeberhan is of the view that[12];

> Traditional Africa is a place of philosophical unanimity allowing no room whatsoever for a Socrates or Descartes. No indigenous African person had

[8] Nduka Otonti, *Western education and the Nigeria cultural background* (London: Oxford University Press, 1964).

[9] Francis O. C. Nwonwu, *Indigenous knowledge systems in Igbo traditional agriculture* (USA: Author House, 2011).

[10] A. K. Tiberondwa, *Missionary teachers agents of colonialism: A study of their activities in Uganda, 1877–1925* (Lusaka: Kenneth Kaunda Foundation, 1978).

[11] Nigerian Ordinance No. 11 1927.

[12] Tsenay Serequeberhan, *African philosophy: The essential readings* (Paragon House, 1991).

> the frame of mind let alone the inclination to detach himself (herself) from the prevailing established beliefs…

According to an African proverb: ‘one person gives birth to a child but one person does not train a child’.[13] In effect, education in the African system had an inbuilt revalidation system of everyone in the community been an examiner of the attitude and behaviour of a child. Within the African human rights systems, education is described from a perspective which takes the community into deep consideration. For instance, Article 11 of the African Charter on the Rights and Welfare of the Child (ACRWC) provides for the core components of African education. It provides:

1. Every child shall have the right to an education.
2. The education of the child shall be directed to:
   (a) the promotion and development of the child’s personality, talents and mental and physical abilities to their fullest potential;
   (b) fostering respect for human rights and fundamental freedoms with particular reference to those set out in the provisions of various African instruments on human and peoples’ rights and international human rights declarations and conventions;
   (c) the preservation and strengthening of positive African morals, traditional values and cultures;
   (d) the preparation of the child for responsible life in a free society, in the spirit of understanding tolerance, dialogue, mutual respect and friendship among all peoples ethnic, tribal and religious groups;
   (e) the preservation of national independence and territorial integrity;
   (f) the promotion and achievements of African Unity and Solidarity;
   (g) the development of respect for the environment and natural resources;
   (h) the promotion of the child’s understanding of primary health care.

[13] Igbo-Eastern Nigerian traditional proverb.

The provision encompasses the fact that the African child most be educated with one purpose, which is to give value to others and the community. This concept is today popularly known as the *Ubuntu* philosophy.[14] A reflection on the provision of the African Children's Charter provision shows the content of the African indigenous style of education; a few of which I discuss below.

5.2.1 *Communalism*

The village square and folklore set-up in Africa was an informal set-up where African indigenous knowledge was hatched and transmitted from generation to generation.[15] During these periods, heroics and means of achieving them were freely thought to everyone present.[16] This represented the fact that no one in African traditional society had the prerogative of existing alone. Jekayinfa reiterates that in communal hunting expedition and farming laid the bond of everyone learning from one another and fostering the oneness of the community rather than otherwise.[17] Aside the learning of skills, economics also grew within the African educational sphere. The *isusu* which represent the thrift society style of today also grew in the African indigenous knowledge system; this was aimed towards assistance and support of family units

5.2.2 *Self-Development for the Good of the People*

The African system of education was laden with techniques of letting the learner have hands on task experience. However, this characteristic

[14] R. H. Bel, *Understanding African philosophy: A cross-cultural approach to classical and contemporary issues* (New York: Routledge); M. B. Ramose, *African philosophy through Ubuntu* (Indian University, 2008).

[15] Chinua Achebe, *There was a country: A personal history of Biafra* (Penguin Press); Ladislaus Semali, "Community as classroom: Dilemmas of valuing African indigenous literacy in education," (1999), http://download.springer.com/static/pdf/500/art%253A10.1023%252FA%253A1003859023590.pdf?auth66=1396781401_6487a0f5e-6f8502a593ae50090baa35e&ext=.pdf (accessed 30 June 2017).

[16] Nnamdi C. Onuora-Oguno and Azubike C. Onuora-Oguno "Uncensor the minstrel, uncage human rights—A case for the actualization of human rights through music genre in Igboland—Nigeria," *Centrepoint Journal of Humanities* 16(1) (2013): 41–60.

[17] Alice A. Jekayinfa, "Indigenous African education," in J. O. Abiri and A. Alice Jekayinfa (eds), *Perspective on the history of education in Nigeria* (Ilorin: Bamitex, 2010).

of the education system was not done for the parochial importance of the individual but rather that of the effective contribution to the community.[18] In most communities, individual had the opportunity of showcasing their talents and others learnt from them.

5.2.3 Moral Content

No individual in African traditional set-up was tutored as a freethinker. This simply implies that within the formal and informal set-up, there was a place for the entrenchment of morals and respect. This is argued ensured that the popular African spirit grew in leaps and bounds because everyone had an incline into the sense of unity and the Supreme Being that orchestrated the fate of man.[19] In Summary, Africa had a highly entrenched system of education which was value laden and prepared its people towards a gradual development. This should have possibly ushered Africa into its 'light' had it not been distorted by the parochial nature of 'western education' pattern.

A major criticism of African concept of education remain its assumed perpetration of cultural practices that were described as been contrary to public policy, morals and good conscience; entrenchment of gender inequality and inability to lead to a more meaningful engagement on the political economy of the present time.[20] While the above criticisms are not ignored, it is contended that new initiatives within the African sphere were sufficient to have allowed a paradigm shift towards enhanced respect and development. The perceived shortfalls were also not peculiar to Africa alone. The pattern of regard for the male child was also one that was captured in the philosophies of Aristotle and Plato.[21]

[18] Ladislaus.

[19] M. B. Adeyemi and A. A. Adeyinka, "The principles and content of African traditional education," *Educational Philosophy and Theory* 35(4) (2003): 425–440; Ikenga Oraegbunam, "The principles and practice of justice in traditional Igbo jurisprudence," (2009), www.ajol.info/index.php/og/article/viewFile/52335/40960 (accessed 23 December 2017).

[20] Martins O. Ejidike, "Human rights in the cultural traditions and social practice of the Igbo of South-Eastern Nigeria," *Journal of African Law* 43(1) (1999): 7–98.

[21] J. Bowen and P. R. Hobson, *Theories of education studies of significant innovation in western education thoughts* (Watson Ferhuson & Co, 1974).

Consequently, the deficiency that is possibly attributed to the African style of education was one that could have been resolved internally.[22] It was based on the perceived weakness that the colonial powers bridged a viable pattern that they found in Africa and completely eroded the qualities of self-worth and dignity of the African by wholly introducing a different style and concept of education. In the following section, the impact of the colonial concept of education is examined.

5.3 Colonial Concept of Education—Salvaging or Destroying African Growth?

The advent of colonial education system was much grounded in Plato's philosophy that the paramount aim of 'education is to turn the soul in the right direction and save it from a life of self-deceit and delusion'.[23] This view is reinforced by the assimilation theory of the French that ensured that educational standards in Africa were at parallel with that in France.[24] The British educational system that was brought to Africa by the early missionaries was no different as it provided only the knowledge necessary for the Crown to get base administrative support in its colonial conquest. In Clignet's view, the parochial nature of western education situation in Africa changed, with more exposure coming from a few African leaders that recognised the disparity in quality of education available in the various colonies. This claim finds support in the various commission reports set up by the colonial governments—especially that sponsored by African Slaves in the Americas.

At best, the Western concept of education laid emphasis on the individual rather than the community. This position is buttressed by the thinking that the extended family concept which is characteristic

[22] Considering the fact that Africans had a well internal mechanism of conflict resolution, it is the view of the authors that whatever deficiencies that were existent in the African system would have gradually been resolved and made way for better patterns.

[23] Olusegun Akinbote, "Childhood education in traditional African societies," http://www.nou.edu.ng/NOUN_OCL/pdf/EDUs/ECE%20110%20CHILDHOOD%20EDUCATION%20IN%20AFRICAN%20TRADITION.pdf (accessed 23 December 2017).

[24] Remi Clignet, "The legacy of assimilation in West African educational systems: Its meaning and ambiguities," *Comparative Education Review* 12(1) (1968): 57–67, The University of Chicago Press on behalf of the Comparative and International Education Society, http://www.jstor.org/stable/pdfplus/1186902.pdf?acceptTC=true&jpdConfirm=true (accessed 20 December 2017).

of the African customary system is not existent in the Western society. Consequently, the African system of education prepared the educated African to be able to take care of his community ensuring its development. Not elevating his individual need above that of the community, but the situation existent today is that 'Western individuality is eating deep into African societies'.[25]

Consequently, I argue that the presumption that the educational activities that existed in African were primitive as the colonial conquest foisted on us was never real. The intellectual capacities of African civilisation as shrouded in the early civilisation cultures of Egypt, Mali and the Benin kingdoms attest to this.[26] The argument that the African educational system is 'meagre and intellectually insufficient',[27] is untrue. One can then argue that the seeming difference in the ideology of the African conception of education and that of the West ushered Africa into a large part of the quagmire Africa is enmeshed in today. In this light, I am of the strong view that a change to the African philosophy and targets of education by colonial entry meant an erosion of the ***ubuntu*** nature of African education. This position is also supported by scholars like Olufowobi who opines that the colonial introduction of their style of education was laden with 'individualistic ethos as against the communalistic lifestyle of Africa'.[28]

In addition, the concept from the Western education style was one that was set out to subjugate the learning and cognitive development of the African. It ensured that Africans were treated as second-class citizens. Rodney captures it succinctly when he posited that:

[25] S. A. Omotoso, "Education and emancipation—An African philosophical perspective," *The Journal of Pan African Studies* 3(9) (2010): 222–231.

[26] H. Jacob, L. Carruthersand, and C. Harri (eds), *African history project, the preliminary challenge*; M. P. Philip and Y. Kwesi, 2004. *African folklore: An encyclopedia* (New York: Routledge, 1997).

[27] John K. Marah, "The virtues and challenges in traditional African education," *The Journal of Pan African Studies* 1(4) (2006): 15–24, http://www.jpanafrican.com/docs/vol1no4/VirtuesAndChallengesTraditionalAfricanEducation_JPASvol1no4.pdf (accessed 20 December 2017).

[28] F. O. Olufowobi, "Effect of traditional African education system on modern vocational training in Nigeria in Ouill pen," *A Journal of Communication, Issues and Events* (5) (2006).

> ... Colonial schooling was education for subordination, exploitation; the creation of mental confusion and the development of underdevelopment'... African society has a population who are 'illiterates' as a result of cultural diffusion established by the colonial imposition...

This situation I opine forms the bedrock for the corrupt nature of African societies, where leaders are now more self-centred than people centred, occasioning the continents' struggles of redefining its developmental challenges.

5.4 Impact of African Style Education on Rule of Law, Governance and Development

As already stated, African states have in most situations continued to rue the negative effects of colonial conquest. It is, however, important that an end to this position be adopted with an inward examination and attempt to fashion a way forward for the Africa of our dreams. It thus remains incontrovertible that from the beginning of post-colonial rule in Africa, there remains a retarded quest towards positive development in the continent.[29] The dearth of rule of law and good governance in the recent past remains the bane of Africa developmental issues and not that of colonial conquest. Imperatively, a brief understanding of the synergy between the trinity is paramount to enable us have a better grasp of the impact an African conceptualisation of education would have in aiding the realisation of the African development.

5.4.1 Rule of Law

The rule of law is that situation in which every society follows the dictates of the law written and unwritten. It goes to speak that no one has the privilege of acting outside the ambit allowed by the law. Every society therefore is meant to operate under the prescribed modus and

[29] Azubike C. Onuora-Oguno, "Nigeria nation at a cross road: Search for democracy amidst the Militarization challenges," *Bayero Journal of International Law and Jurisprudence* 1(1) (2016): 74–100, Published by Department of Jurisprudence and International Law, Faculty of Law, Bayero University, Kano.

maintaining the equilibrium of the state.[30] The concept of the rule of law has some cultural implication, as every society had an inherent system of following cultural norms and practices that ensures its harmonious existence. Thus, in the African society, it was part of the educational curriculum to teach people respect for elders and adherence for cultural norms. A failure to adhere to the laid-down norms attracted penalties as was already established. Some of these punishments included isolation from the society and naming and shaming.

5.4.2 Good Governance

Governance refers to the situation where people in the position of leadership manage the resources of a nation, or community for the greater good of the people.[31] Consequently, good governance suggests a positive management of the available resources for the common good of the people. This concept of governance and good governance does not suggest that the term is a straightforward concept devoid of ambiguity. This is so because the basis of ascertaining the components of good governance is not certain.[32] However, I adopt the concept of good governance as that style of governance in which the leadership is transparent, efficient and accountable. The African Charter on Democracy, Elections and Good Governance identifies accountability and transparency as major component of good governance in States (African Charter). This therefore to my mind is all encapsulated within the ambit of education within the African context.

The African style of education as has been enunciated is laden with transparency and accountability. The well-entrenched concepts of separation of power in Africa reflected in the education concept ensure that learners were educated in line with knowing that they did not possess monopoly of both power and knowledge. The bearers of knowledge in

[30] Antonin Scalia, "The rule of law as a law of rules," *University of Chicago Law Review* 56(4) (1989): 1175–1188; N. L. Amir, G. Chanan, and H. S. Shalom, "Culture rules: The foundations of the rule of law and other norms of governance," *Journal of Comparative Economics* 35(4) (2007): 659–688.

[31] Santisa Carlos, "Good governance and aid effectiveness: The world bank and conditionality" (2001), http://www.sti.ch/fileadmin/user_upload/Pdfs/swap/swap108.pdf (accessed 18 November 2017).

[32] Ved P. Nanda, "The 'good governance' concept revisited," *The Annals of the American Academy of Political and Social Science* 603(1) (2006): 269–283.

the African system therefore took pride in the number of scholars that have mentored and grown to manage the affairs of their own communities. A cross-fertilisation of learning in the fields of economics, traditional medicine and artistry ensured that emissaries were sent from across communities to travel far and near to acquire knowledge for the protection, guidance and enhancement of their various communities.

Hinged on the above propositions, I argue that the African concept of education was laden with the concepts of the respect for the rule of law and norms and also with components of good governance. I now explore further merits that abound in the African system and concept of education.

5.5 African Concept of Education—Any Merits?

The inherent positives in the African style of education find a leaning on the fact that in Africa we are made to pass through various stages of education from cradle to grave. Through the process, we learn not just from communal experiences but also from individual encounters.[33] Interestingly, across African cultures, every child was exposed to intellectual growth, physical strength and respect for one another. All of these acts are found in traditional African histories of both arts and literary works that existed before the advent of the colonial masters.

The African concept of education was tailored in such a way that each individual learnt not just a particular skill but also got inspiration from other fields to enable him have a complete perception of the society as a whole. Consequently, to be a good builder, an individual was to have experiences in forestry related matters, likewise farming with fishing or even indigenous traditional medical knowledge.[34]

It is important to reiterate that the African system of education was not without some irregularities.[35] Like any other system, it had its shortcoming; however, it is paramount that the refocusing of the African system of education to provide the desired African of our tomorrow be embraced. This position is enunciated on the premise that the process of 'indigenous

[33] Jomo Kenyatta, *Facing Mount Kenya.*

[34] J. P. Ocitti, *African indigenous education: As practised by the Acholi of Uganda* (Nairobi: East African Literature Bureau, 1973).

[35] G. J. Dei, "Learning culture, spirituality and local knowledge: Implications for African schooling," *International Review of Education* 48 (2002): 335–360.

education in pre-colonial Africa was intimately integrated with the social, cultural, artistic, religious, and recreational life of the ethnic group'.[36]

As shown in the previous section, the African concept of education had respect and transparency as its major contents and was capable of gradually leading towards a positive African nation if it had been left unadulterated.

5.6 Elevating Education as a Human Right for Effective Development

As I have already advanced in the previous chapters, there is need to ensure that education is treated as a human right, consequently, I briefly argue here on the need to elevate the African concept of education as a fundamental right as means of driving development in Africa.

The African Charter on Human and Peoples' Rights provides for the right to education. The aspiration as set out in Article 1 encouraging States to ensure that they adopt legislative means and other necessary policy to ensure that they realise the rights enshrined in the Charter. With the provision and expansion of the right as stipulated in the African Charter on the Welfare and Rights of Children, the importance of education is reiterated. The Cultural Charter of Africa also recognises the role of education and further goes to stipulate the importance of the content of education been in line with the cultural and religious belief of the people.

The informal and non-formal education sectors in Africa prepared youths to be agents of development, and therefore, the need to harness the skills learnt remains germane in Africa of today.[37] In this light, it is important that the exposure of Africans to the learning process must be protected within a legal framework. The present treatment of education responsibility as a mere obligation is therefore not encouraged. Almost, all African countries provide for the right to education within their various Constitutions but treating them as mere aspiration that should be met. However, South Africa remains an exception with its non-qualification of the right to education; Ghana and Kenya have also currently

[36] Padmore Agbemabiese, "African centred female education before colonization: Exploring the physical, socioeconomic, and spiritual content of girl child educational curriculum," https://www.academia.edu/1483436/African_Traditional_Education_Prior_to_Colonization (accessed 19 December 2017).

[37] A. W. Wood, "Informal education and development in Africa," vol. 10, Institute of Social Studies, vol. 10, the Netherlands (University of Michigan: Mouton, 1974).

followed this path. Like every other rights, in the bill of rights it is one that remain, a mandatory responsibility of the state to ensure its protection, promotion and fulfilment.

It is my contention that with the elevation of education as a right in Africa, then, the pathway to the desired development will become clearer and more realistic. The argument of education becoming a right which is protected within the legal framework is assumed will ensure the creation of quality and maintenance of same. It is noted that quality is at the heart of all education as it enhances both learning and teaching ensuring effective influence for both the learner and the community.[38]

5.7 Conclusions

I have argued in this paper that the idea that education is alien to Africa is an erroneous one. It was established that Africa had a concept of education that was progressively emancipating her from the shackles of poverty as it was laden with the concepts of rule of law and good governance. Thus, with the continued elusiveness of development in Africa and the realisation that education has ability to put Africa on the proper plane for development that is desired, it is pertinent that African education be refocused.

In addition, I have established that the utilitarian nature of African traditional education is needed to drive the development of Africa. Today, the call is for a return to the indigenous education system, albeit in a modified form. The argument is that an education that has the input of all members of the community should be encouraged. It must be understood that this approach will not in any form disadvantage Africa, as the recommendation speaks to the reconceptualisation of content and purpose of education in line with African values and aspirations. Finally, it is concluded that the link between developments hinged on education is an incontrovertible fact[39]; also the positive impact of the African concept of education is laden with the ingredients capable of delivering African development.

[38] D. N. Sifuna and N. Sawamura, *Challenges of quality education in sub Saharan African countries* (UK: Nova Science Publishers, 2010).

[39] K. Kinyanjui, *Education and development in Africa: Theories, strategies, and practical implications* (Occasional paper: Working papers no. 375) (1980), https://opendocs.ids.ac.uk/opendocs/bitstream/handle/123456789/1245/wp375-317594.pdf?sequence=1&isAllowed=y (accessed 20 December 2017).

5.8 Recommendation

With the above conclusions, the question therefore is what ways possible in reconceptualisation of education from African perspectives to provide for the desired African of our dream.

Firstly, it is my considered opinion that the fact that there is an urgent need to ensure the restoration of dignity in the education of Africans. Self-belief is one of major factors that must be restored in the African student to enable him grow in self-worth and appreciate the role that needs to be played in driving an Afrocentric development.

Secondly, there is the need to stem the migration of educational skills from Africa to the world beyond. This is argued from the perspective that numerous African scholars who have sojourned into Western education are not motivated to return to Africa to bring a blend of the experiences learned with the African experiences and see how development can be leveraged on.

Thirdly, it is suggested that education curriculum from the basic education level in all African countries be reviewed so as to provide a basis for the 'reconstruction of education as per community needs'.[40] The need for this is germane as it will enhance the acceptability and adaptability of education by every community while advancing the positive objectives laden in education

Finally, it is recommended that education must be treated as a human right and judicialised with a view of empowering the judiciary to provide a needful check and balance on executive and parliamentary powers in the management of funds and curbing of corruption that remains the bane of development of quality in education in African states.[41]

[40] Adebayo Olukoshi, Opening panel discussant 'Solution to Africa's problem' TMALI book series launch symposium programme, 22–24 August 2013, UNISA Main Campus, Pretoria, South Africa.

[41] Ann Skelton, "The role of the courts in ensuring the right to a basic education in a democratic South Africa: A critical evaluation of recent education case law" (Pretoria: De Jure, 2013), 1–23; Klaud D. Beiter, *The protection of the right to education by international law* (Martinus Nijhoff: The Netherlands, 2006).

CHAPTER 6

Human Right or Human Capital Approach: Walking the Path to Actualisation of Access to Basic Education in Africa

6.1 Introduction

Education is a basic tool with the capability of initiating the enhancement of the status of an individual. It inherently has the capacity to lead to transformation and self-sufficiency. The task of realising education in itself is a daunting one because of the economic and logistical requirements. While the importance of education globally is not in contention, the question of the perspective to recognise it as a fundamental human right or otherwise has remained a huge challenge. This is not withstanding the importance accorded to education in the Millennium Development Goals (MDGs) and the Education For All (EFA) initiatives among others.

Following the concept of rights by Donelly for instance, a right is only so if it does not require been demanded for or put differently it is innate and accrues for the simple reason of human existence.[1] Other scholars like Henys conversely argue that a right can be demanded via what he describes as the struggle theory approach to human rights.[2] In the opinion of Tomasevski, the legal question as it pertains to education is two

[1] Jack Donelly, *Universal human rights in theory and practice* (Cornell University Press, 2003), 1; see also J. Donelly, "The relative universality of human rights," *Human Rights Quarterly* 29(2) (2007): 281–306.

[2] Christof Heyns, "A struggle approach to human rights," in C. Heyns and K. Stefiszyn (eds), *Human rights, peace and justice in Africa: A reader* (PULP, 2006).

A. C. Onuora-Oguno, *Development and the Right to Education in Africa*,
https://doi.org/10.1007/978-3-319-90335-4_6

pronged: the first being the perspective of education as a human right by international law and the second, the perspective of education as a traded service by international trade law.[3]

The doctrine of human capital seeks to analyse goods and services as a premise of human development with utmost financial benefits that can accrue from such services.[4] In this wise, the provision of goods and services must be weighed against the benchmark of cost benefits. Consequently, education if seen as a human capital will require the government to ensure that profit equals or surpasses investments in education. The basic challenge that this portends is that the provision of education will be at some cost or at best subject to a progressive realisation. If this is so, the realisation of education and its already agreed impact will be only to individuals that can afford same.

It is my argument that premised on the very nature of education and seen from the perspective of a social right, its protection, provision and fulfilment engrave it as a fundamental human right. This consequently requires both positive and negative obligations from governments on the one hand and individuals on the other. Considering the obvious benefits of education, its non-realisation will simply ground the violation of every other rights be it that of life, freedom of expression and political participation.

6.2 Social Right Nature of Education

In having a conceptual understanding of social rights, it is important to note that there is a strong responsibility between the State and the individuals. This concept popularly called the social contract theory stipulates that there should be cessation of certain rights by the individuals to the state with the state likewise having the responsibility to promote, protect

[3] See generally, K. Tomasevski, "Globalizing what: Education as a human right or as a traded service?" *Indiana Journal of Global Legal Studies* 12(1) (2005), Article 1; L. Almendarez, "Human capital theory: Implications for educational development," available at http://www.open.uwi.edu/sites/default/files/bnccde/belize/conference/papers2010/almendarez.html (accessed 19 March 2017).

[4] L. Almendarez, "Human capital theory: Implications for educational development," available at http://www.open.uwi.edu/sites/default/files/bnccde/belize/conference/papers2010/almendarez.html (accessed 19 March 2017).

and fulfil the individuals' rights.[5] In addition, it is important to restate that whatever claims that the individual must make should be of a legitimate nature and not otherwise.[6]

In the present discussion, while the individual must obey the laws as stipulated by the State, there is a corresponding obligation to protect the individuals' rights to access education. As obtainable in most sub-Saharan African countries, the right to education is seen merely as a negative right. It is, however, argued that as much as the government owes the individual the obligation not to prevent access to educational institutions it equally owes the duty to ensure the positive responsibility of assuring the availability and accessibility of education.

Arguing in this paradigm, Currie postulates that the States' responsibility to allow 'a prisoner right to a defence counsel also includes the positive right to ensure that if the prisoner does not have ability to retain such counsel; the state must provide free legal aid'.[7] States have a responsibility to 'refrain from interfering in a manner that negatively affects the realisation of a right…or should not prevent poor people from organising to claim their social entitlements'.[8]

Consequently, viewing education as social right, there is a responsibility to ground it as a fundamental human right as this will enable the realisation.[9] In order to achieve this, a minimum core standard has been set by the General Comment No 13 of the ECSR.[10] This approach is important as human rights must be viewed as interrelated with a violation of one meaning the non-realisation of others.[11] In elaborating this, the

[5]For more readings into the social contract theory, see generally, Stuart White, "Review article: Social rights and social contract—Political theory and the new welfare politics," *British Journal of Political Science* 30 (2000): 507–532.

[6]L. H. Piron, "Rights based approaches to social protection," 6, available at www.odi.org.uk/resources/docs/1700.pdf (accessed 11 March 2017).

[7]D. P. Currie, "Positive and negative constitutional rights," *The University of Chicago Law Review* 53(3) (1986): 873–874.

[8]L. H. Piron, "Rights based approaches to social protection."

[9]In Beiter's opinion, education must be seen as a basic need even beyond human rights as it is a major premise of life enhancement. See generally, K. D. Beiter, "The protection of the right to education by international law."

[10]See generally, F. Coomans, "Identifying the key elements of the right to education: A focus on its core content," available at http://www.crin.org/docs/Coomans-CoreContent-Right%20to%20EducationCRC.pdf (accessed 19 March 2017).

[11]L. H. Piron, "Rights based approaches to social protection."

Indian Supreme Court has held that the right to life is intrinsically linked to the right to education.[12] In *Unnikrishnan vs State of Andhra Pradesh*,[13] in the instant case, the Indian Supreme Court found that article 45 of the Indian Constitution is directly linked with the article 21 thereof that enshrines the right to life. The court stated clearly that 'the right to life cannot have any meaning if there is absence of education.'

In South Africa, the courts have also upheld the content of the right to a basic education and also decided severally on the quality thereto in terms of availability, access and adaptability. According to Skelton, reliance on International law commitment of South Africa in line with provisions of the Bill of Rights remains a veritable basis for the realisation of quality in the right to basic education.[14] In addition, the Constitutional Court of South Africa has further hinted on the sanctity of the right to education even as a stand-alone right.[15]

Thus, education as a social right includes the obligation on the government to ensure that availability, accessibility, affordability and adaptability are met.[16] In many sub-Saharan African nations, basic education remains at its lowest ebb with shocking statistics. Government failure to pay teachers' salaries alongside very poor welfare conditions continues to ensure the paucity in quality experienced in schools. This is stated herein to be a direct reason for absenteeism and poor quality of curriculum delivery by teachers.

[12] In *SP Gupta v President of India* AIR (1982) SCC 149 at 189, the Indian Court found that the violation of any constitutional right meant the violation of other rights also enshrined in the Constitution. Consequently, the violation of the right to food, education or even shelter amounts to the violation of the right to life. See also A. Sachs, "Social and economic rights: Can they be made justiciable?" 53 *S.M.U. Law Review* 1381 (2000).

[13] 1993 AIR 2178, 1993 SCR (1) 594; see the full case at http://youthforequality.com/supreme-court-cases/27A.pdf (accessed 17 March 2017).

[14] A. Ann Skelton, "The role of the courts in ensuring the right to a basic education in a democratic South Africa: A critical evaluation of recent education case law," *De Jure* (2013): 5.

[15] See *Minister of Welfare and Population Development v Fitzpatrick* (2000), 3 SA 422.

[16] See generally F. Coomans, "Clarifying the core elements of the right to education," http://www.uu.nl/faculty/leg/NL/organisatie/departementen/departementrechtsgeleerdheid/organisatie/onderdelen/studieeninformatiecentrummensenrechten/publicaties/simspecials/18/Documents/18-03.pdf (accessed 27 May 2017); Beiter, "The protection of the right to education by international law."

Further, the social and economic value of education includes the intrinsic ability to enhance the ability of an 'individual and safe guard the individual from all forms of exploitation and also better appreciation of consumer rights and privileges'.[17] The neglect of the social right nature of education has also occasioned neglect of certain vulnerable groups in the society especially children with disability. The lack of structural and policy framework to drive emerging concepts like inclusive education remains a major pointer to neglect of the social importance of education.[18] The intrinsic ability of education to breach societal inequalities is not contested. Therefore, treating education as a social right to enhance the elimination of inequalities in the society is important.[19]

6.3 Human Capital and Human Right Perspectives of Education

6.3.1 Human Capital

> The human capital model is the basis of neoclassical analysis of labour markets, education and economic growth. However, education policy... has been influenced by models based on screening theory and public choice theory which yield the policy implication that reductions in education spending are generally desirable.[20]

Theories on the concept of human capital seek to balance investment and returns.[21] It seeks to examine the correlation between input and output

[17] I. Robeyns, "Three models of education: Rights, capabilities and human capital," *Theory and Research in Education* 4 (2006): 71.

[18] Azubike C. Onuora-Oguno, Beyond nomenclature: Special education or inclusive education: Advocating quality basic education in Nigeria, presented at the Global Alliance for Justice Education (GAJE), OP Jindal University, India, 2013.

[19] M. C. Nussbaum, "Beyond the social contract: Capabilities and global justice," *Oxford Development Studies* 32(1) (2004): 4.

[20] J. Quiggin, "Human capital theory and education policy in Australia," available at http://www.uq.edu.au/economics/johnquiggin/JournalArticles99/HumanCapitalAustER99.html (accessed 10 March 2017).

[21] F. Lange and R. Topel, "The social value of education and human capital," in E. Hanushek and F. Welch (eds), *Handbook of the economics of education* (Amsterdam: Elsevier, 2006), 459–510. The chapter is also http://www.econ.yale.edu/~fl88/Handbook_Chapter.pdf (accessed 11 March 2017).

and is currently the basis of several Western education concepts.[22] This approach brings to the fore the choice and option to invest either in education or in selected individuals. In relating the concept of human capital to education, it has been postulated that individuals bear the cost of education.[23] While there is a consensus on the benefit of education to increase productivity, the major question is on the reduction in spending and in these circumstances by the government and borne by the individual.

Considering the huge impact of poverty in sub-Saharan Africa, government reduction in funding of education and the continued treating of same as a mere fundamental objective of State policy portends danger. With the impact of globalisation and the advancement of trade, goods and service, education has become a subject of liberalisation.[24] This influences the ability to access education in terms of monetary and fiscal policies of States.[25] A comparison of the human capital approach to education which places obligations on the individual is argued to be akin to the screening model approach.[26] Early scholars had proposed the education of 'gifted' children as 'guardians' of the State as the children deemed not to be gifted had little or nothing to offer the State and constituted mere waste of scarce resources.[27]

This position is critiqued because it falls short of the understanding that the individual should be the major object of receiving a right before proceeding to ensure that others benefit from the same. The human

[22] L. Almendarez, "Human capital theory: Implications for educational development," http://www.open.uwi.edu/sites/default/files/bnccde/belize/conference/papers2010/almendarez.html (accessed 19 March 2017).

[23] G. Mulongo, "Human capital theory in education," http://humancapitaltheoryineducation.blogspot.com/2012/06/human-capital-theory-in-education.html (accessed 19 March 2017).

[24] K. Tomasevski, "Globalizing what: Education as a human right or as a traded service?" *Indiana Journal of Global Legal Studies* 12(1) (2005), Article 1.

[25] K. Tomasevski, "The state of the right to education worldwide free or fee: 2006 global report," http://www.katarinatomasevski.com/images/Global_Report.pdf (accessed 19 March 2017).

[26] S. Brown and J. G. Sessions, "Signalling and screening," in G. Johnes and J. Johnes (eds), *International handbook on the economics of education* (Edward Elgar, 2004), 58.

[27] J. Bowen and P. R. Hobson, *Theories of education studies of significant innovation in western education thoughts* (Watson Ferguson & Co., 1974), 349–350.

capital approach is inclined to consolidate the benefit of education within the economic sector and not the social paradigm.[28] This is posited to be against the right-based perspective canvassed in this paper.

The effect of the human capital approach to issues like education is the fact that it reduces children to mere subjects of education and not objects, which is ideal in ensuring an enhanced capacity for the child.[29] If the provision of education is consequently based as a human capital with the attendant challenges of capital sourcing, diminishing returns and private versus social investment arguments[30] then a whole lot of children in Sub-Saharan Africa will continue to be excluded for accessing education.[31]

6.3.2 *Human Rights*

> The philosophical discussion of human social and welfare rights rarely focuses on the practical delivery and enforcement of asserted rights, generally leaving implementation issues to politicians.[32]

Using the concept of rights in education signifies the presence of obligation and also the ability to make claims when such a right is violated. This seems to be settled in issues as it relates to civic rights but still to be settled with respect to social rights.[33] As argued by Viljoen, the presence of objectives of state principles in most national constitutions should

[28] F. Lange and R. Topel, "The social value of education and human capital," in E. Hanushek and F. Welch (eds), *Handbook of the economics of education* (Amsterdam: Elsevier, 2006), 459–510. The chapter is also available at http://www.econ.yale.edu/~fl88/Handbook_Chapter.pdf, see p. 4 (accessed 11 March 2017).

[29] K. Tomasevski, "Free and compulsory education for all children: The gap between promise and performance right to education," *Primers No. 2* (2001), 10.

[30] G. Psacharopoulos, "Returns to education: A further international update and implications," *The Journal of Human Resources* 20(4) (1985): 584.

[31] This may also be true for the cultural barriers that have ensured early marriage and denial of education for the girl child. See generally, C. Anyanwu and A. C. Onuora-Oguno, "Ten years of the AU protocol on the rights of women in Africa: An overview of the girl child's access to basic education in Africa," in K. Brenda, S. Rainatou, and J. M. Faiza (eds), *Journey to equality: 10 years of the protocol on the rights of women in Africa* (2013), p. 74.

[32] J. Veit-Wilson, "No rights without remedies: Necessary conditions for abolishing child poverty," 3 Heinonline 8 *European Journal of Social Security* 317 (2006).

[33] J. Veit-Wilson, "No rights without remedies: Necessary conditions for abolishing child poverty," 4 Heinonline 8 *European Journal of Social Security* 317 (2006).

necessitate a drive towards owning responsibilities in their realisation and not otherwise trying to oust accountability.[34]

With the already analysed international human rights laws that relate to education examined, it is reiterated here that the need to progress towards a constitutional entrenchment of education as a fundamental right is apt. This position aligns with the proposition of Kumar when he restates[35]:

> The fact that civil and political rights became entrenched in many constitutions and legislation of developing countries, instructively demonstrates that the countries could have taken additional steps to ensure the protection and promotion of economic, social, and cultural rights. The enforcement of economic, social, and cultural rights could provide the precious space and numerous opportunities that would make the enjoyment of civil and political rights socially meaningful and practically significant.

The central nature of education warrants that it is treated as core fundamental right.[36] This position therefore necessitates that education should no longer be only subject to policy implementations and left at the caprice of the legislative and executive, but the role of the judiciary to adjudicate on same be enhanced.[37] Education as intrinsic as it is must be treated as a stand-alone right.[38] As conceptualised by the GC on education, it is understood that education should accrue to a human being as it is a basis of capacity building and for the fact of being human.

[34] Frans Viljoen, *International human rights law in Africa*, 2nd ed. (Oxford, 2012), 551.

[35] C. R. Kumar, "International human rights perspectives on the fundamental right to education-integration of human rights and human development in the Indian constitution," 249 Heinonline 12, *Tulane Journal of International and Comparative Law* 237 (2004).

[36] K. Tomasevski, "Education denied: Cost and remedies" (Zed Books, 2003), 4; The same view is also shared by present UN special rapporteur Kishore Singh on the right to education as he canvasses the viability of judicial enforcement and holding of the state accountable in the manner issues bordering on the right to education is handled.

[37] A. Sachs, "Social and economic rights: Can they be made Justiciable?" 53 *S.M.U. Law Review* 1381 (2000); Fons Coomans, "Justiciability of the right to education," *Erasmus Law Review* 2(4) (2009): 427–443.

[38] See Beiter, "The protection of the right to education by international law," 2006; Martinus Nijhoff, I. Robeyns, "Three models of education: Rights, capabilities and human capital," *Theory and Research in Education* 4 (2006): 74.

It is important to note that a human right perspective to education means 'every child, entitled to decent education, even when one cannot be sure that this education will pay off in human capital terms'.[39]

6.4 Impact of Various Human Capital Economic Policies like Structural Adjustment Policy (SAP) on Access to Basic Education

SAPs are policies by the World Bank (WB) and the International Monetary Fund initiated to regulate trade, business and economic policies on activities ranging from accessing social welfare to infrastructural frameworks. SAP regulates things like education, health and interest rates.[40]

The advent of SAP in most sub-Saharan African countries heralded the inability of individuals to access a lot of social service. SAP introduced reduced budgetary cost and spending on education and practically initiated free but fee-paying education policies.[41] The summary impact of SAP could well be said to have had adverse effect on individuals with women and the girl child—the most vulnerable in these circumstances.[42]

Succinctly put, the adoption of SAP in a country like Zimbabwe meant the 'removal of subsidies in social welfares like health and education among other things thereby making access to education to the average worker a herculean task'.[43] The introduction of SAP simply evolved a human capital perspective to issues like education dwelling on private investment and returns as opposed to the intricacy of the right to education as have already been argued.[44]

[39] Robeyns, "Three models of education: Rights, capabilities and human capital," 75.

[40] S. McGregor, "Structural adjustment programmes and human well-being," *International Journal of Consumer Studies* 29(3) (2005): 171.

[41] K. Tomasevski, "The state of the right to education worldwide free or fee: 2006 global report," available at http://www.katarinatomasevski.com/images/Global_Report.pdf (accessed 19 March 2017).

[42] S. M. Kawewe and R. Dibie, "The impact of Economic Structural Adjustment Programs [ESAPs] on women and children: Implications for social welfare in Zimbabwe," *Journal of Sociology and Social Welfare* 28(4) (2000): 83.

[43] Kawewe and Dibie, "The impact of Economic Structural Adjustment Programs [ESAPs] on women and children: Implications for social welfare in Zimbabwe," 87.

[44] Kawewe and Dibie, "The impact of Economic Structural Adjustment Programs [ESAPs] on women and children: Implications for social welfare in Zimbabwe," 89.

The WB could be argued to be the largest source of educational policies in the world; however, their stringent conditions make access to education difficult.[45] Heyneman notes that 'to access loans countries have agreed to raise education fees, which has exacerbated divisions between rich and poor'.[46] This resulted in the periods during the SAP implementation in most African countries having very low access and quality education with high dropout rates. In addition, the period of the influence of SAP ensured that the WB laid emphasis on the economic justification of support on educational investments. This led to 'prohibition of any assistance to the art, science and faculties of humanities, even libraries, all primary schools…'[47]

The impact of human capital and WB policy on education in sub-Saharan Africa led to the 'education system in developing countries being the exclusive preserve for the elite and imbalanced'.[48] Echoing the views of Samoff, Heynemann states that the 'WB policy acquired a reputation in some academic and NGO circles for abrogating the rights to a free education'[49];

> Structural adjustment is normally associated with the correction of imbalances in …domestic consumption …with deregulation and privatization of the economy…resulting in reduced government funding for public education programmes…budgets available for education…which only some can afford.[50]

[45] S. P. Heyneman, "The history and problems in the making of education policy at the World Bank 1960–2000," *International Journal of Educational Development* 23 (2003): 315; M. Carnoy, "Structural adjustment and the changing face of education," *International Labour Review* 134(6) (1995): 661.

[46] Heyneman, "The history and problems in the making of education policy at the World Bank 1960–2000."

[47] Heyneman, "The history and problems in the making of education policy at the World Bank 1960–2000," 317.

[48] Heyneman, "The history and problems in the making of education policy at the World Bank 1960–2000," 318.

[49] Heyneman, "The history and problems in the making of education policy at the World Bank 1960–2000," 326.

[50] M. Carnoy, "Structural adjustment and the changing face of education," *International Labour Review* 134(6) (1995): 653.

The harshness of SAP as an agent of human capital approach made the 'delivery of education more difficult in developing countries'.[51] Furthermore, the impact of SAP was particularly harmful as the conditions set ensured a truncation of the smooth flow of academic activities in all sectors of education.[52] The drive towards reduced funding of higher education and increased funds for primary education may sound appealing; however[53]; from a right-based approach, this position violates the position of international human rights. This is because access to secondary and tertiary education is encouraged to be embarked on in a progressive manner. The progressive realisation of this does demand a systematic and cogent effort in realising this goal, as captured by Carnoy:

> The combination of economic crisis and structural adjustment results not only in public expenditure cuts but usually also in lowered incomes; in the case of SAPs, it tends to reduce incomes unequally, affecting the poor... concerning education, there is a fall-off in the demand for schooling... structural adjustment can also reduce attendance at school.[54]

Taking into consideration the factors that have inhibited access to education of the girl child in sub-Saharan Africa, it is clear that the human capital ideology would be a veritable basis for the continued exclusion and discrimination of the girl child.[55] In buttressing this position, Robeyns un-assumedly further posits that:

> The problem with human capital model is that it is economistic: the only benefits from education that are considered are an increased productivity... the consequences are that money spent on education...is regarded as better spent on boy than on women.

In addition, the dangers of the human capital approach are the possibility of equating the returns on education on other forms of investments.[56]

[51] Carnoy, "Structural adjustment and the changing face of education," 654.

[52] Carnoy, "Structural adjustment and the changing face of education," 656.

[53] Carnoy, "Structural adjustment and the changing face of education," 662.

[54] Carnoy, "Structural adjustment and the changing face of education," 665.

[55] Anyanwu and Onuora-Oguno, "Ten years of the AU protocol on the rights of women in Africa: An overview of the girl child access to basic education in Africa," 74.

[56] I. Robeyns, "Three models of education: Rights, capabilities and human capital," *Theory and Research in Education* 4 (2006): 74.

It implies understanding that education as a right must be viewed with an 'individual as end point of moral and political justice as opposed to the human capital perception of seeing an individual as inputs for economic production and growth'.[57]

6.5 Courting the Right to Education: Towards Realising Right to Education

Until Constitutions of sub-Saharan African countries protect the right to education, constitutionally they would remain documents 'elevating luxuries over necessities'.[58] Understandably, the arguments against the judicial enforcement of the right to education remain hinged on the three-pronged basis. Mureinik identifies the arguments of expense, indeterminacy and positive as basis on why rights like education should be excluded from judicial enforcement.[59]

The argument that the resolution of ESCR becomes problematic because of 'possible alternatives and that the judiciary remain unqualified to resolve the issues'[60] is no longer tenable. As have been clearly stated by the South African courts in several cases, the justiciability of the right to education has a specific paradigm to ensure both positive and negative enforcement of the right to and in education.[61]

The involvement of the courts in adjudicating on the right to education attests to the centrality of the courts in driving the right to education by relying on global and regional human rights instruments. While the challenges facing justiciability of ESCR are still existent, it is important to reiterate that the involvement of the court in adjudicating

[57] Robeyns, "Three models of education: Rights, capabilities and human capital," 75.

[58] E. Mureinik, "Beyond a charter of luxuries: Economic rights in the constitution," Heinonline 8 *South African Journal on Human Rights* 464 (1992). Mureinik argues here that when someone is hungry, then the person's right to nutrition will be of more importance over the right to vote. This analogy can also be said to the necessity of the right to education as it pertains to the right to vote or rights of freedom of expression.

[59] See generally, E. Mureinik, "Beyond a charter of luxuries: Economic rights in the constitution," Heinonline 8 *South African Journal on Human Rights* 464 (1992).

[60] E. Mureinik, "Beyond a charter of luxuries: Economic rights in the constitution," 492.

[61] See Fons Coomans, "Justiciability of the right to education"; A. Skelton, "How far will the courts go in ensuring the right to a basic education?"; A. Skelton, "The role of the courts in ensuring the right to a basic education in a democratic South Africa: A critical evaluation of recent education case law."

the right to education should not be seen as a means of the 'unqualified judge' interfering with executive economic policies.

This point is well articulated thus[62]:

> ...A court would never be entitled to interfere with a government's honest and rational programme for eradicating starvation simply because it disapproved of the underlying political or economic theory. A court would be bound to respect all the government's choices, whether inspired by Marxism or monetarism; whether social democratic or liberal ...

The role of the judiciary in courting the right to education will be acts of policy review, and as posited by Skelton, the courts role will be that of ensuring that policies are not in any way discriminatory in nature. For instance, in the case of exclusion of pregnant girls in schools in South Africa, the courts have held such policies by school boards to be discriminate and not capable of general limitations and consequently struck out to be a violation of the Bill of Rights.[63] I shall in the next chapter discuss in detail the role of the courts in ensuring the realisation of the right to education.

6.6 Conclusions

From the foregoing, it is concluded that a human capital perception to education will lead to a more deplorable state of access to education in sub-Saharan African countries. Considering the importance of education as a major means of transformation of an individual, the individuals' empowerment and capacity, denial of access to education is a violation of a fundamental right.

In addition, to ensure that the executive ensure the promotion, protection and provision of the right to education, the role of the courts is not to be neglected. Importantly, a human capital perception to education ultimately leads to the violation of the right to education as compared to a human right perception. Finally, the policies that are linked to a human capital perspective like SAP have resulted in denial of access to education, and thus, education must be seen as an intrinsic obligation by governments in Africa.

[62] Mureinik, "Beyond a charter of luxuries: Economic rights in the constitution."

[63] See *Head of Department, Department of Education Vs Free State Province Welkom High School & Governing Body of Welkom High School* Case: CCT 103/12 [2013] ZACC 25.

CHAPTER 7

Comparative Analysis of Jurisprudence Governing Basic Education

7.1 Introduction

The chapter proceeds on the proposition of Skelton that … 'the realisation of the right to basic education is a tripartite function. It requires the role of the legislature in putting adequate laws in place either in terms of policies and more particularly constitutionally. 'The Executive must in turn ensure the will to ensure the realisation and implementation of the legislative outcomes without limitation and budgetary excuses; the judiciary in turn plays the arbiter role in ensuring the proper interpretation and compliance of all the laws and implementation process all geared towards ensuring that the right to a basic education are not compromised in any way'.[1]

The need to examine the role of the judiciary is premised on the fact that the judiciary has the 'ability to ensure the interpretation of the right to access of basic education as well as other rights firmly aided by the expectation of the judiciary defending the core values which are part of world jurisprudence and part of the evolving constitutional development'.[2]

[1] A. Skelton, "How far will the courts go in ensuring the right to a basic education?" *Southern African Public Law* 27 (2012): 398.

[2] A. Sachs, "Social and economic rights: Can they be made justiciable?" *SMU Law Review* 53 (2000): 1388.

A. C. Onuora-Oguno, *Development and the Right to Education in Africa*,
https://doi.org/10.1007/978-3-319-90335-4_7

The UN Special Rapporteur on the Right to Education, capturing the role of the judiciary in advancing the right to education, stated[3]:

> The role of adjudication is to ensure that the right to education as an internationally recognised right as established by numerous treaties and legislation is respected, protected and fulfilled. Its most basic tenets, free and compulsory primary education for all, the progressive realisation of secondary and tertiary education, and the immediate non-discrimination in their application, are universally recognised.

The effectiveness of the role of the judiciary in ensuring the realisation of the right to education is seen from the ground-breaking case of *Brown v Board of Education*[4] in the USA. Be it as it may, *Brown* continues to elicit numerous criticisms and support, but the jurisprudence has helped in enshrining the rights in education which has its core value towards the respect of human dignity and avoidance of inequality and discrimination. Dell succinctly captured the importance of *Brown* by stating that 'the goals in school desegregation suits remained the effective use of the Brown mandate to eliminate state sanctioned segregation'.[5] The case of *Brown* and several others will be examined to ascertain the viability of advocating that Nigerian courts must engage with the issue of the realisation of the right to basic education.

The chapter proceeds firstly by examining the legal framework of basic education in South Africa and India, enumerating some noticeable challenges and then examining the judicial jurisprudence in advancing the realisation of the right to basic education in both jurisdictions.

7.2 Basic Education—A South African Perspective

The basis for the realisation of the right to access to basic education in South Africa is the Constitution.[6] It provides: 'Everyone has the right to a basic education, including adult basic education'.[7] The provision for

[3] K. Singh, "Report of the special rapporteur on the right to education, justiciability of the right to education," A/HRC/23/35, 10 May 2013, para 13.

[4] *Brown v Board of Education* 347 US 483, 1954.

[5] D. A. Bell, Jr., "*Brown v Board of Education* and the interest-convergence dilemma," *Harvard Law Review* (1980): 518, 529.

[6] Constitution of the Republic of South Africa, 1996.

[7] Sec 29(1) South African Constitution.

the right to a basic education is enshrined in chapter two of the Bill of Rights and eliminates the question of its justiciability. The need to bridge the gap created in the education of black South Africans entrenched by apartheid rule is informative in the recognition of education within the Bill of Rights of the South African Constitution. The further ambit of the concept of 'everyone' within the South African jurisdiction, meaning everyone within the country, is also a laudable one. Thus, access to basic education does not discriminate between citizens and non-citizens.

It is my position to concede the fact that the recognition of basic education as compulsory and that of tertiary education to be subject to progressive recognition is an important one, considering the challenges of resources in most African countries. This position is in line with the provision of the ICESCR. Article 2 thereof provides:

> (1) Each State Party to the present Covenant undertakes to take steps, individually and through international assistance and cooperation, especially economic and technical, to the maximum of its available resources, with a view to achieving progressively the full realisation of the rights recognised in the present Covenant by all appropriate means, including particularly the adoption of legislative measures.
> (2) The States Parties to the present Covenant undertake to guarantee that the rights enunciated in the present Covenant will be exercised without discrimination of any kind as to race, colour, sex, language, religion, political or other opinion, national or social origin, property, birth or other status.
> (3) Developing countries, with due regard to human rights and their national economy, may determine to what extent they would guarantee the economic rights recognised in the present Covenant to non-nationals.

Consequently, the cogent efforts to ensure that access to education is fully entrenched as a right in African countries, especially in Nigeria, must be sustained by engaging in both legislative and collaborative initiatives. It is argued that 'basic education does not relate to the number of years of education to which a child is entitled but rather to the adequacy of the education'.[8]

[8] This view is expressed by Berger and Wolman and is re-echoed by Skelton. See Skelton (n. 1 above), 403–404.

The emergence of the term 'basic education' within the South African jurisdiction is rooted in the work of the 'technical committee that supported the 1993 negotiations that led to the interim Constitution'.[9] Calderhead opines that the couching of the section on basic education in the South African Bill of Rights is a direct offshoot of the influence of the provisions of various international law instruments, particularly with respect to the World Declaration on Education.[10]

In restating the purpose of basic education in South Africa, Calderhead echoes the provisions of the White Paper on Education and Training,[11] drawing a direct link with the purposes obtainable in international law. In giving credence to this approach, the South African Constitution provides that recourse must be had to international law in the interpretation of the provision on the right to education.[12] A direct significance of this is that, when faced with issues bordering on the right to education, the provisions of international law on the right to education will take precedence over South African law and policies.[13]

This is a sharp contrast with the position in Nigeria, where recourse is singularly had to the constitutional provision that treats the right to access of basic education as a mere fundamental principle of state objective. The general consensus in both India and South Africa is enshrined in the judiciary, which insists that the 'state refrains from engaging in acts that are capable of depriving an individual the minimal core decencies of life'.[14] The drive towards the realisation of the right to education stems more from the 'growing acceptance all over the world that certain core fundamental values of a universal character should penetrate and suffuse all governmental activity, including the furnishing of the basic conditions for a dignified life for all'.[15]

[9] Calderhead.

[10] As above. See generally C. Simbo, "Defining the term 'basic education' in the South African Constitution: An international law approach," *Law, Democracy and Development* 16 (2012).

[11] White Paper on Education and Training Notice 196 of 1995 Department of Education, Parliament of the Republic of South Africa, Cape Town, 15 March 1995, WPJ/1995, http://www.education.gov.za/LinkClick.aspx?fileticket=855fT9w3A2U%3D&tabid=191&mid=484 (accessed 26 February 2017).

[12] See sec 39(1)(b) of the South African Constitution.

[13] Calderhead, 9.

[14] Sachs, "Social and economic rights: Can they be made justiciable?"

[15] As above.

In addition to the above, South Africa, as a signatory to all major global and regional law instruments that provide for the right to basic education, strives to keep to its obligations. Apart from the legal provisions, there is also legislation providing for the right to basic education.[16] The Department of Basic Education (DBE) is saddled with the responsibility to enhance the realisation of the right to basic education.[17]

While the position of basic education is lauded in South Africa, scholars have reservations on some major challenges that still face the sector. The right to basic education and ensuring its quality in South Africa is a major concern. For instance, it is on record that[18]:

> The attempts of students from sprawling informal settlements and poor townships and rural areas to link poverty to the obstacles that prevent them from accessing and receiving quality education has become a feature of community struggles in the past year in South Africa.

From the above, it is clear that a major challenge is that of content, which is directly linked to quality. The reality of the need to ensure that the content of basic education is of a quality nature and to ensure that within the scope, the best interests of the child are enhanced and protected continues to be a huge source of concern in the South Africa.[19]

[16] See generally http://www.education.gov.za/DocumentsLibrary/Legislation/Acts/tabid/185/Default.aspx (accessed 26 February 2014); South African Schools Act 84 of 1996 available at http://www.education.gov.za/LinkClick.aspx?fileticket=808cFmkP8U4 (accessed 26 February 2017).

[17] The DBE is tasked with providing primary and secondary education. See generally http://www.education.gov.za/TheDBE/AboutDBE/tabid/435/Default.aspx (accessed 26 February 2014).

[18] C. A. Spreen and S. Vally, "Education rights, education policies and inequality in South Africa," *International Journal of Educational Development* 26 (2006): 353.

[19] For divergent comments and opinions on the state and quality of basic education in South Africa, see generally K. Wilkinson, "Why the matric pass rate is not a reliable benchmark of education quality," http://africacheck.org/reports/why-the-matric-pass-rate-is-not-a-reliable-benchmark-of-quality-education/ (accessed 26 February 2014); S. Van der Berg, S. Taylor, and M. Gustafsson, "Improving education quality in South Africa. Report for the National Planning Commission September 2011," http://resep.sun.ac.za/wp-content/uploads/2012/10/2011-Report-for-NPC.pdf (accessed 26 February 2017); S. Woolman and B. Fleisch, *The constitution in the classroom: Law and education in South Africa 1994–2008* (2009).

This challenge is further expressed in the fact that the ambit of basic education as envisaged by section 29(1) is directly tantamount to ensuring quality education.[20] Consequently, the task of ensuring quality and quantity in South Africa still looms large.[21]

Another factor is that of the issue of separation of powers. The balancing of the responsibility expected of the various arms of government has been a challenge which to a large extent is the reason for the current case law from South Africa to be settled. This is because the fear of breaching the separation of power concept has also been laid to rest in some of the roles courts have played in South Africa. Consequently, the status of socio-economic rights generally in South Africa has found grounding in the understanding that rights are indivisible in nature. It is believed in the South African jurisprudence that, although 'socio-economic rights are not universally accepted as fundamental rights, they are at least to some extent justiciable; and at the very minimum can be negatively protected from invasion'.[22]

In South Africa, while it is accepted that the executive and the legislature have inherent powers to administer the states resources, it is noted that the role of the judiciary is also very important. As argued by Mubangizi, '[i]t is mainly through judicial enforcement that the realisation and enjoyment of socio-economic rights takes place'.[23] This position is echoed by Brand when he asserts that the judiciary can effectively drive the protection of economic, social and cultural rights through its ability to interpret legislation.[24]

[20] Calderhead above 161–164.

[21] Simbo above. Simbo queries the act of awarding marks by the *Umalusi* unexplained manner of adding marks to matric students. It is stated: 'There seems to be an unwelcome practice by *Umalusi* of adjusting final marks for matriculants … without justifying such adjustments'.

[22] *Re Certification of the Constitution of the Republic of South Africa*, 1996 (4) SA 744 (CC) in J. C. Mubangizi, "The constitutional protection of socio-economic rights in selected African countries: A comparative evaluation," *African Journal of Legal Studies* 2 (2006): 5.

[23] As above.

[24] D. Brand, "Introduction to socio-economic rights in the South African Constitution," in D. Brand and C. Heyns (eds), *Socio-economic rights in South Africa* (2005), 1–15.

In Nigeria, the judiciary also wields the same power and exercises it by the doctrine of judicial precedence while exercising its interpretative role of legislations. However, the dearth of jurisprudence on economic, social and cultural rights, especially the right of access to basic education, raises concern, driving the hope that the outcome of this book will engineer a turnaround for the better.[25]

Thus, it is a safe conclusion to assert that 'the Constitutional Court of South Africa can and has played an important role in the judicial enforcement of socio-economic rights in South Africa'.[26] According to Sachs, J.:

> I think that just about everyone agree that shelter, education, nutrition, clean water, and basic health services should be universally available. That is no controversy… what is controversial is whether claims to such decencies should be regarded as enforceable fundamental rights in the constitutional order in a way similar to civil and political rights.[27]

The situation in India presents an interesting and similar context. While the directive principles of state policies existed, the India Supreme Court has gone on to 'use the directives of state policy as a means of interpreting the justiciable rights with accusations that they smuggled socio-economic rights in through the back door'.[28] This position seems to be supported by Viljoen, when he reiterates the fact that the inclusion of economic, social and cultural rights as directive principles in the Constitution must have some effect.[29] Viljoen goes further to opine that 'directive principles are to serve as part of public policy to guide

[25] See generally, I. Imam, "The myth of judicial activism in Nigeria: Making sense of Supreme Court judgments," http://unilorin.edu.ng/publications/imami/THE%20MYTH%20OF%20JUDICIAL%20ACTIVISM%20IN%20NIGER%20N0%202.pdf (accessed 26 February 2017); O. A. Obilade, *The Nigerian legal system* (1979). As canvassed by Imam, the ability of the court to deviate from existing decisions provides the court with an opportunity of laying down new precedents to be followed and relied on (see Imam above 5). C. A. Obiozor, "The constitutional vesting of judicial powers in the judicature in Nigeria. The problem with section 6(6)(d) of the Constitution 1999," *Nigeria Institute of Advanced Legal Studies (NIALS) Law and Development Journal* (2010): 218–230.

[26] Mubangizi above.

[27] Sachs, "Social and economic rights: Can they be made justiciable?"

[28] As above.

[29] Viljoen, *International human rights law in Africa* (2012), 551.

the authorities and agencies…to achieve these principles progressively legislative or otherwise but only enforcement is outlawed'.[30]

Seeking to enshrine not just the right to education, but all other economic, social and cultural rights, all African Constitutions[31] would not be an easy task to accomplish as even South Africa faced the same challenges during the drafting of its current Constitution. As posited further by Sachs, J., '[t]he great battle was not so much over whether social and economic rights should be incorporated, but over how they should be incorporated: as justiciable rights in the ordinary way, or as mere directives of state policy'.[32] The positive is that, despite the challenges, economic, social and cultural rights are contained in the South African Bill of Rights, and the South African Constitutions are today lauded as one of the most progressive in the world.

In addition, an important standard worthy of emulation is the content of the right to basic education within the South African jurisdiction. As succinctly put by Calderhead[33]:

> The point here is that it may well be a mistake to equate the content of the right with what government has either enacted or chosen to set out in white papers…s 29(1)(a) on the other, support a position which refuses to defer to government's contentions regarding the scope of the right.

It is also important to note that there is no limitation of the right to basic education, even subject to the limitation clause found in the South African Constitution.[34] Skelton is of the view that[35]:

[30] F. Viljoen, *International human rights law in Africa* (2012), 552.

[31] This is the chapter that houses the rights that are generally perceived to be justiciable.

[32] Sachs, "Social and economic rights: Can they be made justiciable?"

[33] Calderhead above 16.

[34] Sec 36 of the South African Constitution provides for a limitation of the rights provided for in the Bill of Rights. However, Calderhead opines that this position does not extend to the right provided in Sec 29(1)(a). See generally Calderhead (n. 11 above) 36. See also *Augusto v Electoral Commission* 1999 (3) SA 1 (CC). In this case, the Constitutional Court found that government's inability to fulfil a particular right will not be a sufficient basis for the government to invoke the limitation clause of the Constitution.

[35] Skelton (n. 1 above); A. Skelton, "The role of the courts in ensuring the right to a basic education in a democratic South Africa: A critical evaluation of recent education case law," *De Jure* (2013): 3.

> s29 (1) (a) guarantees the right to a basic education and not merely access to the right; the State must provide education, and not merely to take reasonable legislative and other measures within available resources, to achieve the progressive realisation of this right.

In buttressing this viewpoint, it has been held that[36]:

> To understand the nature of the right to 'basic education' under section 29(1) (a) unlike some of the other socio-economic rights this right is immediately realisable. There is no internal limitation requiring that the right to be 'progressively realised' within 'available resources' subject to 'reasonable legislative measures'.

Despite the above *dictum*, it is important to reiterate that in the event of remedial awards by the court,[37] the executive has opportunities of contributing to ensure the realisation of the right.[38]

Thus, unlike in Nigeria, where it is legislation that is the fulcrum of the realisation of the right to basic education,[39] the Constitution is the

[36] *The Governing Body of the Juma Musjid Primary School v Essay (Centre for Child Law as Amicus Curiae)* 2011 7 BCLR 651 (CC) para 37.

[37] Sec. 172 of the South African Constitution provides for the remedy powers of the courts. It provides: '(1) When deciding a constitutional matter within its power, a court (a) must declare that any law or conduct that is inconsistent with the Constitution is invalid to the extent of its inconsistency; and (b) may make any order that is just and equitable, including (i) an order limiting the retrospective effect of the declaration of invalidity; and (ii) an order suspending the declaration of invalidity for any period and on any conditions, to allow the competent authority to correct the defect. (2) (a) The Supreme Court of Appeal, the High Court of South Africa or a court of similar status may make an order concerning the constitutional validity of an Act of Parliament, a provincial Act or any conduct of the President, but an order of constitutional invalidity has no force unless it is confirmed by the Constitutional Court [para (a) substituted by sec 7, of the Constitution Seventeenth Amendment Act of 2012]. (b) A court which makes an order of constitutional invalidity may grant a temporary interdict or other temporary relief to a party, or may adjourn the proceedings, pending a decision of the Constitutional Court on the validity of that Act or conduct. (c) National legislation must provide for the referral of an order of constitutional invalidity to the Constitutional Court. (d) Any person or organ of state with a sufficient interest may appeal, or apply, directly to the Constitutional Court to confirm or vary an order of constitutional invalidity by a court in terms of this subsection'.

[38] Skelton above.

[39] The UBEC ACT 2004 is the law that enshrines the protection of the right to basic education in Nigeria.

fulcrum in South Africa. It is, therefore, believed that this provides a strong basis for the litigation bordering on the realisation of the right to basic education within the South African jurisdiction, and other African countries should emulate this.

However, the questions that beg for an answer are whether the courts have played any significant role in this regard, and to what extent the courts should embark in pursuit of the realisation of the right to basic education. In answering these questions, a major challenge, as envisaged by Skelton, is establishing the ambit of basic education and the proprietary of the court delving into issues of quality. However, Skelton posits that:

> Even if we have not established what a basic education consists of, the fact that some children enjoy a dramatically better standard of education would certainly be simple to demonstrate, based on infrastructure, conditions, class sizes, and indicators such as test scores.[40]

Consequently, the courts are empowered to make a comparison in terms of equality in ensuring that the provision of basic education is devoid of all signs of inequality.[41] This situation is still very prevalent in Africa with the unequal treatment and provision of education to areas classified as hard to reach areas.[42]

It is important to note that the 'judicial power of the Constitutional Court to strike down laws as invalid if they are in conflict with the Constitution is an essential part of a constitutional democracy'.[43] This consequently empowers the judiciary in the exercise of its oversight function on both the legislature and the executive in the implementation of execution of laws and policies that hinge on the realisation of the right to basic education. It is also noted that, in line with the doctrine of the separation of powers, the judiciary is expected to exercise sufficient limits and caution by ensuring that it does not violate or go overboard in

[40] Skelton.

[41] Calderhead below 47.

[42] The Mbamili region of Anambra State represented in the Anambra West Local Government area represents one of such localities that can benefit from the jurisprudence in this case. During the course of the LLD research, the author took a tour of the entire local government producing a documentary on the state of basic education in the region.

[43] Calderhead above 393.

adhering to the doctrine of separation of power, as espoused in the case *of Premier, Mpumalange v Executive Committee of State-Aided Schools, Eastern Transvaal*.[44]

7.3 Basic Education—An Indian Perspective

At independence, the right to education was provided for in the Indian Constitution as a mere fundamental objective of state principles.[45] Article 45 provides for education: 'The state shall endeavor to provide within a period of ten years from the commencement of the Constitution for free and compulsory education for all children until they complete the age of 14'. The challenge of placing an age restriction on the realisation of basic education is already espoused above.

From the period leading up to 1947, the state of education remained abysmal in India, but current statistics show some hope in the growth of the percentage of children able to access basic education.[46] Presently, Article 21(A) of the Indian Constitution recognises the right to basic education as a fundamental right. Article 21(A) provides that '[t]he state

[44] 1999 (2) SA 91; 1999 BCLR 151. In this case, the crux of the matter was for the court to determine procedural fairness on matters that involved issues on budget allocation. While the matter was hinged on the challenges of constitutional and social transformation as pertains to racially divided schools and the need for increased funding, it also dealt with ensuring that both white schools and other schools were equally furnished with same facilities and quality teachers. The applicants consequently prayed the court to approve 'provincial legislation for budget which expressly appropriated finds for payments of bursaries'. The court in paragraph 41 held that 'In determining what constitutes procedural fairness in a given case, a court should be slow to impose obligations upon government which will inhibit its ability to make and implement policy effectively (a principle well recognised in our common law and that of other countries). As a young democracy facing immense challenges of transformation, we cannot deny the importance of the need to ensure the ability of the executive to act efficiently and promptly'.

[45] N. Singal, "Inclusive education in India: International concept, national interpretation," *International Journal of Disability, Development and Education* 53(93) (2006): 351.

[46] UNICEF statistics show that presently only about 1.6 million Indian children are out of school. See http://www.uis.unesco.org/Education/Documents/fs-25-out-of-school-children-en.pdf (accessed 8 April 2017). While Nigeria ranks as the number one country with the highest number of out of school girls, India is ranked third, while South Africa is not in the worst 10 categories. See http://www.worldbank.org/education/edstats, VI Issue 2 (accessed 8 April 2017).

shall provide free and compulsory education to all children of the age of 6–14 in such a manner as the state may by law determine'.

The statistics on children who are able to access basic education differ from one region to another, in India it is said[47]:

> The Indian scenario is too complex and varied to be effectively captured through aggregate national figures in relation to the availability of schooling facilities across the country and their optimum use for educating all children. At one end of the spectrum, there is Kerala with practically every child completing elementary school and transitioning to secondary school; and almost every school having at least five teachers and five classrooms. At the other end, there is Bihar where only one out of two children in the relevant age group is in school; the majority of children entering school fail to complete an elementary cycle; many schools are understaffed; and teachers are often untrained and given little academic support.

The above captures the challenges of quality which are also akin to the situation in Africa generally. The difference remains that in both South Africa and India, the progressive improvement in the level of access and quality has some judicial flavour and is not just left to the whips of the political class.

The task of realising and enhancing the right to access of basic education in India became a national project as early as 1960. According to Govinda and Madhumita, three factors are crucial to achieving the goal, namely[48]:

i. increased direct involvement of the central governments in strengthening the infrastructure and delivery of elementary education;
ii. new dimension to multi-layered planning and implementation framework;
iii. social mobilisation.

[47] R. Govinda and M. Bandyopadhyay, "Access to elementary education in India. Country analytical review," *National University of Educational Planning and Administration* 3 (2008).

[48] As above. In addition, it is noted that for social mobilisation to be effective, the communities alongside the traditional rulers must all be engaged and carried along so as to ensure that policies and strategies adopted are both acceptable and relevant to the community in fashioning out a model of basic education that will be generally accepted; further details on this concept are discussed on pages 94 and 95 of the thesis.

The interplay of the three identified factors is conceded to be pivotal to ensuring the realisation of the right to access of basic education.

The structure of education in India is divided into the 10-2-3 system. The first 10 years represents 'a broad-based general education for all pupils'.[49] In this structure, the first 8 years represents the basic education paradigm and is ranged between the ages of 6–14. In addition, the basic education bracket is divided into two broad perspectives, with the first 5 years termed 'lower primary' and the last 3 'upper primary'.[50] It is noted that some variation exists with some of the various states adopting different patterns in order to suit the specific needs of their regions.[51]

Schools in India are run by government, private organisations and NGOs. The Education Guarantee Scheme (EGS) is a scheme that is put in place to ensure that the education of children in the hard to reach areas is achieved.[52] A sharp contrast with the situation in Nigeria is that the government-run schools continue to provide greater quality and are more accessed by the majority of children in India.[53] This is not the case in Nigeria as most parents presently send their children to privately run education institutions. The effect of this is that the quality in the government-run schools has dropped significantly. Neglect and infrastructural depreciation and poor quality of teachers are added disadvantages.

Also, the reliance on persuasion rather than compulsion has been shown to achieve greater results in India as opposed to the Nigerian situation, where some states have resorted to the use of force in ensuring attendance.[54] The Indian government, with the support of NGOs, operates both the EGS and also the Alternative and Innovative Education (AIE) schemes. The main objectives of the model are to fashion a workable means of ensuring that education is adaptable in all senses.[55]

[49] Indian National Policy on Education (n. 56 below).

[50] As above.

[51] Govinda and Bandyopadhyay above; Singal above.

[52] Govinda and Bandyopadhyay.

[53] As above. A contrary view is shared by R. C. Gretchen, B. R. Betsy, and M. Karthik, "A profile of the Indian education system," paper prepared for the New Commission on the Skills of American Work Force (2006), 4.

[54] N. Juneja, "Constitutional amendment to make education a fundamental right issue for follow-up legislation," 23–24, http://www.nuepa.org/Download/Publications/Occasional%20Paper-33njuneja.pdf (accessed 8 April 2017).

[55] Govinda and Bandyopadhyay.

The role of the Indian courts, like their South African counterparts, in bolstering the frontier of access to basic education cannot be overlooked. The Indian Supreme Court has found that education is a fundamental right that must be treated as such and not just a mere fundamental objective of state principle. In the case of *UnniKrishnan JP v State of Andhra Pradesh & Ords*,[56] the Court found that the right to education was akin to the right to life. This case and a number of other cases are discussed in detail in the later. In the following section, the Indian Education Act, which is a follow-up to the constitutional requirement for education, is discussed.

7.3.1 The Right of Children to Free and Compulsory Education in India (RTE ACT)[57]

With the wording of Article 21(A) of the 86th amendment of the Indian Constitution, requiring that education be treated as a fundamental right and no longer as a fundamental objective of state policy, the need for defining the ambit of the phrase 'by law' became necessary. This led to the enactment of the RTE Act.[58] The Act provides for access to a neighbourhood school until a child attains the age of 14.[59] This provision, it is argued, enhances access to basic education in terms of the 1–3 km distance advocated under international human rights law.[60] It further provides for the exclusion of all forms of fees by a child.[61]

The Act places responsibilities on parents, teachers and governments; it respects the rights to education of a child, shielding them from discrimination, degrading and inhuman treatment.[62] By virtue of the Act, the central government of India reserves a greater responsibility of ensuring compliance on the provision of education in India. With the coming into place of the RTE, it is heart-warming to note that India has[63]

[56] SC 2178 (1993).

[57] Act 35 of 2009.

[58] The RTE Act, http://eoc.du.ac.in/RTE%20-%20notified.pdf (accessed 8 April 2014).

[59] Sec 3(1).

[60] G. Betcherman, J. Fares, A. Luinstra, and R. Prouty, "Child labour, education, and children's rights", Social Protection (2004) Discussion Paper Series, 18, http://www.ilocarib.org.tt/projects/childlabour/library/educationchildrenrights.pdf (accessed 14 April 2017).

[61] Sec 3(2).

[62] Secs 15–17. Note that ch IV of the Act specifically includes the protection of the rights of the child.

[63] Right to education, http://mhrd.gov.in/rte.

> moved forward to a rights-based framework that casts a legal obligation on the Central and State Governments to implement this fundamental child right as enshrined in the Article 21A of the Constitution, in accordance with the provisions of the RTE Act.

While the push for a greater number of children accessing education in India remains high, it is also to be noted that, like Nigeria and South Africa, India continues to face the challenges of quality and examination malpractices. Apart from the issue of quality, discrimination is another major challenge that plagues the seemingly worthy approach to the access of basic education in India.[64]

Regarding the education of Children with Disabilities (CWD), India has adopted a dual approach solution to this: Special and Integrated Schooling.[65] However, in compliance with their treaty obligation under human rights law,[66] India is gradually concentrating efforts towards 'focusing on educating children with disabilities in the mainstream, this has gathered further momentum as a result of a range of developments at the international and national level'.[67]

7.4 South Africa and India—Ahead?

With particular reference on the structure to basic education in South Africa and India analysed above, a peculiar thread is identified. In both countries, unlike in Nigeria, the right to education has metamorphosed from a mere fundamental objective of state principles to being a fundamental human right. The constitutional recognition of the right to education as justiciable has thus encouraged the development of the jurisprudence on issues relating to education. This has also enhanced the participation of NGOs in engaging in public interest litigation (PIL) and the role of the National Human Rights Commissions of South Africa and India. It is thus safe to conclude that in both legislative and judiciary participation in enhancing access to basic education, India and South Africa are ahead.

[64] Singal above.

[65] As above.

[66] See generally the Salamanca Declaration of 1994 and also the CRPD.

[67] Singal above.

An identified factor influencing the scenario above is the place of public interest litigation. The growth of PIL in India is traceable to the era 'from 1975–1977, occasioned by the impact of colonial rule and wide spread state repression and governmental lawlessness... this in addition encouraged the judges of the Indian Supreme Court to openly disregard the Anglo-Saxon procedure in providing access to justice'.[68] Consequently, it can be argued that the level of poverty and violation of the rights of individuals is at the bedrock of the evolution of PIL in India. This situation provides a sufficient basis for Africa to embrace PIL towards realising economic rights and particularly the right to basic education. It is noted here that India like Nigeria for instance inherited the same technicalities of the Common Law and still embraced judicial activism as a means to ameliorate the situation of such rights like the right to education.[69] Also the development of PIL in India is attributed to the engagement of both fundamental rights and objective of state principles described as 'conscience of the constitution',[70] by the judiciary that saw both as needful in enforcing the rights of individuals.

In the case of South Africa, Badwaza highlights numerous challenges confronting access to Justice and judicial engagement as factors that account for the growth of PIL.[71] Also, important is the fact that despite the challenges that are identified, the desire to ensure the realisation of equality and drive for social change was also a strong basis for the evolution of PIL in South Africa.[72] As identified by Klaaren, Dugard and

[68] http://www.legalserviceindia.com/article/l273-Public-Interest-Litigation.html (accessed 15 October 2017).

[69] See generally A. R. Thiruvengadam, "Swallowing a bitter PIL? Reflections on progressive strategies for public interest litigation in India," in O. Vilhena, U. Baxi, and F. Viljoen (eds), *Transformative constitutionalism: Comparing the apex courts of Brazil, India and South Africa* (2013).

[70] For a more detailed history of the evolution of PIL in India, see generally, S. Deva, "Public interest litigation in India: A critical review," *Civil Justice Quarterly* 21(1) (2009); M. K. Sadual, "Public interest litigation in India: Pros and cons," *International Journal of Humanities & Social Science* IV (2015): 38; A. H. Desai and S. Muralidhar, "Public interest litigation: Potential and problems," in B. N. Kirpal, et al. (eds), *Supreme but not infallible-essays in Honour of the Supreme Court of India* (2000), 159.

[71] Y. M. Badwaza, "Public interest litigation as practiced by South African human rights NGOS: Any lessons for Ethiopia?" Unpublished LLM dissertation submitted to the University of Pretoria, 11, http://repository.up.ac.za/bitstream/handle/2263/1135/badwaza_ym_1.pdf?sequence=1 (accessed 15 October 2017).

[72] Y. M. Badwaza above 1.

Handmaker, the growth of PIL in South Africa has some leanings on the transformative constitution of South Africa and the impact of apartheid in the country.[73] Gloppen further attributes the responsiveness of the courts in South Africa as an encouraging factor for the growth of PIL in South Africa.[74]

From the above, it is clear that the role of both NGOs and the courts is instructive for African nations (Uganda, I agree, is beginning to show great strides towards engaging PIL in advancing the rights and developments).

7.4.1 *Jurisprudence on the Right to Education—South Africa, India and Select Jurisdictions*

Since this section is committed to deciphering the wisdom in encouraging the justiciability of the right to basic education, it is paramount to determine the question of principle set forth in *Brown*[75] and to ascertain the impact of the judicial involvement on economic and social rights, such as education.

The *Brown* case[76] was predicated on the aspiration to ensure the American Declaration of Independence that 'all men are born equal'. Following on the several amendments, notably the 14th Amendment, the situation of African Americans remained gloomy as their rights in education, not to be discriminated against remained entrenched.[77] The *Brown* case represents a 'consolidation of several cases which though hinged on different facts had a central issue of state sponsored

[73] See generally, J. Klaaren, J. Dugard, and J. Handmaker, "Public interest litigation: Introduction," *SAJHR* 27 (1) (2011); For further insight, see generally Public interest litigation and social change in South Africa: Strategies, tactics and lessons, http://www.atlanticphilanthropies.org/sites/default/files/uploads/Public-interest-litigation-and-social-change-in-South-Africa.pdf (accessed 15 October 2017).

[74] S. Gloppen, "New frontiers of social policy," conference paper on Public Interest Litigation, Social Rights and Social Policy, Arusha, 12–15 December 2005.

[75] *Brown v Board of Education* above.

[76] A brief summary of the facts of the case is hinged on the inability of a mother to send her child to a school which was a distance from their home. However, she was not allowed by state law to send the child to the school which was close by her home as this was exclusively for white children.

[77] http://www.uscourts.gov/educational-resources/get-involved/federal-court-activities/brown-board-education-re-enactment/history.aspx (accessed 9 April 2014).

discrimination based on race' as the underlying basis for discrimination.[78] After years of inability to reach a decision, in 1954 Justice Warren read the lead judgment that found that 'separate but equal has no place in public education'.[79]

Since the decision in *Brown*, reactions to the potency of courts getting involved in issues concerning education have continued to be discussed.[80] Interest on the veracity of the decision of the court has been captured by Bell, Jr. when he argues that '[b]lack children could possibly be achieving quality education had they remained in black schools segregated from the whites'.[81] According to Bell[82]:

> Demographic patterns, white flight, and the inability of the courts to effect the necessary degree of social reform render further progress in implementing *Brown* almost impossible.

Considering the basis for the decision in *Brown*, as captured by Warren J., it is opined that despite the criticisms and seeming shortfalls in the implementation of *Brown*, enhancing equality in the education sphere is central to ensuring that education achieves the objective of upholding human dignity. In the words of Warren[83]:

[78] The cases are listed as *Brown v Board of Education of Topeka*; *Briggs v Elliot*, *Davis v Board of Education of Prince Edward County (VA)*, *Boiling v Sharper and Gebhart v Ethel*. See generally http://www.uscourts.gov/educational-resources/get-involved/federal-court-activities/brown-board-education-re-enactment/history.aspx (accessed 9 April 2017).

[79] http://www.uscourts.gov/educational-resources/get-involved/federal-court-activities/brown-board-education-re-enactment/history.aspx (accessed 9 April 2014).

[80] See generally J. T. Patterson, *Brown v Board of Education: A civil rights milestone and its troubled legacy* (2001). It must also be stated that, despite the fact that the USA does not have the right to access of basic education enshrined in its Constitution, the political will to ensure that every child is not deprived of this is encouraging. Interactions had with colleagues during the American Society of International Law 109 Annual meeting in Washington, DC April 8–11 show that the level of commitment by the various states in America seemingly forecloses the need for legislation on this.

[81] Bell above.

[82] As above.

[83] http://www.ushistoryatlas.com/era9/USHAcom_PS_U09_brown_R2.pdf (accessed 9 April 2017).

> Today, education is perhaps the most important function of state and local governments. Compulsory school attendance laws and the great expenditures for education both demonstrate our recognition of the importance of education to our democratic society. It is required in the performance of our most basic public responsibilities, even service in the armed forces. It is the very foundation of good citizenship. Today it is a principal instrument in awakening the child to cultural values, in preparing him for later professional training, and in helping him to adjust normally to his environment. In these days, it is doubtful that any child may reasonably be expected to succeed in life if he is denied the opportunity of an education. Such an opportunity, where the state has undertaken to provide it, is a right which must be made available to all on equal terms.

It is, however, agreeable that the role of the courts is germane and pivotal to ensuring that the right to access of basic education is achieved. While there was a genuine pitfall in the implementation of the decision of the *Brown* case, the recommendation of Mbazira is important. According to Mbazira[84]:

> An effective remedy is therefore one that embraces and considers the problems that are likely to be encountered at the implementation stage. The court should look at the end results of its remedy and consider its long term effectiveness.

Effectively, the flaws in the manner and pattern of the US court in *Brown* not laying down cogent and definite means of realising the judgment should not in any way be a discouraging factor. It is important to follow Mbazira's approach by ensuring that remedies called for by courts are not impossible and do not place overtly unachievable responsibilities on the shoulders of the executive.

The position of Mbazira is further supported by McConnachie and McConnachie[85] when they find that 'Litigation alone will not fix the systemic problem of inadequate school facilities or the broader problems

[84] C. Mbazira, "Litigating socio-economic rights in South Africa: A choice between corrective and distributive justice," (2009), 118.

[85] C. McConnachie and C. McConnachie, "Concretising the right to a basic education," *South African Law Journal* 129 (2012): 561, 588.

in the education system'[86] Despite this caution, then I subscribe to the viability of litigation in driving a change in the systemic improvement in holding both the state and individuals responsible in enhancing the realisation of the right to education. This view is in line with the position of Thiruvengadam when the importance of the role of judges is restated thus[87]:

> ...judges abandon the command and control strategies that are currently on display...judges should instead be encouraged to adopt a far more modest, facilitative role, where the focus is on the citizens who suffer, the social movements who organise their interests, and the lawyers who represent them...

In the following cases discussed, it will be shown how the South African Constitutional Court and the Indian Supreme Court have tried to achieve this balance in the several decisions they have issued. In some of the cases, the bargain model has been encouraged by the courts to ensure that the resultant effect of the litigant's aspiration is eventually met over a period agreeable to all parties in a pending suit.[88]

7.5 South African Jurisprudence on Education

Despite the historical context of education in South Africa, South Africa has made tremendous legislative and judicial gains in ensuring enhanced access to basic education. The cases analysed below capture the fact that the judiciary in South Africa and India has taken poignant steps to assist enhanced access to basic education. Summarily, the judiciary has played a role in ensuring the elimination of all forms of discrimination in education, ensuring that policies are followed actively to necessitate proper realisation, ensuring that the role of teachers is enhanced by remuneration worthy of their calling, ensuring that the rights of the child trump

[86] McConnachie and McConnachie, above 557. See also F. Viljoen, "The justiciability of socio-economic and cultural rights: Experience and problems," in Y. Donders and V. Volodin (eds), *Human rights in education, science and culture: Legal developments and challenges* (2007), 53.

[87] A. R. Thiruvengadam, 528.

[88] For discussion of the bargain model in litigation of ESCR, see Mbazira (n. 96 below), 183.

all other rights in upholding the best interests of the child[89] and ensuring that the central government's supervisory roles are well entrenched so as to provide a check for the actions of provincial and local authorities. Finally, the judiciary has also ensured that the right to a basic education elicits both a positive right from the government and a negative obligation, making this both a horizontal and vertical responsibility.

i. *The Head of Department: Department of Education, Free State Province v Welkom High School & Harmony High* (the *Welkom* case)[90] (Access to Basic Education and the Constitution)

The *Welkom* case hinges on the administrative role of a school governing board as provided for under the South African Schools Act 84 of 1996.[91] It is also noted that the case is a consolidation of separate cases involving different schools, in the instant case, Welkom and Harmony High Schools. As provided for by the Act, the principal and the School Governing Board (SGB) has the responsibility to lay down the moral rules for the school and make such other decisions as it may deem fit.[92] The case further addresses the question of non-discrimination and equal access of education of the girl child, especially on such circumstances as occasioned by gender and sex issues.

In the instant case, Rampai J. of the Free State High Court found that the Head of Department acted *ultra vires* in insisting that a school principal carries out orders that are contrary to the rules as adopted by the school governing body. He found[93]:

[89] The concept of the best interest of the child as adopted in this thesis means decisions that are taken concerning a child's access to education. It is advanced that the right to access of basic education of a child should surpass any other competing rights and obligations. For a further and general detail on the concept of the best interest of the child, see the following, Y. Dausab, "The best interest of the child," http://www.kas.de/upload/auslandshomepages/namibia/Children_Rights/Children_h.pdf (accessed 13 October 2015); UNHCR Guidelines on Formal Determination of the Best Interests of the Child Provisional Release, May 2006; T. Hammarberg, "The principles of the best interest of the child-what it means and what it demands from adults," https://wcd.coe.int/ViewDoc.jsp?id=1304019 (accessed 13 October 2015).

[90] Case 766 and 767/2011.

[91] http://www.education.gov.za/LinkClick.aspx?fileticket=808cFmkP8U4 (accessed 30 April 2017).

[92] Sec 20.

[93] Para 2(a) amended High Court Order.

> For as long as the pregnancy policy remains in force, the first respondent is interdicted and restrained from directing the school principal to act in a manner contrary to the policy adopted by the school governing body.

The fact of the case deals with the adoption of a pregnancy policy for learners by the Welkom and Harmony High School boards. The said policy was purportedly adopted in accordance with 'National Department of Education's Measures for the Prevention and Management of Learner Pregnancy, which were published in 2007 and intended to assist public schools in managing learner pregnancies as and when they occurred'.[94]

The first instance was the decision suspending access to education of a pregnant learner from 2010 to 2011 after said leave of absence would have been observed by the learner towards the term of the pregnancy and nurturing the baby. On appeal from the parents to the Minister for Basic Education in the Free State and the Human Rights Commission of South Africa, the principal of the school was instructed to rescind the expulsion decision of the learner.

In the second instance, the Harmony school policy of not allowing pregnant learners to have access to school in the same year of pregnancy was also in issue and the principal was asked to rescind the decision by the Head of Department of Basic Education. It is instructive to note that the principals had been advised to absorb the learners pending such a time as the court decision is determined.[95] Following the decision of the High Court, the South African Human Rights Commission was subsequently admitted as *amicus curiae* alongside the Centre for Child Law.[96]

The main argument as advanced by the *amicus* was on the discriminatory nature of the policy against pregnant learners. Hinged on the provision of the Schools Act to promote the interests of the school and to enhance quality learning experiences of learners, the matter was set forth for appeal. Hinging their argument on the doctrine of collateral challenge, the SGB argued that it was open to pregnant learners to challenge the validity of the policy against them and not that of Members of

[94] Para 3.

[95] This position further reinforces the role the court can play in ensuring that interim measures are put in place and followed in the bid to ensure that no child is deprived of the right of access to basic education.

[96] Para 7.

Executive Council for Education (MEC). MEC in its position sought to enforce its constitutional obligation to protect the right to a basic education of learners as provided under section 29 of the Constitution.

The Supreme Court of Appeal found that a public officer could only make decisions as it is empowered by the law. In the instant case, the Head of Department for Education (HOD) was not legally empowered to revoke the decisions of the SGB. However, it could seek other options open to it to review an administrative decision via the court. Contrary to the opinion of the Supreme Court of Appeal, the Constitutional Court opined[97]:

> In *Ermelo* the Supreme Court of Appeal held that the function of determining a language policy for a school belonged to the governing body of the school alone and the HOD had no power whatsoever to revoke that function under the Schools Act and his only remedy was judicial review. This Court disapproved of that view and reasoning. In the present case the Supreme Court of Appeal also adopted the reasoning that the power to determine a learner pregnancy policy belonged to the school governing body alone and that the HOD's remedy, if he was unhappy about it, was a judicial review to have the policy set aside. Just as this Court disapproved of that reasoning in *Ermelo*, I am of the opinion that in the present matter that reasoning should also be rejected.

Thus, while upholding the laid-down administrative procedure, a violation of the constitutional right to access basic education was found by the decision of the principal despite acting in line with the SGB policy. In the words of the learned judge, it was stated:

> I find that these policies *prima facie* violate constitutional rights and thus order that they be reviewed in the light of the considerations set out in this judgment. Further, I order the respondent schools to engage meaningfully with the Free State HOD in the process of revising their pregnancy policies and to furnish copies of the revised policies to this Court.

The *Welkom* case thus advances the centrality of the right in education. It must be noted that administrative bureaucracies should not be relied on to limit or encroach on the right to education. This decision and reasoning can be expanded to cover prompt decisions by administrators on

[97] Para 263. WELKOM case, http://www.saflii.org.za/za/cases/ZACC/2013/25.html (accessed 16 April 2017).

matters that will affect access to education. It is my conviction that the reasoning in this case will assist situations where several bottlenecks stand in the way of ensuring access to education.

ii. *Member of the Executive Council for Education in Gauteng Province, Head of Department: Gauteng Department of Education, District Director Johannesburg East D9: Gauteng Department of Education v Governing Body of the Rivonia Primary School Ms Cele, Mr Mackenzie Ms Drysdale* (*Rivonia* Case)[98] **(Right of Access)**

The *Rivonia* case captures the challenge presented by limited economic resources available to the different class groups in South Africa. The gap created by apartheid and huge income differences brings to the fore the challenge in fulfilling the constitutional provision enshrined in section 29 of the South African Constitution. It also captures the salient importance of having the best interests of the child in mind when determining the use of economic resources in realising the right to a basic education. The *Rivonia* case further espouses the responsibilities of authorities[99] saddled with the obligation to provide education and the desire of parents to ensure that education of their children is not denied on any basis. Apart from the parents, the Centre for Child Law, the Suid-Afrikaanse Onderwysers Unie and Equal Education were admitted in the case as *amici curiae*.

The summary of the facts of the *Rivonia* case deals with the non-placement of a learner who was interested in Grade 1 placement in a school near Johannesburg. Citing filled quota that was set at 120 people by the school authority, the learner was placed on a waiting list. The parents of the learner, not being satisfied with the decision of the school governing board and the various government authorities, lodged a complaint with the Gauteng HOD. The Gauteng HOD subsequently ordered that the admission policy of the school be overturned and that the child be admitted, but this was refused by the school principal. The learner was eventually placed in the school by the Gauteng HOD.

[98] Case CCT 135/12 [2013] ZACC 34.

[99] Gauteng Department of Education; Member of the Executive Council for Education in the Province of Gauteng; Head of the Department of Education in the Province of Gauteng; District Director Johannesburg East D9.

The school approached the High Court to contest the contravention of section 5(5) of the South African Schools Act that empowered the school's governing body to take decisions on administrative needs of the school. The court found in favour of the Gauteng HOD, stating that it had the powers to determine the admission capacity of the school and ensuring that the right to a basic education of a child is not denied. However, on appeal, the Supreme Court of Appeal found otherwise, stating that the actions of the Gauteng HOD were arbitrary. The decision of the Supreme Court of Appeal was hinged on the reasoning that[100]

> it would be inappropriate for the Department to be vested with a power to use the additional capacity at Rivonia Primary, because that capacity had been created through additional funds raised by the Rivonia Governing Body. It would be a disincentive for parents to contribute to school funds if the increased capacity created by these funds could be used to accommodate more learners than the Rivonia Governing Body wanted to admit.

In the Constitutional Court, the Court in its wisdom distilled that the prime role of a school's governing board was to 'give effect to the constitutional right to education'.[101] It further recognised the role of the Minister of Basic Education to provide some form of uniformity in the administration of running of basic education.[102] This is notwithstanding the role various tiers of government have in the administration of education.[103]

The Constitutional Court examined issues of procedural fairness and cooperation between the parties in the case. It reached varying conclusions in the different roles wrongly played by the parties. The Constitutional Court distilled a very crucial issue, 'the best interests of the child and the impact of the relief sought[104] by the

[100] Para 25.

[101] Para 35.

[102] Para 38.

[103] As is the case in Nigeria, the involvement of local, state and federal governments in education administration should therefore ensure that the minister at the central level shows some form of control over the administration of basic education notwithstanding the administrative decisions of the states and local governments.

[104] The school had requested that the child be placed in another school pending when the governing board deems it fit to admit the learner to the Rivonia School.

school'.[105] Consequently, based on the best interests of the learner, the Constitutional Court upturned the decision of the Supreme Court. It found that the question of access to education should be handled based on the best interests of a child over and above other administrative and procedural flaws that arise out of uncooperative situations between schools.

The *Rivonia* case also raises interesting perspectives to issues surrounding the administration and realisation of access to basic education. As in the *Welkom* case, the courts upheld the best interests of the child high and above administrative clogs. I advocate that the jurisprudence from the case will assist in eliminating lack of political will or religious restrictions that affect access to basic education. *Rivonia* will also be instrumental in ensuring that the consistent impasse suffered during the various spates of strikes in education sector will be eliminated.

iii. *Juma Musjid Primary School and Others v Essay NO and Others* (Right of Availability)

The *Juma Musjid* case[106] deals with the question of availability. In this case, a public school operating on a private property was successfully evicted by the owners of the property, Juma Musjid Trust. The basis of the case was grounded on the failure of the MEC for Kwazulu-Natal to conclude a proper tenancy agreement. The court of first instance rightly found that the right of the trustee to own property was constitutional but it went further to weigh the right to property and the best interests of the child in terms of section 29 of the Constitution, read with section 28 of the Constitution.

The Juma Musjid School was established as a public school with Islamic flavour in 1957 with some expenses paid by the trustee with an understanding of possible refunds by the MEC. Part of the establishing agreement included a clause 14 which was subsequently not adhered to.[107] Following several notices and breached understanding by the MEC on concerns of the trust, relating to rentals and costs incurred, the trust approached the High Court for redress.

[105] Para 76.

[106] (2011) 8 BCLR 761 (CC).

[107] Para 11.

The High Court upheld the application of the trust and consequently sanctioned the eviction order against the respondents. The decision of the High Court was grounded on common law and also a failure to keep to tenancy obligations. The High Court further found[108]:

> The Trust owes no constitutional obligation to the first respondent or to the learners at the school. It has its own constitutional rights to property recognised in terms of section 25 of the Constitution. The obligation to provide compulsory education is an obligation of the Department of Education.

Furthermore, the High Court found that relief from the parents could only be sought against the MEC and not the owners of the property, insisting that closure and eviction of the school from the private property did not constitute a closure of the school as MEC could make alternative arrangements to relocate the school to another premises.

The decision of the High Court was contested by MEC on the premises that the trust was carrying out a public function in line with the South African Promotion of Administrative Justice Act (PAJA).[109] It was further argued that the best interests of the learners were not properly taken into consideration. The MEC consequently prayed for the suspension of the eviction order until MEC was able to find alternative solutions.

The Constitutional Court delineated the core issue of negative responsibility on individuals, precedence of the best interests of the child and property rights.[110] The Constitutional Court laid down the basis of core content of the right to a basic education as envisaged within the Constitution. In its wisdom, it restated that[111]:

> a 'basic education' under section 29(1)(a). Unlike some of the other socio-economic rights, this right is immediately realisable. There is no internal limitation requiring that the right be 'progressively realised' within 'available resources' subject to 'reasonable legislative measures'. The right

[108] Para 21.

[109] South African Promotion of Administrative Justice Act, http://www.justice.gov.za/legislation/acts/2000-003.pdf (accessed 30 April 2017).

[110] Para 31.

[111] Para 37.

> to a basic education in section 29(1) (a) may be limited only in terms of a law of general application which is 'reasonable and justifiable in an open and democratic society based on human dignity, equality and freedom'. This right is therefore distinct from the right to 'further education' provided for in section 29(1) (b). The state is, in terms of that right, obliged, through reasonable measures, to make further education 'progressively available and accessible.

In addition, the Court restated the obligation of South Africa under regional and global international law instruments.[112] It thus upheld the significance of basic education stressing the challenges of inadequacy which ultimately affect access to basic education. In addition, the guilt of any parent or person that obstructs access to basic education of a child was highlighted by the Court.[113] The Court consequently found that, while the MEC had failed in its positive obligation to provide, promote, protect and fulfil the right to basic education of a child, the trust also had a negative responsibility to ensure that the access to basic education of the child is not obstructed.

In reaching this decision, the Constitutional Court read the provisions of section 8 of the South African Constitution[114] in line with section 29, finding that the purpose of section 8(2) is[115]

> not to obstruct private autonomy or to impose on a private party the duties of the state in protecting the Bill of Rights. It is rather to require private parties not to interfere with or diminish the enjoyment of a right.

[112] Para 40.

[113] Para 44.

[114] Sec 8 of the Constitution deals with the application and binding nature of the Bill of Rights. It provides: '(1) The Bill of Rights applies to all law, and binds the legislature, the executive, the judiciary and all organs of state. (2) A provision of the Bill of Rights binds a natural or a juristic person if, and to the extent that, it is applicable, taking into account the nature of the right and the nature of any duty imposed by the right. (3) When applying a provision of the Bill of Rights to a natural or juristic person in terms of subsection (2), a court - (a) in order to give effect to a right in the Bill, must apply, or if necessary develop, the common law to the extent that legislation does not give effect to that right; and (b) may develop rules of the common law to limit the right, provided that the limitation is in accordance with section 36(1). (4) A juristic person is entitled to the rights in the Bill of Rights to the extent required by the nature of the rights and the nature of that juristic person'.

[115] Para 58.

The decision of the High Court was set aside as it did not take into full consideration the best interests of the child. While still granting that the trust takes possession of its property, time was given for MEC to make alternative arrangements to ensure that access to education of the learners is not compromised.

iv. *The Centre for Child Law and Others v The Minister of Basic Education and Others*[116] (Availability)

The underlying principle in this case is the importance of the availability of teachers as core components of realising the right to basic education.[117] Primarily, the case concerns the fundamental right to education of children in public schools, especially in the Eastern Cape province of South Africa. The applicants in this case sought a compelling order on the respondent to ensure the availability of sufficient teachers for schools. In order to achieve this, the remuneration of teachers, the employment of teachers and administrative support for teaching and non-teaching staff are well entrenched.

A core aspect of the case includes the role of national government to ensure that the provincial and local councils do all in their power to ensure that constitutional obligations are met.[118] In addition, the sacking of about 4000 teachers attributed to a lack of management was also a basis for contention. Other negative effects that hampered access to education were blamed on lack of funds for programmes on transport, feeding and nutrition.[119]

[116] Case 1749/2012.

[117] Para 12.

[118] See sec 100 of the Constitution: '(1) When a province cannot or does not fulfil an executive obligation in terms of the Constitution or legislation, the national executive may intervene by taking any appropriate steps to ensure fulfilment of that obligation, including (a) issuing a directive to the provincial executive, describing the extent of the failure to fulfil its obligations and stating any steps required to meet its obligations; and (b) assuming responsibility for the relevant obligation in that province to the extent necessary to (i) maintain essential national standards or meet established minimum standards for the rendering of a service; (ii) maintain economic unity; (iii) maintain national security; or (iv) prevent that province from taking unreasonable action that is prejudicial to the interests of another province or to the country as a whole'. Para 6.

[119] Para 13.

It was alleged that the Eastern Cape Department failed to carry out its obligation effectively by providing for an 'effective and efficient budgeting to support pedagogic cum administrative processes in schools'.[120] This was captured in the failure to provide funding for the operations of the schools and shortage of teachers in schools.[121] The effect of the totality of the facts stated above was that the realisation of the right to a basic education was not only breached, but other fundamental rights were contravened.[122]

The learned trial judge found that efficient measures must be in place to ensure that budgetary issues do not obstruct the execution of the constitutional rights of the respondents, especially pertaining to the realisation of the right to education. In the *dictum,* the Court opined:

i. The respondents are obliged to ensure the post-establishments for both non-teaching and teaching staff for 2013 for public schools and fill same[123];
ii. Appoint educators on a temporary basis pending the permanent appointment of all vacant substantive posts …[124];
iii. Pay salaries of all educators which the respondents have failed to pay[125];
iv. Reimburse all funds spent by schools in paying educators hired privately that have provided the required services.[126]

The judgment thus captures another important role of the judiciary in ensuring that the objectives that are set out by the executive and the legislature are implemented. Efficiency and implementation therefore provide a means via which the right to education must be realised. This case provides an avenue for individuals who are saddled with the responsibility of implementing policies to be held responsible when they fail to do so. Also, the case can provide a leverage to tackle challenges of

[120] Para 15.
[121] Para 17.
[122] Para 21.
[123] Para 34.
[124] Para 35(3).
[125] Para 35(4).
[126] Para 6.

corruption that is already identified to be one of the major obstacles to the realisation of the right to basic education. It is therefore advanced that an official who fails by omission or commission to ensure that budgetary obligations or administrative responsibility are upheld could be held liable by the law.

v. Western Cape Forum for Intellectual Disability v Government of the Republic of South Africa and Another (Access)

The Western Cape Forum comprises of several NGOs working on education for disabled persons. This case considers the issues of economic obligations and the role of education of children with disabilities. The applicants challenged the disparity based on financial support for the education of children with disabilities as opposed to children without disabilities. Furthermore, the distinction between funding and eventual access to education of children with severe disabilities differed from access to education of children with mild disabilities; this was also advanced by the state as a basis for differential funding of the schools.

While the government accepted the challenges on which the case was grounded, they contended based on the entrenchment of disparity as an offshoot effect of apartheid. In addition, the government further argued a gradual improvement and increase of the number of children able to access education as a reason for inability to increase funding of private NGOs supporting the education of children with disabilities. Furthermore, the usefulness of education to the learners in question was also put forward as it was argued that education could actually do them no good. According to Murungi, the instant case brought to the fore varying obligations of the state to promote, fulfil and honour its treaty obligations, especially the provisions of Article 24 of the Convention on the Rights of Persons with Disabilities (CRPD).[127]

The Court in its wisdom rightly scaled the obligation and onus to provide and ensure the realisation of the constitutional right to a basic education to be more on the state as against the obligation on individuals and NGOs.[128] The Court found that 'it is unreasonable for a private

[127] N. Murungi, "The duty to provide basic education for children with severe and profound intellectual disabilities," http://reference.sabinet.co.za/webx/access/electronic_journals/esrrev/esrrev_v12_n3_a4.pdf (accessed 17 April 2017).

[128] Para 24.

entity…to be forced to bear the burden which should be borne by the state'.[129] The reasoning here resonates with the *dictum* of the Court in the case of *Juma Musijid* discussed above. Furthermore, the reliance on White Paper 6 on inclusive education,[130] which did not contemplate the education of children with severe disabilities, was rejected by the Court in respect of the treaty obligations of South Africa. Particularly, the provision of Article 23 of the CRC provides[131]:

> A mentally or physically disabled child should enjoy a full and decent life, in conditions which ensure dignity, promote self-reliance and facilitates the child's active participation in the community.

The reasoning of the Court in this case is advanced inherently capable of ensuring collaboration between private agencies involved with the education of persons with disabilities. In Nigeria, some disability homes face extinction because of challenges of funds. The Court further relied on the provisions of the African Children's Charter,[132] the revised European Social Charter[133] and the Optional Protocol of the CRPD to arrive at a conclusion. Leaning on the reasoning in the *Paul O Donoghue v The Minister for Health, Minister for Education & Others*,[134] the Court construed the obligation on the government to ensure the provision of education for any child to mean and include 'achievement of fullest potentials'. Thus, the constraint of economic and competing national needs was rejected by the Court.[135]

The courts went further to link the budgetary obligation of the government to the question of equality between all individuals. In this way, any concentration on a group of individuals on the circumstances of birth and physical condition was construed to be tantamount to discrimination and denial of equality in access to basic education.[136]

[129] As above.

[130] http://www.dhet.gov.za/LinkClick.aspx?fileticket=gVFccZLi%2Ft-I%3D&tabid=191&mid=484 (accessed 17 April 2017).

[131] Para 20.

[132] Arts 11 and 13.

[133] Art 15.

[134] (1993) IEHC 2.

[135] Para 26.

[136] Para 27.

In holding the Western Cape government liable for a breach of their obligation to fulfil the access to basic education of children, the Court rightly put forward the provision of interim measures towards, ensuring that the realisation of the right to basic education is achieved. This approach as already advocated provides the court with an opportunity to monitor the progress and steps taken by the executive to realise the constitutional rights of the affected learners.

vi. MEC for Education: KwaZulu-Natal and Others v Navaneethum Pillay and Others[137] (Acceptability)

The nose ring case represents the position of courts on the rights to education. In this case, the elimination of any form of discrimination based on the grounds of religion was rejected. In the instant case, the learner, Sunali Pillay, wore a nose ring to school in line with her religious obligation. However, as had been established by the SGB, learners were not allowed to wear such ornaments to school. The mother of the leaner subsequently took the matter to court, alleging unfair discrimination based on her choice of religion.

The court of first instance found in favour of the school, while the High Court found in favour of the learner. The decision to stop the learner from wearing her religious ornament was declared void as it was contrary to the South African Constitution, notwithstanding the argument of the respondent that enforcing the claimed right of equal treatment by Pillay would eventually amount to discrimination against other learners, and that the act of wearing of a nose stud was voluntary.

When confronted with the case in the Constitutional Court, Justice Lang, in delivering the lead judgment, opined that[138]

> the rule prohibiting the wearing of jewelry had the potential for indirect discrimination because it allowed certain groups of learners to express their religious and cultural identity freely, while denying that right to others.

The question of discrimination resonates in several community schools in Nigeria. Religion-based discrimination and ethnic-based discrimination

[137] Case CCT 51/06.

[138] Media Summary, http://www.saflii.org.za/za/cases/ZACC/2007/21media.pdf (accessed 18 April 2014).

are top among this. The resultant effect is a lack of zeal to access education institutions by learners from poor communities.[139]

7.6 Indian Jurisprudence on Education

The role of the courts in India in driving the right to access of basic education can be summed up in these words[140]:

> The Indian Supreme Court has created major reforms in the protection of human rights. Taking a judicial activist role, the Court has put itself in a unique position to intervene when it sees violations of these fundamental rights.

The interventions of the courts in India provide the basis of understanding that the right education is intrinsic and interlinked with such rights like the right to life. The courts as will be shown in the following cases have adopted two programmatic approaches: the first deals with the question of education as a fundamental right and the second with the safety of education institutions and protection of access to education of marginalised groups.

The role of the courts has, however, not been without some criticism as it has been argued to be able to subject the judiciary to 'judicial excess and rather not a beacon of hope for the oppressed'.[141] As already argued, the role of the judiciary in the South African situation has shown that the fears of the judiciary engaging in overarching decisions are expellable. An important point to note is the willingness of the Indian judiciary to adjudicate on the right to access of basic education even before

[139] This was part of the information gathered by the author during his tour of the Anambra West local government area education institutions in 2012. It was observed that children from the area (mostly poor) avoided school because they were abused as never doing well by teachers. The same response was also gathered by the author in 2008 during his research on access to education of indigenous people in Uganda with a particular focus on the Batwa. See generally A. C. Onuora-Oguno, "Access to education of indigenous people in Uganda. A case study of the Batwa," unpublished LLM thesis, University of Pretoria, 2008, http://repository.up.ac.za/bitstream/handle/2263/8005/azubike.pdf?sequence=1 (accessed 24 April 2014).

[140] A. Rosencranz and M. Jackson, "The Delhi pollution case: The Supreme Court of India and the limits of judicial power," *Columbia Journal of Environmental Law* 28 (2003): 223, 224.

[141] As above.

the recognition in Article 21(A) of the Indian Constitution. While it is my opinion that the specific mention of the right to education as against other economic, social and cultural rights is linked to the pivotal and the intrinsic nature of education, scholars like Killander perceive it as incidental.[142]

Against this backdrop, the following cases from the Indian jurisdiction are examined.

i. *Society for Unaided Private Schools of Rajasthan VUOI & Another*[143] (Affordability)

This case dealt with the applicability of the application or otherwise of the RTE Act 2009 with unaided non-minority schools in India. The courts, in considering the legality of the RTE Act to ensure equality in education, established the role of parents, teachers, pupils and ultimately the government as major actors. In addition, the vital role of basic education was well articulated stressing the issues of access to 'neighbourhood schools'. In interpreting the wording of the Act, the court opined that[144]:

> The word 'Free' in the long title to the 2009 Act stands for removal by the State of any financial barrier that prevents a child from completing 8 years of schooling. The word 'Compulsory' in that title stands for compulsion on the State and the parental duty to send children to school. To protect and give effect to this right of the child to education as enshrined in Article 21.

From the above dictum of the court, it is decipherable that the onus to protect, promote and fulfil the right to education of a child is hinged both horizontally and vertically. It enunciates the importance of quality education in equal terms to all children. Furthermore, the court found that all forms of hindrance in terms of fee or for fee education must be abhorred to ensure the full realisation of the child's right to education.

[142] During an interaction between M. Killander and M. Hansungule, Centre for Human Rights, 2 April 2015.

[143] Writ Petition (C) 95 OF 2010.

[144] Writ Petition (C) 95 of 2010.3, http://www.lawyerscollective.org/files/Right%20to%20Eduucation.pdf (accessed 22 April 2017).

The provisions of sections 5 and 6 of the RTE Act further espoused definite obligations on the Indian government to ensure the access component of basic education by ensuring that such schools are within a reasonable distance from the community. A timeline is envisaged to ensure that the progressive realisation of measurable steps is implemented by a well-structured follow-up mechanism. It is based on realising these measures that the court, as advanced, is recommended to act as the unbiased arbiter between the institutions, individuals and parents.

In the event where schools that are unaided take responsibility for children, the government is statutorily mandated to ensure the reimbursement of such expenditures to the tune of monies spent on per child basis.[145] Consequently, the court found that provisions that ousted support for some minority schools were contrary to the Constitution and also the RTE Act.[146] The decision in this case resonates to some extent the decision in the *Western Forum* case in South Africa. The role of the government as the sole responsibility owner in ensuring the implementation and the realisation of the right to a basic education cannot be overlooked despite the involvement of private juristic bodies in the education industry.

Thus, the role of the court in the case enunciates the interpretative role of the court in giving an elaborate definition of the meaning and the scope of both law and policy that touches on the right to education. Consequently, it dispels the fears that the court would interfere with obligations or tasks that are not properly suited within their competence.

ii. Mohini Jain v State of Karnataka[147] (Access)

This case, although not dealing with basic education, strictly brings to the fore two pivotal comments on the right to education: first, the elimination of fees capable of hindering access to education; second, and the elimination of discrimination in education. However, it must be underscored that the role of higher education, in itself, albeit progressive, is determined by the calibre of people churned out from the basic education sector. This has a direct impact on the availability of well-skilled teachers that are engaged in the delivery of quality basic education.

[145] Sec 12(2) RTE Act.

[146] See the provisions of the RTE Act secs 12(1)(c) and 18(3).

[147] 1992 AIR 1858, 1992 SCR (3) 658.

Capturing the pivotal role of higher education and primary education, Dlamini Zuma argues that 'no country can develop based on primary education alone' arguing for a holistic re-conceptualisation of the entire education paradigm in Africa.[148]

In the instant case, the petitioner, Miss Mohini Jain, was obligated to pay an amount of money to enable her to gain access to study for the MBBS degree. The said amount was over and above what was tenable and payable by students from Karnataka. Consequent upon her parents' failure to make tuition payments and provide bank guarantees, admission was denied. It was argued by the respondent that the distinction was a meritorious one as students were placed on 'government seats' depending on grades obtained.[149]

In the Court's wisdom, some questions were set down for the determination[150]:

i. 'right to education' guaranteed to the people of India under the Constitution? If so, did the concept of 'capitation fee' violate same?
ii. Whether the charging of capitation fee in consideration of admissions to educational institutions was arbitrary, unfair, unjust and as such violated Article 14 of the Constitution?

Considering the provisions of the right to education under the Indian Constitution, the court's finding from the perspective of the dignity of man being inviolable was premised on the opinion that education was the bedrock of achieving dignity. The court found that[151]

> it was with that hope that Articles 41 and 45 were brought in Chapter IV of the constitution. An individual cannot be assured of human dignity unless his personality is developed and the only way to do that is to educate him...

The above decision was further predicated on the fact that 'it is the duty of the state to respect and protect the right to education'.

[148] N. C. Dlamini Zuma, Chairperson of African Union Commission lecture "The role of research universities such as the University of Pretoria in the development of Africa," lecture delivered at University of Pretoria, 24 April 2014.

[149] Para 659.

[150] Para 660.

[151] Para 667(f).

It is noted that, despite the fact that at the time of the instant case, the right to education was contained as a mere fundamental of state objective which was deemed non-justiciable. The courts were courageous enough to advance that the inclusion of the right in the Constitution was not a 'mere pious provision'.[152] The court went further to state strongly that[153]:

> The 'right to education', therefore, is concomitant to the fundamental rights enshrined under Part III of the Constitution. The State is under a constitutional mandate to provide educational institutions at all levels for the benefit of the citizens. The educational institutions must function to the best advantage of the citizens. Opportunity to acquire education cannot be confined to the richer section of the society.

The charging of capitation fees was eventually declared to be null and void,[154] a violation of the constitutional right to education and a commitment by the government not to sell education. It was stated that '[c]apitation fee is nothing but a price for selling education. The concept of "teaching shops" is contrary to the constitutional scheme and is wholly abhorrent to the Indian culture and heritage'.[155] The question that also begs for an answer is whether the concept of 'teaching shops' is obtainable within the Nigerian education sphere. Following the analogy drawn by Zuma above, it is important to note that the argument of which is more important may be one of the egg or chicken argument. With the existence of 'teaching shops' at the tertiary level in Nigeria, the quality of teachers that are churned out to engage in basic education is increase in quantity but with pure lack of quality.

iii. *Unnikrishnan JP v State of Andhra Pradesh*[156] (Access and Pivotal Nature of Education)

This case brought to the fore the inalienable nature of rights. The case enunciates further the intrinsic nature of the right to education as

[152] Para 667(h).

[153] Para 668(e).

[154] Para 672(g).

[155] Para 670(c).

[156] 1993 AIR 217, 1993 SCR (1) 594.

encompassing even the right to life. The case called for the interpretation of Articles 41[157] and 45[158] of the Indian Constitution in line with Article 21[159] thereof.

The case was a consideration of the legality of charging capitation fees. Recalling the wisdom of the court in the *Mohini Jahin* case, it is worth noting that the charging of any fees has the capability of limiting access to education, especially considering the level of poverty in developing states, and Nigeria in particular. However, the distinction between higher education and basic education was also drawn by the court. Importantly, it must be underscored that the pivotal nature of education was held to be paramount and not violable.

In articulating the role the court must play in the realisation of the right to education, it was stated that the court 'must monitor the progressive realisation' as advanced in Article 45 of the Constitution and ensure it is followed up.[160] In this wise, it is also encouraging to note the diction of the court in comparing fundamental rights and fundamental directives of state objectives[161]:

> Since fundamental rights and directive principles are complementary to each other, there is no reason why this fundamental right cannot be interpreted in this manner.

This position finds some credence in the arguments of Viljoen in his discussion of the supposed roles of fundamental objectives of state principle already canvassed in this thesis.[162]

[157] The state shall, within the limits of its economic capacity and development, make effective provision for securing the right to work, to education and to public assistance in cases of unemployment, old age, sickness and disablement, and in other cases of undeserved want.

[158] The state shall endeavour to provide, within a period of ten years from the commencement of this Constitution, for free and compulsory education for all children until they complete the age of fourteen years.

[159] The State shall provide free and compulsory education to all children of the age of six to fourteen years in such manner as the state may, by law, determine.

[160] Para 713(e). In paras 716(d)–(f), the court absolves itself of attempting to show priority. However, this position is assumed not coherent with the particular importance attached to basic education as contained in the ICECSR and also as seen in the South African situation. Importantly, however, the role of the court in ensuring that the argument of progressive realisation is not rhetoric is lauded and should also be seen to guide the judiciary in Nigeria in ensuring that economic, social and cultural rights are achieved over stipulated periods.

[161] Para 719(h).

[162] Viljoen 551.

iv. Avinash Mehrotra vs Union of India & Ors[163]

The case dealt with the need to ensure the establishment of safe schools. After a fire incident, the case was initiated as PIL. It raised the challenge and neglect of government to ensure that school safety and regulation are maintained in India.[164] The main prayer of the petitioner was for the court to find that 'each and every child of this country can receive good education free from fear of safety and security'.[165] The court found among several holding that[166]:

i. Before granting recognition or affiliation, the concerned State Governments and Union Territories are directed to ensure that the buildings are safe and secured from every angle and they are constructed according to the safety norms incorporated in the National Building Code of India.
ii. All existing government and private schools shall install fire extinguishing equipments within a period of six months.
iii. The school buildings be kept free from inflammable and toxic material. If storage is inevitable, they should be stored safely.

The present case is instructive in examining the safety of Nigerian schools especially in the light of circumstances surrounding the disappearance of the Chibok girls from a school dormitory.

With cases discussed from both the South African and Indian courts, it is important to discuss the jurisprudence of supranational judicial and quasi-judicial bodies. The discussion of these institutions within the African human rights system is important as it provides a leeway through which the right to basic education may be pursued within the African system, even if the Nigerian judicial system does not open up to the channel to advance same.[167]

[163] (2009) 6 SCC 398.

[164] See paragraph 7 at http://indiankanoon.org/doc/232115/.

[165] See paragraph 8 at http://indiankanoon.org/doc/232115/.

[166] See paragraph 40 at http://indiankanoon.org/doc/232115/.

[167] A. C. Onuora-Oguno, "Seeking solace from a distance, jettisoning national courts: Reliance on supra-national judicial bodies to realise economic, social and cultural rights (ESCR)," paper presented at the American Society of International Law Conference, 8–11 April 2015, Washington, DC, USA.

As already discussed, the ECOWAS Court has upheld and reiterated the importance and justiciability of the right to education in the *SERAP v FGN case.*

7.7 Conclusion

This chapter concludes by echoing the position of Skelton when she opines[168]:

> The legal claim that the right to a basic education is immediately enforceable does not wave a magic wand...the delivery of basic education to all...there are huge backlog in infrastructure, there is an ever increasing demand for more schools and classrooms amongst a socially and geographically mobile population, there are concerns about quality.

From the various decisions emanating from the South African and Indian, it is discernable that the role of the courts in driving the realisation of the right to basic education is very paramount. The recognition of the right to education in the South African and Indian Constitutions is an example worthy to be emulated towards realising the right to basic education and development.

The courts in South Africa and India have contributed immensely in developing the jurisprudence on education. The role of the judiciary, according to Skelton, is captured thus[169]:

> The courts have played an important role in the progress being made with regard to children's right to a basic education in South Africa. Measured against the interlinked principles of availability, accessibility, acceptability and adaptability, the case law of the past few years has shown some significant advancement...the courts have outlined State and private responsibilities in not hampering the right to basic education.

[168] A. Skelton, "The role of the courts in ensuring the right to a basic education in a democratic South Africa: A critical evaluation of recent education case law," *De Jure 4* (2013).

[169] As above.

CHAPTER 8

The African Human Rights Response to Access to Basic Education

8.1 Introduction

In this chapter, I consider some jurisprudence emanating from the African human rights architecture. This is needful in the light that in certain circumstances, recourse may be had to supranational judicial institutions in a bid to uphold the rights of individuals. An increasing wave of public interest litigation is on going in several African nations with Uganda and Ghana taking some front row in the pattern of what we have seen in South Africa. The main purposes of the analysis here is to provide, national NGOs an insight into how to engage with the jurisprudence of the African Union human rights institutions and provide a guideline on how the several treaties that states are party too can be engaged national in driving development anchored on the respect to the right to education.

8.2 Expert Committee on the Rights and Welfare of the Child (Committee)

i. *Centre for Human Rights (University of Pretoria) and La Rencontre Africaine Pour La Defence Des Droits De L'homme (Senegal) v Government of Senegal*[1] **(Access and Best Interests of the Child)**

This case borders on a complaint instituted based on a claim by parents on their inability to send their children to government schools and rather

[1] Communication 001/Com/001/2012.

A. C. Onuora-Oguno, *Development and the Right to Education in Africa*,
https://doi.org/10.1007/978-3-319-90335-4_8

send them to assumed Quranic schools. It was advanced by the complainants that over '100,000 children aged between 4 and 12' are routinely forced by their instructor's *marabouts* to engage in street begging.[2] It was submitted before the Committee that the Act, having lasted over a long period, contravened the Penal Code of Senegal and also a failure to rely on Article 74 of the respondent state Constitution; should ground the admissibility of the case before the Committee. The present communication was subsequently found admissible by the Committee, stating:

> The African Committee of Experts on the Rights and Welfare of the Child notes and concludes that the communication submitted by the authors has fulfilled all the admissibility conditions as laid down in the Committee's Guidelines on Consideration of Communication; and it is accordingly declared admissible.

While the admissibility of the communication is founded on grounds of compliance with the procedure of submitting communications before the court, it is envisaged that the decision on the merits will advance the responsibility of the state to protect the right to education of the *talibees* in Senegal. This anticipation is hinged on the fact that access to basic education must be protected and promoted by states, ensuring that funds do not inhibit a child's ability to access schools in African states. The challenge of funds is linked to the effort of eradicating poverty in African states. Poverty is identified to be a major premise on which children are either unable to enrol or drop out of school. According to Molokwu[3]:

> Extreme poverty and hunger are major problems that the Nigerian government has not been able to solve. Past governments between 1972 and now have mounted at least eight projects that were meant to alleviate poverty… The link between poverty, hunger and human development is very significant. Indeed, poverty and hunger are the exact opposite of human development. All the attributes of human development are deprived by poverty. Poverty is lack of job. Poverty is hunger, poor health, *low education*, low self-esteem, lack of adequate housing, lack of land, inability to cloth oneself/family low economic status.

[2] Paras 2–3.

[3] N. Molokwu, "The challenges of reducing poverty in Nigeria: Repositioning home economics for sustainable education" (2010), http://www.educationforsustainabledevelopment.org/papers/202.doc (my emphasis) (accessed 25 April 2017).

However, the fact that the case is considered admissible before the commission must encourage individuals, and other NGOs (interested in PIL) to approach the Committee with various issues hinging on the obligation of the government to the provision of basic education.

ii. *Nubian Minors v Kenya*[4] (Access, Availability and Acceptability)

In this case, the Nubian children faced severe challenges which, among others, included discrimination and inability to access basic education. Hinged on the alleged violation of Articles 3 and 6 of the African Children's Charter, the Nubian children were denied access to equal education within Kenya. Article 3 provides:

> Every child shall be entitled to the enjoyment of the rights and freedoms recognised and guaranteed in this Charter irrespective of the child's or his/her parents' or legal guardians' race, ethnic group, colour, sex, language, religion, political or other opinion, national and social origin, fortune, birth or other status.

Article 6 provides:

> 1. Every child shall have the right from his birth to a name.
> 2. Every child shall be registered immediately after birth.
> 3. Every child has the right to acquire a nationality.
> 4. States Parties to the present Charter shall undertake to ensure that their constitutional legislation recognises the principles according to which a child shall acquire the nationality of the state in the territory of which he has been born if, at the time of the child's birth, he is not granted nationality by any other state in accordance with its laws.

Despite the finding of the Kenyan Human Rights Commission (KHRC) that the act of the government was nothing but 'an institutionalised discrimination',[5] the ultimate effect of this action was that the Kenyan

[4] Communication 002/2009.

[5] Kenyan National Human Rights commission, *An identity crisis? A study on the issuance of national identity cards in Kenya*, http://citizenshiprightsinafrica.org/docs/KNHRC-ID-Report-2007.pdf (accessed 25 April 2017).

government 'fails to provide equal access to education and healthcare, condemning Nubian children to a life of poverty'.[6]

The violation and entrenchment of denial of education were enunciated on the fact that 'the number of schools provided for the Nubian children and poor funding of their education amounted to a denial of access to education'.[7]

The African Committee of Experts on the Rights and Welfare of the Child (African Children's Committee) found, among other things, that the Kenyan government must ensure that a swift response to the issues that affected the access to education of the Nubian children was addressed. Importantly, these provisions must be 'administrative, short and long term in nature'.[8] A core component of the decision of the Committee as advanced in the instant case is that[9]:

> A state may not be able to justify a policy that encourages disparity or double standards in the provision of essential services. Considering the fact that registration at birth is crucial for the enjoyment of many other services, the Nubian children would seem to have been implicitly excluded from benefiting from some of the essential services they ordinarily should have been entitled to.

From the two cases discussed above, it is clear that the African Children's Committee is open to advance the realisation of issues hinged on the best interests of the child. It therefore projects a fertile place for NGOs and other parties interested in public interest litigation to test the many challenges confronting the realisation of the right to access of basic education.[10]

[6] http://www.ihrda.org/2011/03/kenya-violates-african-children%E2%80%99s-charter-as-nubian-children-suffer-discrimination-and-statelessness/ (accessed 25 April 2014).

[7] Para 65.

[8] E. Durojaye and E. A. Foley, "Making a first impression: An assessment of the decision of the committee of experts of the African Children's Charter in the Nubian children communication," *African Human Rights Law Journal* 12 (2012): 567.

[9] Durojaye and Foley, 575.

[10] It is noted that under the communication procedure before the African Commission and the Court, individuals and NGOs are entitled to bring complaints. See generally M. Hansungule, "African courts and the African Commission on human and peoples' Rights," 250, http://www.kas.de/upload/auslandshomepages/namibia/Human_Rights_in_Africa/8_Hansungule.pdf (accessed 24 April 2017).

In addition, as a quasi-judicial body, the Committee has further crystallised the role that national human rights institutions can play in ensuring the positive implementation of administrative measures, policy and legal directive towards the realisation of the right to education.[11]

8.3 African Commission on Human and Peoples' Rights

The African Commission on Human and Peoples' Rights (African Commission) is another quasi-judicial body within the African human rights structure. The commission is saddled with the responsibility of interpreting the rights contained in the ACHPR. While conceding the indivisibility of human rights, the African Commission has faced some challenges in its development of economic, social and cultural rights within the African human rights system.[12] The ACHPR, being the basic document that stipulates the functions of the African Commission, saddles it with the responsibility of providing both promotional and protective mandates. Article 45 provides that the functions of the commission shall be:

1. to promote the human and peoples' rights and in particular:
   (a) to collect documents, undertake studies and research on African problems in the field of human and peoples' rights, organise seminars, symposia and conferences, disseminate information, encourage national and local institutions concerned with human and peoples' rights and, should the case arise, give its views or make recommendations to governments;

[11] Challenges that the implementation of the decision of the Committee has been enunciated and the judiciary remains the ultimate arbiter in the event of disputes and failure to implement decisions. See A.G. Assefa, "Will Nubian children have to go to the African Court?," 24 April 2014, http://africlaw.com/2012/04/13/will-nubian-children-have-to-go-to-the-african-court/; Durojaye and Foley (in 172 above), 576–578. Katema has argued that seeking non-legal means for the resolution of developmental rights will have better results if not done legally, especially under authoritarian rule. However, it is important to note here that, with the increase in democratic rule within African states and Nigeria especially, the courts should remain the last arbiter for the dispensation of justice. See generally W. Katema, "How are rights claimed under an authoritarian rule? A case study of Operation Murambatsvina (clear the filth) in Zimbabwe," (2005), https://www.google.com/url?sa=t&rct=j&q=&esrc=s&source=web&cd=3&cad=rja&uact=8&ved=0ahUKEwj0jsSg4PjaAhWKFSwKHdhyCssQFgg1MAI&url=https%3A%2F%2Fthesis.eur.nl%2Fpub%2F7149%2FWashington%2520Katema%2520HDS.pdf&usg=AOvVaw0cnOX-oMLn4Yp4DB6Jd2g8a (accessed 28 April 2017).

[12] M. Ssenyonjo, "The economic, social and cultural rights jurisprudence of the African Commission: 30 years since the adoption of the African Charter," *Netherlands Quarterly of Human Rights* 29 (2011): 358.

(b) to formulate and lay down principles and rules aimed at solving legal problems relating to human and peoples' rights and fundamental freedoms upon which African Governments may base their legislation;
(c) to co-operate with other African and international institutions concerned with the promotion and protection of human and peoples' rights.

2. Ensure the protection of human and peoples' rights under conditions laid down by the present Charter.
3. Interpret all the provisions of the present Charter at the request of a state party, an institution of the OAU or an African Organisation recognised by the OAU.
4. Perform any other tasks which may be entrusted to it by the Assembly of Heads of State and Government.

It is based on this that the commission is well positioned to entertain complaints from individuals and other recognised entities. Discussed below are few instances that the ACHPR engaged with the subject of access to education.

i. *Zimbabwe Lawyers for Human Rights, Human Rights Trust of Southern Africa v The Government of Zimbabwe Forced Evictions Hopley–Porta Farm and Hatcliffe Communities*[13] (Access and Availability)

This case, while not dealing specifically with the realisation of the right to education, inferred it implicitly. The case was about the forced eviction of some indigenes residing in the Porta farm area. The complainant in the case sought the African Commission to hold the government of Zimbabwe liable for violating the right to education, among other rights. It was argued by the complainant that the natural consequence of the eviction was that evicted children would be unable to access school. They further claimed that the planned relocation of the Caledonia farm violated their rights to access basic amenities as amenities like schools, health care and sanitary facilities were not available at the proposed site of relocation.

[13] Communication 314/05.

It was the African Commission's finding that forced evictions should be done in line with General Comment 4.[14] Paragraph 8(b) thereof provides for 'availability of services, materials, facilities and infrastructure'; education lacking in this respect consequently aided the decision of the commission. It can be inferred, therefore, that governments must ensure that in all developmental initiatives, the provision of educational infrastructure is crucial and important. This also suggests the importance of access to educational institutions within a reasonable walking distance. The point here is that the commission is disposed to entertain issues hinged on questions of access to education directly or indirectly if approached.

ii. *Free Legal Assistance Group, Lawyers' Committee for Human Rights, Union Interafricaine des Droits de l'Homme, Les Témoins de Jehovah v Zaire*[15] (Acceptability)

This complaint was hinged on the alleged persecution of any group of people based on their religious beliefs, in this instant case, the Jehovah's Witness group in Zaire. The allegation spanned from the exclusion from 'persecution of the Jehovah's Witnesses, including arbitrary arrests, appropriation of church property, and exclusion to access education'.[16] The commission, besides the referral of the grave human rights violations to the Assembly of Heads of States, also embarked on an on-site visit.[17] Subsequently, a violation of the right to education as enshrined in Article 17 of the ACHPR was found against Zaire. In the wording of the commission, '[t]he closure of universities and secondary schools as described in Communication 100/93 constitutes a violation of article 17'.[18]

[14] ESCR Committee 13 December 1991, E/1992/23 General Comment 4, 'The Right to Adequate Housing (art 11(1) of the Covenant)', http://www.refworld.org/docid/47a7079a1.html (accessed 29 April 2017).

[15] Communication 25/89, 47/90, 56/91, 100/93 (1995), http://www1.umn.edu/humanrts/africa/comcases/25-89_47-90_56-91_100-93.html, http://www1.chr.up.ac.za/index.php/browse-by-institution/achpr-commission/266-drc-free-legal-assistance-group-and-others-v-zaire-2000-ahrlr-74-achpr-1995.html (accessed 29 April 2017).

[16] Para 3.

[17] Para 6.

[18] Para 48.

An important inference from the above case would, for instance, be the closure of all primary schools in Anambra State of Nigeria and also the various closures of schools in Nigeria. In Anambra State, learners were unable to attend school for an academic session, thereby jostling the academic progress of pupils. This suggests that if various institutions that have the capacity of seeking such redress are enlightened on the mechanisms available, more and proper accountability can be advanced in ensuring that the right to basic education is realised in Nigeria.

iii. *Kevin Mgwanga Gumne et al. v Cameroon*[19] (Acceptability)

This communication was rooted on several grievances that were traced to the 1961 independence of Cameroun. The Southern Cameroun alleged several violations leading up to marginalisation by the French-speaking area of the country. This violation spanned from economic to political marginalisation. It was further alleged specifically that[20]

> the Francophones have monopolistic control of the Ministry of National Education. That the Respondent State has underfunded primary education in Southern Cameroon, it failed to build new schools, understaffed primary schools, and it is closing all teacher training colleges. They allege further that the Respondent State 'Cameroonised' the GCE from the University of London, leading to mass protests which forced government to create an independent GCE Board. That, upon unification, diplomas awarded by the City & Guild, a technical education institution based in England, were replaced by the Certificat d'Aptitude Professionale (CAP) and the BAC Technique. These measures have resulted in persistent high levels of illiteracy in many areas in Southern Cameroon.

Cameroun in its response to the complaint refuted the claimant's claim, stating that it had on some occasions expended more funding on the region than other regions. In addition, the state argued that its non-recognition of the Bamenda University of Technology was purely based on the fact that it did not meet the stipulated requirement.[21]

[19] Communication 266/2003 (2009), http://www.achpr.org/files/sessions/45th/comunications/266.03/achpr45_266_03_eng.pdf (accessed 29 April 2017).

[20] Para 10.

[21] Para 146.

The decision of the African Commission in this communication was that it did not find the government of Cameroun to be in violation of the right to education. However, it is important to note that this decision was not hinged on the inability of the commission to determine the scope of the right to education.[22] The commission's decline to find a violation was found on the complainant not using the provisions of Rule 119(3)[23]:

> All explanations or statements submitted by a State party pursuant to the present Rule shall be communicated, through the secretary, to the author of the communication who may submit in writing additional information and observations within a time limit fixed by the Commission.

The commission in its *dictum* found that[24]:

> Concerning the alleged refusal to grant authorisation for the registration of the Bamenda University of Science and Technology, the Respondent State stated that the said university did not fulfil conditions for establishment of private universities. The Complainant did not show whether the criteria were met by the Bamenda University of Science and Technology or not. The Commission reiterates that for it to make finding on any allegations, the Parties have to provide it with the necessary information. Rule 119 of the Rules of Procedure of the Commission (which govern this communication) require parties to furnish explanation or statements, including additional information.
>
> The Complainants should have done so under Rule 119(3) of the Rules of Procedure. The Commission allowed Parties to make oral submission in this particular case. The Complainants did not substantiate the allegations. For the above reasons, the African Commissions finds that there is no violation of Article 17(1) of the Charter.

[22] It is argued by Ssenyonjo that this could be the case for the failure in the present communication. See M. Ssenyonjo, "The economic, social and cultural rights jurisprudence of the African Commission: 30 years since the adoption of the African Charter," *Netherlands Quarterly of Human Rights* 29 (2011): 379. It must be taken into account that the provision of Article 60 of the Charter allowing the Commission to draw inspiration from international law on human rights from both the African system, the UN system and other regional human rights systems. See Viljoen, 215.

[23] http://caselaw.ihrda.org/doc/1995_acmhpr_rop/view/119 (accessed 29 April 2017).

[24] Paras 148–149.

It is assumed that had the complainant adhered strictly to the available rules of procedure, the decision of the commission could have been different. It is important, therefore, that proper training and capacity building for any individual or institution wishing to engage the mechanism of not just judicial or quasi-judicial bodies be seen as paramount. As this is not the responsibility of the state, it behoves the CSO community to ensure that they are armed with the requisite knowledge of the process of litigating issues hinged on public interest.

Thus, the African Commission, from the cases discussed above, shows a willingness to engage on the alleged violation of the right to education as enshrined in the ACHPR. As rightly argued by Ssenyonjo, '[t]he approach by the Commission is in line with the developments towards increased justiciability of ESC at both international and domestic levels'.[25] The African Commission's approach has been 'that of progressive and generous interpretation, relaxing traditional standing requirements, minimising the effect of claw-back clauses and reading into the Charter some important economic rights'.[26] Finally, on the importance of engaging the Commission on an interpretation of the provision of economic, social and cultural rights, especially the right to education, Viljoen advances that '[t]he Charter does not base fulfilment of any of its provisions dependent on available resources or progressive realisation'. In addition, he posits that despite the reliance on the argument of progressive realisation, it is not applicable to a definite and instant realisation of the right to education.[27] This interpretation has been advanced earlier in this chapter as applicable in South Africa and thus should provide a positive direction for Nigerian authorities towards its pursuit of the realisation of the right to basic education.

8.4 The African Court on Human and Peoples' Rights

The African Court is the first judicial body established by the African Union. Recently, the Court has been empowered to have a criminal chamber that will adjudicate on international criminal law. The major mandate of the Court is to complement the African Commission. Article 2 of the Court Protocol provides:

[25] Ssenyonjo, 384.

[26] Viljoen, 296.

[27] As above.

> The Court shall, bearing in mind the provisions of this Protocol, complement the protective mandate of the African Commission on Human and Peoples' Rights (hereinafter referred to as 'the Commission') conferred upon it by the African Charter on Human and Peoples' Rights (hereinafter referred to as 'the Charter').

The protective mandate of the African Commission is as provided in Article 45(2) of the ACHPR targeted towards ensuring that the rights provided in the Charter are respected and remedies are granted when violations occur. The jurisdiction of the Court is as provided in Article 3 of the Protocol, which provides:

> The jurisdiction of the Court shall extend to all cases and disputes submitted to it concerning the interpretation and application of the Charter, this Protocol and any other relevant Human Rights instrument ratified by the States concerned.

From the foregoing, it can be inferred that, since the sources of laws applicable before the Court are 'the provisions of the Charter and any other relevant human rights instruments ratified by the states concerned',[28] the chances of the Court adjudicating on the right of access to basic education are high. It is noted, however, that while access to the Court as stipulated under Article 5(3), which provides:

> The Court may entitle relevant non-governmental organisations (NGOs) with observer status before the Commission, and individuals to institute cases directly before it, in accordance with article 34 (6) of this Protocol.

The limitation of the provision of Article 36(6),

> [a]t the time of the ratification of this Protocol or any time thereafter, the State shall make a declaration accepting the competence of the Court to receive cases under article 5 (3) of this Protocol. The Court shall not receive any petition under article 5 (3) involving a State Party which has not made such a declaration.

It is envisaged that with the complementary role of the African Commission, the possibility of testing the disposition of the Court

[28] Article 7 of the protocol to the African Court.

towards the right to access of basic education and other economic, social and cultural rights is promising.

8.5 Lessons from the UK

Concern for the quality of education in the UK has been a priority over the years,[29] necessitating the drafting of the White Paper on Schools Achieving Success.[30] The questions surrounding education law range from 'liability of truant children; parents' right to redress and before which body, funding of schools and religious owned institutions and the legal rights of disabled pupils and pupils with learning disability'.[31]

The White Paper laid emphasis on the literacy and numeracy ability of the child,[32] and the continued sustenance of the ability of the child through secondary education.[33] According to Ruff, '[t]he content of education law has increased the level and impact of litigation on issues hinged on education by using judicial reviews and specialist tribunals'.[34]

The need to encourage the involvement of courts on issues of education is important, as this will ensure the timely dispensation of administrative responsibilities of individuals. The use of judicial review of decisions taken by various authorities on matters that affect access to education would be encouraged.[35] Various tribunals, like the Special Educational Needs Tribunal (SENT), have entertained several cases in Britain on matters hinging from school admissions, discrimination and exclusion policies.[36]

Discussed in the following section are a few cases from within the UK.

[29] See generally D. Gillard, "Education in England: A brief history," http://www.educationengland.org.uk/history/chapter10.html (accessed 30 April 2014).

[30] Cm 5230, http://planipolis.iiep.unesco.org/upload/UK/UK_Schools_achieving_success.pdf (accessed 30 April 2017).

[31] A. Ruff, *Education law, text, cases and materials* (2005), 1.

[32] Para 1.3.

[33] Para 1.4.

[34] Ruff (n. 212 above), 12.

[35] Ruff, 29.

[36] Ruff, 1.

i. *Mandla v Dowell Lee*[37] (Acceptability)

The case deals with the wearing of turbans and cutting of hair in line with the customary practice of the Sikhs. As in with the South African nose ring case,[38] this case raised issues of discrimination and equality. The court, considering the Race Relations Act of 1976, found[39]:

> Gurinder Singh cannot comply with the school rules without becoming a victim of discrimination.

The decision in the above case is akin to the decision in the Nose Ring case in South Africa. It goes to ground the need to ensure that the religious belief of learners must be respected and protected with the education sphere.

ii. *Wandsworth London Borough Council v A (2000)*[40] (Availability)

This case deals with the protection of teachers from the actions of parents. The headmaster of the school had barred a parent from interfering with the professional conduct of teachers in the school. The decision was taken based on the provisions of Section 547 of the Education Act of 1996. The case brings to the fore the importance of professionalism of teachers in Nigeria and elevating their dignity in labour. While the case was not favourably considered by the court, it is important to point out that this was hinged on the fact that the headmaster failed to give the parent a fair hearing. The positive aspect from the case remains the fact that abusive attitude of teachers by parents can be curtailed.[41]

[37] (1983) 2 AC 548, http://www.hrcr.org/safrica/equality/Mandla_DowellLee.htm (accessed 30 April 2014).

[38] See *MEC for education: KwaZulu-Natal and Others v Navaneethum Pillay and Others* below page 194.

[39] http://www.equalrightstrust.org/ertdocumentbank/Microsoft%20Word%20-%20 Mandla.pdf (accessed 30 April 2017), http://www.hrcr.org/safrica/equality/Mandla_DowellLee.htm (accessed 30 April 2017).

[40] RLR 257.

[41] Ruff (n. 212 above), 30; M. Fordham, *Judicial review handbook: Case synopses short case summaries* (2008), 11.

iii. *Nwabudike v Southwark London Borough* (Availability)

The case represents the responsibility placed on teachers and school authorities to ensure the safety of pupils within the school vicinity. While in the instant case it was found that the school was not liable for negligence having taken necessary steps to ensure the protection of students, it presents a form of checks and balances for school authorities and their employees to ensure that necessary measures are adopted to ensure the safety of children within the school premises. Interestingly, the abduction of over 250 girls from a school in Chibok, north-east Nigeria[42] presents a good example. In these circumstances, who should the parents of the girls hold liable? Are they able to approach the courts for redress?

From the foregoing jurisprudence examined, I classify the lessons learnt into three. The first is that African judiciary can lean on the innovative means relied on by their counterparts in India to circumvent the limitation of the challenge of non-justiciability. Second, the legislature should take a bold and definite step to recognise the right to access of basic education as a fundamental right, as done in India and also in South Africa. Third, NGOs should engage the legal frameworks both at the national, regional and global levels to build jurisprudence towards getting the judiciary to play a definite role in enhancing access to basic education.

8.6 Conclusion

The African Commission and the African Children's Committee have relied on the ACHPR and other international law instruments to develop the jurisprudence on the subject of access to education and development.

Importantly, the cases discussed in the chapter show the role of individuals, NGOs, academic institutions and national human rights institutions towards engaging with judicial and quasi-judicial institutions in driving the right to education. Finally, the cases discussed have not overtly upheld claims against states or individuals, but rather followed the due process of interpreting laws, policies and legislation towards providing a direction in the quest of realising the right to education.

[42] Chibok abductions: Nigeria girls taken abroad', http://www.bbc.com/news/world-africa-27206449 (accessed 30 April 2014); Issues in the Chibok school girl's abduction http://nigeriamasterweb.com/paperfrmes.html (accessed 30 April 2017).

CHAPTER 9

Repositioning Institutions for Realisation of the Right to Basic Education

9.1 Introduction

As identified from the start of this book, the quest to realise access and enhance development can only be achieved via a synergy between the law and institutions. I have shown my bias extensively for the judiciary as an institution and aligned with the theory of Skelton on the extent of the courts involvement in realising not just the right to education but other socio-economic rights. I have also underscored the fact that the court is not allowed or more appropriately incapable of getting involved in matters without a triggering process. Individuals, CSO's and other agencies must be involved in this process. Having argued for a reconceptualising of education from an African perspective, it is also my opinion that traditional institutions and the communities must also get involved in the drive for development via access to education.

9.1.1 National Human Rights Commissions (NHRC)

The NHRC is an institution that is set up to entertain public complaints and ensure that the rights of persons are not blatantly violated either by other individuals or state agencies. In South Africa and Kenya,[1]

[1] See generally http://www.knchr.org/Portals/0/Articles/KenyaNationalCommissiononHumanRights_Act_No14of2011.pdf?ver=2016-08-01-132051-907 (accessed 18 January 2018).

A. C. Onuora-Oguno, *Development and the Right to Education in Africa*,
https://doi.org/10.1007/978-3-319-90335-4_9

the human rights commissions have shown great resolve in the protection of the rights of citizens. In Ghana for instance, Asibo is of the view that the deficiencies found in the scope of the efficiency of the Ghana Ombudsman informed the formation of the Commission on Human Rights and Administrative Justice by the 1992 Ghana Constitution.[2] The main of the commission like that in Nigeria, South Africa is 'checking and redressing incidents of maladministration and promotion of human rights'. It is also enabled "to investigate complaints of violations of fundamental human rights and freedoms, injustice and …"[3]

In Nigeria, the NHRC, established by the NHRC Act,[4] has the core responsibility for promoting and protecting human rights in Nigeria. In addition, the NHRC[5]

> serves as an extra-judicial mechanism for the enhancement of the enjoyment of human rights. Its establishment is aimed at creating an enabling environment for the promotion, protection and enforcement of human rights. It also provides avenues for public enlightenment, research and dialogue in order to raise awareness on human rights issues.

Established during the military regime of General Sanni Abacha, the early days of the NHRC were not without challenges.[6] From the core mandates of the NHRC, it is informative to question to what extent the NHRC has advanced the frontiers of realising the right to basic education in terms of its public enlightenment, dialogue and, more so, enforcement. It must be recalled that part of the aspiration of setting up the NHRC was to ensure and encourage 'extra-judicial realisation of human rights'. Furthermore, in its preamble, it is reiterated that the NHRC is created in[7]

[2] Sam K. Asibuo, "The role of the commission on human rights and administrative justice (CHRAJ) in promoting public service accountability under Ghana's fourth republic," http://unpan1.un.org/intradoc/groups/public/documents/CAFRAD/UNPAN017693.pdf (accessed 18 January 2018).

[3] Sam K. Asibuo above; see generally http://cfnhri.org/members/africa/ghana (accessed 18 January 2018) for the full mandate of the CHRAJ.

[4] National Human Rights Commission Act, 2010. Cap N46 LFN 2004.

[5] http://www.nigeriarights.gov.ng/the-commission (accessed 1 May 2017).

[6] K. R. Salman, "The effectiveness of the Nigerian National Human Rights Commission in human rights protection," unpublished PhD thesis, available at http://www.rksalman.com.ng/publications/RK_Salman_PhD_Thesis_Abstract.pdf (accessed 1 May 2017).

[7] National Human Rights Commission Act, 1995, "Supplement to Official Gazette Extraordinary," no. 28, vol. 82, 6 October 1995, Part A.

furtherance of the above objectives and in its determination to provide a forum for public enlightenment and dialogue on and to limit controversy and confrontation over allegations of human rights violation by public officers and agencies and to reaffirm the sacred and inviolable nature of human and other fundamental rights.

The judicial powers of the NHRC are also recognised and understood by its officials as they have at various times pledged to collaborate with other judicial institutions to drive the realisation of human rights.[8]

The enabling Act of the NHRC provides that the commission shall[9]:

(a) deal with all matters relating to the protection of human rights as guaranteed by the Constitution of the Federal Republic of Nigeria, the African Charter, the United Nations Charter and the Universal Declaration on Human Rights and other international treaties on human rights to which Nigeria is a signatory;
(b) monitor and investigate all alleged cases of human rights violations in Nigeria and make appropriate recommendations to the federal government for the prosecution and such other actions as it may deem expedient in each circumstance;
(c) assist victims of human rights violations and seek appropriate redress and remedies on their behalf;
(d) undertake studies on all matters relating to human rights and assist the federal government in the formulation of appropriate policies on the guarantee of human rights;
(e) publish regularly reports on the state of human rights protection in Nigeria.

The wording of section 5(a) suggests that the NHRC has the foothold to rely on the already discussed regional and global human rights instruments. However, it seems that the NHRC has yet to explore this option of assisting the Nigerian child in realising the right to basic education. A perusal of the annual report of the NHRC does not provide any

[8]This commitment was made by the Secretary-General of the NHRC during a visit to the ECOWAS Court. See "The National Human Rights Commission of Nigeria (NHRC) to partner with ECOWAS," available at http://www.courtecowas.org/site2012/index.php?option=com_content&view=article&id=161:nationa-human-rights (accessed 1 May 2017).

[9]Section 5.

information on the use of the discussed mechanisms at both the global and the regional level to pursue the realisation of the human right to basic education.

One major factor that affects the efficiency of the NHRC is the poor level of awareness among practitioners and even the citizens. During my earlier research, my interaction with a number of legal practitioners exposed this shortcoming. The majority of young lawyers interacted with during the 2014 Nigerian Bar Association Conference in Owerri show little knowledge of the mandate of the NHRC. It is important, therefore, that the NHRC will liaise with institutions like the Nigerian Law School (NLS) to include the study of the functions and mandate of the NHRC in its curriculum. The same approach is recommended for the Council of Legal Education (CLE) and the National University Commission (NUC). The need for this is suggested as it will provide emerging lawyers with knowledge on how to explore the options of enhancing the realisation of the responsibilities of the NHRC.

Despite this seeming, shortcoming, I recognise the fact that there are some positive steps taken by the institution. For instance, the NHRC's aspiration to push the FGN to treat economic, social and cultural rights as fundamental rights is reiterated thus[10]:

> The former are justiciable rights, i.e. citizens could go to court to enforce them if denied. The latter rights are however non-justiceable, i.e. these sets of rights are not enforceable in the court. They are aspirations attainable if and when the state has the resources. However, the Commission believes the two sets of rights are both fundamental and complementary. This is because the right to life, for instance, is meaningless without gainful employment or food to sustain life in the first place. The Commission has made a strong case for the upgrading of economic, social and cultural rights to fundamental rights. Human rights are interdependent, interrelated, indivisible and universal.

The above resolve seems not to be a proactive one as the NHRC to date has not found the FGN liable for the violation of such rights as the right to education. The NHRC is therefore encouraged to follow the steps of the South African Human Rights Commission (SAHRC) and IHRC and seeks to enhance the jurisprudence on the right to a basic education.

[10] http://www.nigeriarights.gov.ng/your-rights (accessed 1 May 2017).

It can be inferred that the NHRC continues to face the challenges of being swayed by the political class. However, in a bid to describe the NHRC, Odinkalu presents it as follows[11]:

> It is not an opposition party, it is not the Salvation Army and it is not a government promotion agency.

While the above captures the supposed nature of the NHRC, it is opined that the NHRC should be the hope of the common man, but it has failed to provide solace in this respect. This is because, by virtue of its mandate, the NHRC should indeed provide succour for the common man by advancing both civil and social rights.

The need and importance of strengthening the NHRC can be deciphered from the words of Odinkalu as stated above. The commission must therefore proceed on the premise of knowing that its mandate is to serve the peoples of Nigeria and not to serve as a government agency. Learning from the mandate and operations of the IHRC,[12] the HRC in Africa will be further strengthened to advance the realisation of human rights. For instance, the IHRC is empowered to 'enquire *suo motu* or on a petition presented to it by a victim or any person on his behalf or on a direction of order of any court'.[13] In addition, the IHRC is also empowered to 'intervene in any proceeding involving any allegation of a violation of human rights pending before a court with the approval of such court'.[14] Furthermore, the IHRC has a premise of undertaking initiatives to ensure that human rights are realised by the actions of the IHRC when the Act provides for an unqualified mandate. It reads 'such other functions as it may consider necessary for the protection of human rights'.[15]

A similar provision is also found in the SAHRC Act.[16] In reiterating the constitutional mandate of the SAHRC, it is provided that the

[11] Interview monitored on Channels TV, 19 April 2014. Human Rights Act, 1993 (amended 2006).

[12] Human Rights Act (n. 24 below).

[13] Indian Human Rights Act, 1993 (amended 2006), section 12(a).

[14] Indian Human Rights Act, section 12(b).

[15] Indian Human Rights Act, section 12(j).

[16] The commission was inaugurated on 2 October 1995 under the Human Rights Commission Act 54 of 1994 and as provided for by the Constitution of the Republic of South Africa Act 200 of 1993.

SAHRC shall 'take steps and secure appropriate redress where human rights have been violated'.[17] The provisions of the IHRC and the SAHRC are argued to have positioned them to actively engage in seeking redress for violations of the right to education in India and South Africa while holding public officers that have the responsibility of ensuring the implementation of education policies liable, mandated to ensure compliance and ensure fairness in procedural issues bordering on education.

The NHRC must therefore show some resolve to follow suit in this step. To achieve this, it is suggested that the NHRC can lean on the overarching provision of its Act that provides 'do such other things as are necessary or expedient for the performance of its functions under this Act'.[18] However, it seems that the NHRC might be curtailed in its judicial activities as it appears to be more geared towards only promotional activities. This position is envisaged as that the NHRC is required to make recommendations to the FGN when it finds any violations.

To be able to make these findings, the NHRC must commence entertaining matters hinged on the right to basic education. More sensitising is needed to the public for them to be aware to pursue the protection, fulfilling and promotion of the right to access basic education.

Furthermore, the NHRC Act empowers it to[19]:

> Refer any matter of human rights violation requiring prosecution to the Attorney-General of the Federation or of a state as the case maybe.

The snag with the above provision is that, considering that the state most often than not is the subject of a violation of rights cannot be a judge in its own case. The rationale here is that, if basic education is construed as a human right, the government must be held responsible, and this cannot be achieved by referring same back to the government. Holding the government accountable for snags in the provision of basic education comes with treating same as a human right concern. Tomasevski opines:

[17] SAHRC Act 54 of 1994, section 2(c).

[18] NHRC Act, section 5(a).

[19] NHRC Act, section 5.

> The human right approach priorities law in holding governments accountable for their pledges, individually and collectively...once a pledge becomes a human right obligation; failure to attain agreed ends by specified means becomes a violation, to be redressed by compensating the victims and ensuring that it does not happen again.[20]

Thus, the NHRC should make definitive findings and statements on the subject of basic education. Besides the above reasoning, subjecting the finding of the NHRC to executive review will also ensure the non-fulfilment of state obligations. This is because, considering the challenges of lack of political will by states, the FGN will be unwilling to prosecute defaulters, especially if they are linked to the political class.

The NHRC can also borrow a leaf from the IHRC and SHRC by actively exploring its judicial mandates as it is able to embark on inquiry as a judicial body.[21] However, the exercise of these duties by the NHRC is criticised by some lawyers. According to Olatoke, the NHRC powers to conduct judicial hearings or issue statements that are aimed to have judicial flavours are flawed as it is not empowered by the Constitution to act as a judicial body.[22] The Kenya Commission on Human Rights created by section 253 of the Kenyan Constitution empowers it in section five to act in any manner that will give effect to its duty in the protection of human rights.[23] The status of the IHRC is not in doubt as it is provided by the enabling statute that '[e]very proceeding before the Commission shall be deemed to be a judicial proceeding'.[24] The relationship between the courts of India and the IHRC is also well stipulated with the power of the IHRC to transfer cases to other courts in India that may also have jurisdiction to handle such complaints brought before it.

[20] K. Tomasevski, *Education denied—Costs and remedies* (2003), 101.

[21] NHRC Act, section 6.

[22] J. Olatoke (Senior Advocate of Nigeria) conversation during the session on Nigerian National Human Rights Commission, Nigerian Bar Association annual national conference, Owerri, 24–29 August 2014.

[23] http://www.knchr.org/Portals/0/Articles/KenyaNationalCommissiononHumanRights_Act_No14of2011.pdf?ver=2016-08-01-132051-907 (accessed 18 January 2018).

[24] Indian Human Rights Act, 1993 (amended 2006), section 13(5).

Furthermore, the need to empower the NHRC is also advocated by FIDH when it found[25]:

> The NHRC does not have sufficient institutional safeguards, investigative powers or authority to compel authorities to respond to its queries. It is also reported that, while its investigative mechanism looks effective, its functioning is compromised by a serious lack of capacity and resources.

So noting that the human rights commissions provide a good ground for the resolution of human rights, it is underscored that more needs to be done still if its full potential will be realised. According to Ojukwu, the NHRC will only realise its potential when lawyers engage it and aid it in building jurisprudence that will help the advancement of social rights.[26] It is therefore argued that the NHRC must activate and engage the provisions of section 6(g):

> Liaise and co-operate, in such manner as it considers appropriate, with local and international organisations on human rights with the purpose of advancing the promotion and protection of human rights.

It is opined here that, while no clear examples are available on the circumstances in which this provision has been relied on to drive realisation of economic, social and cultural rights, the NHRC should, based on this, cooperate with other institutions discussed in this research with the aim of alleviating the non-availability of access to basic education in Nigeria.

[25] FIDH, *Nigeria: Defending human rights: Not everywhere, not every right*, International Fact-Finding Mission Report (2010).

[26] T. Ojukwu, Director Monitoring National Human Rights Commission, speaking during a session titled 'Is the National Human Rights Commission another court—A review of the scope of the National Human Rights Act' held at Owerri during the 2014 NBA annual conference, raised the challenges that still confront the commission in realising its mandate, but stressed the need that the NBA needs to sensitise its members and encourage them to engage the commission. Responding to questions from the author on the NHRC embarking of promotional activities hinged on basic education or other social rights, the Director responded that the institution, while not having done so at present, hoped to carry out such activities provided the necessary legal scope and institutional funding existed to enable the NHRC make its presence felt all over the federation.

9.2 Enhancing Access to Education—Engaging Traditional Institutions

The roles of the traditional rulers in aiding the implementation of government policies continue to thrive today and are pivotal in the quest to realise an improved access to education.[27] This can be ascribed to the respect that is placed on traditional institutions in African.[28] A clear example is what transpired in Nigeria. At the advent of colonial rule in Nigeria, the British engaged two styles of governance. In the north, the indirect rule held sway, while in the south, the rule was by a direct means.[29] The success of indirect rule was very prominent because of the influence of the emirs and other traditional leaders who also doubled as religious leaders.[30]

As already discussed in the above section on the general importance of ensuring that each community becomes part of education policy and implementation plans, the role of the institution of traditional rulers must as a necessity be well involved in this quest.[31] UNICEF has laudably engaged in this approach and it continues to achieve some positive results.[32] In addition, it will be helpful if the traditional rulers are able to

[27] It is noted that the indirect rule was not an easy ride for the colonialist as it was only settled for after protracted conflict that involved the disposition of some emirs causing them to loose influence and eventually realising the pivotal role that the traditional leaders would play in assisting the British achieve their aims. See generally J. T. Fowoyo, "Transforming the Almajiri education for the benefit of the Nigerian society," *Journal of Educational and Social Research* (2013): 68.

[28] See generally C. I. Ejizu, "African traditional religions and the promotion of community-living in Africa," available at http://www.afrikaworld.net/afrel/community.htm (accessed 21 October 2017).

[29] See generally, "Colonialism and the African experience," available at http://www.pearsonhighered.com/assets/hip/us/hip_us_pearsonhighered/samplechapter/0205208606.pdf (accessed 26 October 2015).

[30] F. A. Salamone, "The social construction of colonial reality: Yauri Emirate," *Journal of Legal Pluralism* (1987): 47.

[31] See for a further acceptance of the collective role of communities in achieving developments and increase in social needs, I. E. J. Emeh, I. J. Eluwa, and F. O. Ukah, "A rural-community development in Nigeria: Group dynamics perspective," *Interdisciplinary Journal of Contemporary Research* (2012): 1090.

[32] UNICEF, "Working with traditional rulers to achieve the rights of children," available at http://www.unicef.org/nigeria/media_3328.html (accessed 21 October 2017). In communities like Daura and Kaduna the engagement of traditional rulers have helped to ensure the prevention of polio and also the increased regard for the education of the girl child.

influence the various *Ulmas*,[33] to support the activities of the government in mainstreaming the already established *Almajiri* system of education.[34] This view is advanced will aid the increase of respect for the current form of basic education while also ensuring that the concept of acceptable curriculum is well entrenched.[35] As rightly observed by Baba, this engagement could be fruitful as there still remain some form of apathy among various *Ulma's* and their respect for Western education. Baba found that[36]:

> While some *Ulama* seek engagement with the state and its modern structures, others prefer to maintain a distance in the hope that doing so will help them preserve the teachings and ideals of Islam.

Consequently, the role of the traditional rulers cannot be overlooked in the proposed synergy between the law, the state and community in enhancing access to basic education and development in.

9.3 Engaging the Elephant in the Room Towards Increasing Access to Basic Education

> And let's not forget about the poorest and most marginalised children, particularly girls and those with disabilities, who are still missing out completely – the daily realities of poverty and discrimination combining to prevent them from realising their right to education.[37]

The above reality presents a certain obstacle to the realisation of the right of access to basic education and development in Africa. While corruption takes its toll on the available resources committed to education by the government, it is important to concede the fact that economic challenges

[33] Islamic word for Arabic scholar.

[34] See generally H. I. Okonkwo and I. M. Alhaji, "Contemporary issues in Nomadic, Minority and Almajiri education, problems and prospects," *Journal of Education and Practice* 5 (2014): 13.

[35] N. M. Baba, "Islamic schools, the Ulama, and the state in the educational development of Northern Nigeria," *Bulletin de l'APAD* [En ligne], 33(2011), mis en ligne le 22 mars 2012, Consulté le 20 October 2015. http://apad.revues.org/4092.

[36] As above.

[37] European Year of Development Report, available at https://europa.eu/eyd2015/en/plan-international/posts/financing-right-education (accessed 25 April 2017).

are present.[38] This is done against the backdrop that, despite the eulogising of the benefits of education, it will only amount to 'lame-duck if it is not backed up by the necessary funding'.[39]

As previously stated, it is important, therefore, to envisage how the elephants in the room have influenced issues of education.

The role and effect of policies such as SAP in introducing fee-paying education has already been. Thus, the role of the World Bank and its capitalist approach to education is criticised. This position is further supported by Sarelin by noting that 'today there is no commitment to the right to education by international financial institutions such as the World Bank or the International Monetary Fund (IMF)'.[40] It is noted, however, that in recent years the World Bank has begun to contribute to education financing in developing countries.[41]

Consequently, the need to ensure that more funds are contributed without unnecessary conditions is apt in enhancing the realisation of access to education. International non-governmental organisations and other donor agencies are pivotal in the quest to make education available. It is, reiterated that the challenge does not stop with donations but with ensuring that the funds donated are effectively managed and utilised to achieve its end point. This, therefore, calls for the prominent role of the various arms of government to ensure appropriate policies, the execution and interpretation of laws towards the promotion and protection of the right to access of basic education.

9.3.1 Synergy Towards Strengthening Institutions: Realising Basic Education in Nigeria

The relevance of economic, social and cultural rights is central to ensuring human dignity. However, the commitment of states to their

[38] See generally "Accelerating progress to 2015 Nigeria," available at http://educationenvoy.org/wp-content/uploads/2013/07/NIGERIA-UNSE-FINAL.pdf (accessed 25 April 2017).

[39] European Year of Development Report.

[40] A. L. Sarelin, "The right to education from a developing country perspective," KIOS thematical reports (2006): 11.

[41] See generally "Human rights-based approach for education for all," 60, available at http://www.unicef.org/publications/files/A_Human_Rights_Based_Approach_to_Education_for_All.pdf (accessed 25 April 2017).

enforcement and implementation has remained rhetoric.[42] The continued 'sad state of affairs' regarding the right of access to basic education and development is based on the continued neglect of the substantial nature of economic, social and cultural rights.[43] The basis for the continued neglect of economic, social and cultural rights in African countries has hinged on economic challenges and the lack of political will to follow through on state obligations under international law.

However, the challenges are far beyond the question of financial challenges and more on political will. Despite the clear challenge of economics, the failure of governance, as showcased by inept leadership and corruption, remains more problematic. As identified by Agbakwat[44]:

> One cannot deny the reality of Africa's grim economic situation, which remains a significant constraint on the financial abilities of African states. Although blame is often placed on this economic situation, the lack of political will and the corruption of the ruling elite have also played a large role in preventing an equal emphasis on enforcement of ESCR as of civil and political rights.

Not overcoming the challenge of inept and corrupt leadership has dire consequences for the realisation of economic and social rights. Agbakwat is of the opinion that[45]:

> Corrupt leaders steal by rejecting policies that would better spur development and promote ESCR in favour of policies that bring greater profits their way through businesses, investments, or unscrupulous cohorts. The interests of the people are pursued only to the extent that they coincide with the selfish interests of those in power...

In addition, a further challenge identified is the lack of promotional activities.[46] Institutions like the NHRC among others have persistently

[42] S. C. Agbakwat, "Reclaiming humanity: Economic, social, and cultural rights as the cornerstone of African human rights," *Yale Human Rights & Development Law Journal* 5 (2002): 177.

[43] As above.

[44] As above.

[45] As above.

[46] As above.

failed to embark on sufficient promotional activities to enable the general populace to become aware of their mandates. Consequently, the approach of increasing the promotional mandate is advocated.

The judiciary is identified to be in a position to aid the synergy through this channel. This is enunciated by Christiansen when she posits that[47]:

> While acknowledging the inability of judicial action to fully remedy endemic social injustice, the courts can nonetheless empower popular movements, non-governmental organisations, and activists with their rulings.

This approach will build a synergy between the various institutions, and in addition, it will enhance the participation of NGOs and other public interest and religious organisations. This will further bolster the fronts of promotion of awareness and public sensitisation as the public will be well aware of their rights.[48] If cooperation is achieved, it will inform other suggested means of ensuring the realisation of the right to basic education. This is by relying on the doctrine of a minimum threshold.[49]

The doctrine of minimum threshold deals with ensuring that the deprived and minority areas that are lagging behind in the access to education receive a greater boost in ensuring that the level of access to education in such areas is enhanced. Presently in Nigeria, the continued development of the *Almajiri* education system is a step in the right direction, but requires the elimination of the clogs of corruption

[47] E. C. Christiansen, "Using constitutional adjudication to remedy socio-economic injustice: Comparative lessons from South Africa," *Journal of International Law & Foreign Affairs* 13 (2008): 369, 402.

[48] See generally the *Berea Township* Case CCT 24/07, available at http://www.saflii.org/za/cases/ZACC/2008/1.html (accessed 29 September 2014). In this case, community engagement was enhanced by the ruling of the court that encouraged the government to liaise with the inhabitants of occupiers of 51 Olivia Road, Berea township, and 197 Main Street, Johannesburg, on their planned eviction. If this level of cooperation becomes manifest in Nigeria, then communities and other public interest bodies will be able to demand the meeting of set minimum core thresholds from governments. See generally E. C. Christiansen, "Adjudicating non-justiciable rights: Socio-economic rights and the South African Constitutional Court," available at http://digitalcommons.law.ggu.edu/cgi/viewcontent.cgi?article=1141&context=pubs (accessed 7 July 2017).

[49] Agbakwat above.

and lack of political will. The minimum core threshold has been found to be ineffective in holding states responsible for providing resources below the set out acceptable standards.[50] In this regard, Nigeria will be expected to have a minimum facility standard for all its basic educational institutions that is able to aid the quality of education. When this is done effectively, the political practice of celebrating when amenities are provided will be eliminated as the populace will be aware that this is an obligation required by government.

With the foregoing, an important basis of ensuring the strengthening of the institutions involved in the education is to ensure proper funding. The place of funding in education is not one that is subject to controverted interpretation. For instance, the importance of ensuring that funding of the girl child's education is well captured in the African Women's Protocol. The Women's Protocol provides in article 10(3):

> States Parties shall take the necessary measures to reduce military expenditure significantly in favour of spending on social development in general, and the promotion of women in particular.

Education as a social right falls within this category envisaged by the Protocol. Article 12 of the Women's Protocol provides in very certain terms the importance of encouraging state parties to strive towards the realisation of the right of the girl child to education.

I also identify other means of realising the right to education and development outside the ambit of the law and I discuss a few below.

9.3.2 *The Collective Responsibility Approach*

Here, I reflect on two reasoning, the first is as advanced by Hansungule for prominent African individuals to shun corruption and to strive to give back to the community by engaging their wealth and supporting education initiatives. Akinola's perception supports the proposition of Hansungule. According to Akinola, collective responsibility has the ability to fill in gaps of social and infrastructural decays in the various communities.[51] The second is further premised on the non-legal means of realising economic,

[50] As above.

[51] S. R. Akinola, "Coping with infrastructural deprivation through collective action among rural people in Nigeria," *Nordic Journal of African Studies* (2007): 32.

social and cultural rights. It is reiterated that education is a fundamental condition for an informed society, an essential means of enhancing the spread of knowledge and the foundation for the efficient application and distribution of natural resources.[52] Consequently, basic education aims at delivering a foundation programme of learning that equips the pupil with the capacity to engage in some form of lifelong enterprise.[53]

In relying on the collective responsibility model to enhance access to basic education, it is recalled that before the introduction of Western education, there already existed viable indigenous learning systems.[54] Education was in the mainstream of day-to-day life. Kaunga is of the firm view that[55]

> education was relevant because it served the needs of communities to survive, to be safe from enemy attacks, and to be in harmony with each other and with nature. Most of all, education mirrored and affirmed the distinct cultural identity of communities.

Parents and communities must therefore not wholly abdicate their responsibility to aid the development of an acceptable model for Nigerian basic education. As also pointed out, the lack of willingness on the part of parents to approach lawyers individually, the NHRC and NGOs to initiate judicial processes to protect their rights to education remains worrisome. It is again echoed here that the African Children's Charter provides for parental responsibility to ensure that the rights of the child are realised. Thus, a collective response is required to advance the best interests of the child. The show of communal willingness is advanced able to eliminate the excuses of government's failure and inability to improve access to education of children purely on the excuse that communities are categorised as hard-to-reach and live areas, as the communities are able to demand the minimum threshold expected of the government in its duties.

[52] F. Faller, "Universal primary education in sub-Saharan Africa: Achievable or impossible target," in F. Nwaonu (ed), *Millennium development goals: Achievement and prospects of meeting the targets in Africa in universal primary education* (2008): 37.

[53] Faller above 40.

[54] J. Ole Kaunga, "'Indigenous peoples' experiences with the formal education system: The case of a Kenya pastoralist," *Indigenous affairs* (2005): 33.

[55] As above.

Involvement of the community will ensure that teachers posted to such areas are well-oriented and informed of the environmental challenges of communities and how to respond to these.[56] Another impact communal involvement will have is that they will be able to urge the government to embark on skill acquisition workshops. Skills acquired will empower parents to sustain their families without demanding much support from their children, thus encouraging them to remain in school and eliminating the challenges of child labour and reduce non-completion rates in schools. In addition, it is opined that for education to be revamped African communities, parents, teachers and pupils[57] must all work in perfect harmony to ensure the restoration of the right to education.

9.4 Conclusions

It is important that all available means are explored by all stakeholders to ensure that the right to access of basic education is realised, not minding the means of seeking the remedies, judicial or non-judicial.[58] The approach in exploring non-judicial means to realising the right to education may include the design of an acceptable African educational model different from the received *cum* perceived Western style of education.[59] It is important that cooperation needs to be followed through if the situation of education and development would improve. The role of NGOs in contributing to the promotional knowledge of the right to access of basic education is an important one. The NHRC needs to up its approach to the implementation of its mandate by embarking on its promotional mandates to the public. A strong synergy need to be established between the judicial and non-judicial entities that can influence the realisation of education and thus drive development in Africa.

[56] Faller above 63.

[57] For further reading on the impact of collective responsibility and its possible impact on the outcome of education, see generally V. E. Lee and J. B. Smith, "Collective responsibility for learning and its effects on gains in achievement for early secondary school students," *American Journal of Education Volume* (1996): 103.

[58] See generally C. Mbazira, *You are the 'weakest link' in realising socio-economic rights: Goodbye strategies for effective implementation of court orders in South Africa* (2008).

[59] Agbakwat above.

CHAPTER 10

Conclusions and Recommendations

I set out to establish that access to education is important if development of any society will be achieved. I argued that relying on international human rights laws, cooperation between institutions and relying on some identified non-legal means access to education can be enhanced. I argued also that there is need to ensure that the accessed education has a quality value and is inclusive in nature. I identified factors responsible for the poor state of access to basic education in Africa, citing religion, corruption, culture and lack of political will to be major reasons for the poor state. In response to the challenges, I argued that there was the obvious need to ensure that an African educational philosophy must be deliberately evolved to ground acceptance. In addition, it was found that the indispensability of the right to access basic education was a fulcrum to realising other human rights and that, besides Western philosophies, Africans had a basis for its own philosophy of education. In addition, it was also concluded that international human rights law must be engaged so as to protect groups against the actions and omissions of government.

Another pivotal finding is that the content of education as advanced by Coonmans places both a positive and negative responsibility on the state. This position is supported by the arguments of Beiter and Tomasevski. Hinged on the argument of the scholars above, I argued that, aside the obligation on the state, the question of the right to access basic education as envisaged by human rights law also envisaged both horizontal and vertical obligations.

A. C. Onuora-Oguno, *Development and the Right to Education in Africa*,
https://doi.org/10.1007/978-3-319-90335-4_10

Furthermore, while examining the concept of the 4A theory of education as advanced by Tomasevski, found that the nature of the philosophy of education as advanced by the colonialists was fundamentally flawed. Scholars like Fafunwa and Ikejiani argued that the acceptability and adaptability of education as advanced Africans raised suspicions.

Leaning on the various decisions of the courts in South Africa and India, I advanced the role the courts should play to provide legal direction towards realising the right to education. The role of the court is pivotal in ensuring that access to basic education is made available and adequate, I aligned strongly with the thoughts of Mubangizi, that the judiciary remains a strong basis on which economic, social and cultural rights will be realised. Examining the various cases in South Africa, like the Welkom case, the Western Forum case and the Juma Musjid case, among others, it was advanced that the other judiciaries in Africa had a veritable basis to act as a checks and balances for the executive in ensuring the promotion, protection and provision of the right of access to basic education. The Text Book case provides another important perspective, providing direction and ensuring that officials have space to carry out their duties. Most important is ensuring that the Courts constrain themselves to issuing remedies that are implementable.

India provides a good innovative paradigm for the African judiciaries. In Unni Krishnan J.P. v State of Andhra Pradesh & Ors, the Indian Courts equated the right to education to the right to life. I argue that Courts should follow this innovative means of driving the realisation of the right to education. In addition, the jurisprudence in Society for Unaided Private Schools of Rajasthan VUOI & Another provides a good jurisprudence for the protection of minority groups in accessing education.

The developing jurisprudence before regional and sub-regional bodies provides a viable example towards elaborating the question of litigations on the right to education. Reigniting the arguments of Ssenyonjo and Viljoen, I opined that African countries should be barred from continuing to place the right to access of basic education in chapter two of the Constitution. It was concluded that the recognition of the right of access to basic education is instant and not subject to progressive realisation. This conclusion is further supported by the position of Beiter and Tomasevski.

Selected Bibliography

Books

Achebe, C. (1983). *The trouble with Nigeria*. Enugu: Fourth Dimension.

Adegbija, E. E. (2004). *Multilingualism: A Nigerian case study*. Trenton, NJ: Africa World Press.

Aldrich, R. (1982). *An introduction to the history of education*. London: Hodder and Stoughton.

Aronin, L., & Singleton, D. (2012). *Multilingualism: Impact studies in language and society*. Amsterdam: John Benjamins Publishing.

Austin, J. (2012). *The province of jurisprudence determined. The Law Book Exchange*, first published (1832). London: Richard Taylor.

Beiter, K. D. (2006). *The protection of the right to education by international law*. Leiden and Boston: Martinus Nijhoff.

Biny, A. (2011). *The political and social thoughts of Kwame Nkrumah*. Basingstoke: Macmillan Press—Palgrave.

Bowen, J., & Hobson, P. R. (1974). *Theories of education studies of significant innovation in Western education thoughts*. Brisbane: Watson Ferguson & Co.

Deshowitz, A. (2004). *Rights from wrongs—A secular theory of origins*. New York: Basic Book.

Donnelly, J. (1993). *International human rights*. Boulder: West View Press; Denver: University of Denver.

Ehrlich, E. (2009). *Fundamental principles of the sociology of law*. Cambridge: Harvard University Press.

Fafunwa, A. B. (1974). *History of education in Nigeria*. London: George Allen & Unwin.

A. C. Onuora-Oguno, *Development and the Right to Education in Africa*,
https://doi.org/10.1007/978-3-319-90335-4

Fajan, A. (1978). *Education in Nigeria 1842–1939 (A historical analysis)*. Ibadan: Longman.

Fisher, A. (2004). *The content of the right to education—Theoretical foundations* (Centre for Human Rights and Global Justice Working Paper Economic, Social and Cultural Rights Series No. 4). New York.

Fodor, J. A. (1975). *The language of thought*. Cambridge: Harvard University Press.

Fordham, M. (2008). *Judicial review handbook: Case synopses and short case summaries* (5th ed.). Oxford, UK: Hart Publishing.

Freeman, M., & Mindus, P. (Eds.). (2013). *The legacy of John Austin's jurisprudence*. New York, USA: Springer.

Grube, G. M. A. (1931). *The Cleitophon of Plato, classical philology*. Chicago: University of Chicago Press.

Heyns, C. H., & Stefiszyn, K. (Eds). (2006). *Human rights, justice and peace in Africa: A reader*. Pretoria: Pretoria University Law Press.

Ijaduola, K. O. (1998). *Education in Nigeria: An historical perspective*. Ijebu Ode: Lucky Odoni Publishers.

Kaime, T. (2009). *The African Charter on the Rights and Welfare of the Child—A socio-legal perspective*. Pretoria: Pretoria University Law Press.

Kenyatta, J. (1979). *Facing Mount Kenya: The traditional life of the Gikuyu*. African Writers Series. London: Heinemann.

Locke, J. (1954). *Essays on the law of nature*. London: Oxford University Press.

Mbazira, C. (2009). *Litigating socio-economic rights in South Africa: A choice between corrective and distributive justice*. Pretoria: Pretoria University Law Press.

Mbiti, J. S. (1989). *African religions and philosophy* (2nd ed.). Portsmouth, Botswana: Heinemann Educational.

Nair, P. S. (2011). *Human rights in a changing world*. New Delhi, India: Kalpaz.

Nanda, S. (1900). *Cultural anthropology*. Ohio: Cengage Learning.

Nanda, S., & Warms, R. (2010). *Cultural anthropology*. Ohio: Cengage Learning.

Nduka, O. A. (1964). *Western education and the Nigerian cultural background*. Ibadan: Oxford Press.

Ngugi, W. T. (1981). *Decolonising the mind: The politics of language in African literature*. Dar es Salaam: East African Educational Publishers.

Ngugi, W. T. (2009). *Re-membering Africa*. Dar es Salaam: East African Educational Publishers.

Nolan, A. (2011). *Children's socio-economic rights, democracy and the courts*. Oxford: Bloomsbury.

Norberto, B. (1993). *Thomas Hobbes and the natural law tradition*. Chicago: Chicago University Press.

Nwonwu, F. O. C. (2011). *Indigenous knowledge systems in Igbo traditional agriculture*. Bloomington, USA: AuthorHouse.

Obilade, A. O. (1979). *The Nigerian legal system.* London: Sweet and Maxwell.
Olivas, M. A., & Scheider, G. R. (Eds.). (2008). *Education law stories.* New York: Foundation Press.
Olowu, D. (2009). *An integrative rights-based approach to human development in Africa.* Pretoria: Pretoria University Law Press.
Owomoyela, O. (1979). *African literatures: An introduction.* Waltham: Crossroads Press.
Podgorecki, A., & Whelan, C. J. (1981). *Sociological approaches to law.* London: Guilford.
Stumpf, C. A. (2006). *The Grotian theology of international law.* Berlin, Germany: Walter de Gruyter.
Thio, L. (2005). *Managing Babel: The international legal protection of minorities in the twentieth century.* Leiden: Martinus Nijhoff.
Tomaševski, K. (2001). *Removing obstacles in the way of the right to education.* Primers No. 1. Gothenburg: Novum Grafiska AB.
Tomaševski, K. (2003). *Education denied—Costs and remedies.* Cape Town: ZED Publishers.
Verheyde, M. (2006). *A commentary on the United Nations convention on the rights of the child, Article 28—Right to education.* Leiden: Martinus Nijhoff.
Viljoen, F. (2012). *International human rights law in Africa* (2nd ed.). London: Oxford University Press.
Wellman, C. (1985). *The theory of rights.* Lanham: Rowman & Allanheld Publishers.
Woolman, S., & Fleisch, B. (2009). *The constitution in the classroom: Law and education in South Africa, 1994–2008.* Pretoria: Pretoria University Law Press.
Zuker, M. A. (2002). *Education law* (3rd ed.). Toronto: Carswell.

Book Chapters

Arinze-Umobi, C., & Iguh, A. (2010). The Nigerian girl child: Rights to education and the nexus with national development. In C. Ikekonwu (Ed.), *Child education in Africa.* Enugu: Catholic Institute for Development, Justice & Peace (CIDJAP) Press.
Azikiwe, N. (1965). Foreword. In O. Ikejiani (Ed.), *Education in Nigeria.* New York: Praeger.
Bowels, S., & Gintis, H. (2010). Broken promises: School reform in retrospect. In S. F. Semel (Ed.), *Foundations of education: The essential texts.* Abingdon, UK: Routledge.
Brand, D. (2005). Introduction to socio-economic rights in the South African constitutions. In D. Brand & C. Heyns (Eds.), *Socio-economic rights in South Africa* (pp. 1–15). Pretoria: Pretoria University Law Press.

Coomans, F. (1995). Clarifying the core elements of the right to education. In F. Coomans & F. Van Hoof (Eds.), *The right to complain about economic, social and cultural rights*. Utrecht: SIM.

Desai, A. H., & Muralidhar, S. (2000). Public interest litigation: Potential and problems. In B. N. Kirpal, et al. (Eds.), *Supreme but not infallible—Essays in honour of the Supreme Court of India*. New Delhi: Oxford University Press.

De Varennes, F. (2012). Equality and non-discrimination: Fundamental principles of minority language rights. In J. Castellino (Ed.), *Global minority rights*. Dartmouth: Ashgate.

Faller, F. (2008). Universal primary education in sub-Saharan Africa: Achievable or impossible target. In F. Nwaonu (Ed.), *Millennium development goals: Achievement and prospects of meeting the targets in Africa in universal primary education*. Pretoria: African Institute of South Africa.

Fyle, C. N. (2003). Language policy and planning for basic education in Africa. In A. Ouane (Ed.), *Towards a multilingual culture of education*. UNESCO Institute for Education. https://www.unesco.org/education/uie/pdf/uiestud41.pdf. Accessed 10 Sept 2013.

Grobbelaar-Du Plessis, I., & Van Reenen, T. (2011). Introduction to aspects of disability law in Africa. In I. Grobbelaar-Du Plessis & T. Van Reenen (Eds.), *Aspects of disability law in Africa*. Pretoria: Pretoria University Law Press.

Hanson, J. W. (1965). Developing a federal plan for education. In O. Ikejiani (Ed.), *Education in Nigeria*. New York: Praeger.

Hays, J. (2003). Indigenous rights in education: The SAN of Southern Africa in local and global context. In R. Hitchcock & D. Vinding (Eds.), *Indigenous peoples' rights in Southern Africa*. Copenhagen: IWGIA.

Heyns, C. H. (2006). A "struggle approach" to human rights. In C. Heyns & K. Stefiszyn (Eds.), *Human rights, peace and justice in Africa: A reader*. Pretoria: Pretoria University Law Press.

Howard, R. (2006). The full-belly thesis: Should economic rights take priority over civil and political rights? Evidence from sub-Saharan Africa. In C. Heyns & K. Stefiszyn (Eds.), *Human rights, peace and justice in Africa: A reader*. Pretoria: Pretoria University Law Press.

Ikejiani, O. (1965). Background to the problems of Nigerian education. In O. Ikejiani (Ed.), *Education in Nigeria*. New York: Praeger.

Jekayinfa, A. A., & Kolawole, D. O. (2010). Conceptual background to education in Nigeria. In Abiri & A. A. Jekafinfa (Eds.), *Perspective on the history of education in Nigeria*. Ilorin: Bamitex.

Kalusa, W. T. (2000). Indigenous education in pre-colonial Africa. In H. T. Msango, E. C. Mumba, & A. L. Sikwibele (Eds.), *Selected topics in philosophy and education*. Lusaka: University of Zambia.

Liebenberg, S. (2004). The interpretation of socio-economic rights. In S. Woolman, T. Roux, & M. Bishop (Eds.), *Constitutional law of South Africa* (2nd ed.). Pretoria: Pretoria University Law Press.

Lindholm, T. (1985). Coming to terms with traditions. In H. Hoibraden & I. Gullvag (Eds.), *Essays in pragmatic philosophy*. Norway: Norwegian University Press.

Lundy, L. (2005). School children and health: 'The role of international human rights law. In N. Harris & P. Meredith (Eds.), *Children, education and health: International perspectives on law and policy*. Dartmouth: Ashgate.

McClain-Nhlapo, C. (2011). Foreword. In I. Grobbelaar-du Plessis & T. Van Reenen (Eds.), *Aspects of disability law in Africa*. Pretoria: Pretoria University Law Press.

Meyer, J. W., & Ramirez, F. O. (2000). The world institutionalisation of education. In J. Schriewer (Ed.), *Discourse formation in comparative education*. Frankfurt: Peter Lang.

Osler, A. (2012). Universal Declaration of Human Rights and education. In J. A. Banks (Ed.), *Encyclopaedia of diversity in education*. London and Los Angeles, CA: Sage.

Ravitch, D. (2010). The democratic-liberal tradition under attack. In S. F. Semel (Ed.), *Foundations of education: The essential texts*. Abingdon, UK: Routledge.

Shestack, J. J. (2006). The philosophy foundations of human rights: Concept and language of human rights and related ideas. In C. Heyns & K. Stefiszyn (Eds.), *Human rights, peace and justice in Africa: A reader*. Pretoria: Pretoria University Law Press.

Sow, D. F. (1996). The rights of children in the African judicial systems rights. In E. Verhellen (Ed.), *Understanding children's rights*. Collected papers presented at the first International Interdisciplinary Course on Children's Rights: University of Ghent.

Stamatopoulou, E. (2007). What are cultural rights? The normative content of the right to participate in cultural life. In *Cultural rights in international law article 27 of the Universal Declaration of Human Rights and beyond*. Leiden: Martinus Nijhoff.

Stephen, B. O. (2011). Reforming the mother tongue content of Nigerian education for sustainable national empowerment. In A. R. Lawal, et al. (Eds.), *Education reforms in Nigeria—Past, present and future*. Ibadan: Stirling-Holding.

Thio, L. (2007). The implementation of minority rights within the United Nations Human Rights Regime. In L. Thio (Ed.), *Managing Babel: The international legal protection of minorities in the twentieth century*. Leiden: Martinus Nijhoff.

Thiruvengadam, A. R. (2013). Swallowing a bitter PIL? Reflections on progressive strategies for public interest litigation in India. In O. Vilhena, U. Baxi, & F. Viljoen (Eds.), *Transformative constitutionalism: Comparing the Apex courts of Brazil, India and South Africa*. Pretoria: Pretoria University Law Press.

Tomasevesk, K. (2004). The right to education: Mission to the United Kingdom. In A. Fisher (Ed.), *The content of the right to education—Theoretical foundations* (Centre for Human Rights and Global Justice Working Paper Economic, Social and Cultural rights Series No. 4). New York: New York University Press.

UNESCO. (2008). *Inclusive dimensions of the right to education: Normative bases.* Concept Paper prepared for the eighth and ninth meetings of the joint expert group UNESCO (CR)/ECOSOC (CESCR) on the monitoring of the right to education.

Unterhalter, E. (2005). Ensuring a fair chance for girls, global campaign for education. In S. Aikman & E. Unterhalter (Eds.), *Beyond access transforming policy and practice for gender equality in education* (p. 51). Oxford: Oxfam GB.

Veriava, F., & Coomans, F. (2005). The right to education. In D. Brand & C. Heyns (Eds.), *Socio-economic rights in South Africa.* Pretoria: Pretoria University Law Press.

Wakefield, L., & Murungi, N. (2011). Domesticating international standards of education for children with intellectual disabilities: A case study of Kenya and South Africa. In I. Grobbelaar-Du Plessis & T. Van Reenen (Eds.), *Aspects of disability law in Africa.* Pretoria: Pretoria University Law Press.

Yoloye, A. E. (2004). The relevance of universal basic education in the development of the primary education system in Nigeria. In T. L. Adepoju (Ed.), *Planning and implementation of universal basic education in Nigeria.* Ibadan: Education Industries Nigeria Ltd.

Journal Articles

Aboluwodi, A. (2015). Political will and strategic planning in the implementation of universal basic education in Nigeria: The Obafemi Awolowo example. *Journal of Education and Research, 5*(1), 41–55.

Adams, S. C., Jr. (1960). Nigeria: Where education has not kept pace with politics. *Education and Independence the Phi Delta Kappan, 41*(4), 162–168.

Adegbite, W. (2011). Languages and the challenges of education. *Nigeria Journal of the Nigeria English Studies Association (JNESA), 14*(1), 12–24.

Adeleke, G. O. (2012). Prosecuting corruption and the application of plea bargaining in Nigeria: A critique. *International Journal of Advanced Legal Studies and Governance, 3*, 53–70.

Adewale, T. M., Ajayi, K. O., & Enikanoselu, O. A. (2005). Trends in the federal government financing education in Nigeria. *Journal of Education Management*, 35–41.

Agbakwat, S. C. (2002). Reclaiming humanity: Economic, social, and cultural rights as the cornerstone of African human rights. *Yale Human Rights & Development Law Journal, 5*, 177–216.

Aihie, O. N. (2009). Prevalence of domestic violence in Nigeria: Implications for counselling. *Edo Journal of Counselling, 2*(1), 1–8.

Akinola, S. R. (2007). Coping with infrastructural deprivation through collective action among rural people in Nigeria. *Nordic Journal of African Studies, 16*, 30–46.

Akyeampong, K., Sabates, R., Hunt, F., & Anthony, J. (2009). Review of research on basic education provision in Nigeria. ESSPIN, Centre for International Education: University of Sussex, pp. 1–67. Available at https://www.academia.edu/257936/Review_of_Research_on_Basic_Education_Provision_inNigeria. Accessed 23 Oct 2013.

Aluede, R. O. A. (2006). Universal basic education in Nigeria: Matters arising. *Kamla-Raj Journal of Human Ecology, 20* (2): 97–101.

Aluede, O. (2009). The teacher matters: Strategies for making the teaching profession more relevant in the Nigerian educational system. *International Journal of Educational Sciences, 1*(1), 39–44.

Aluede, O., & Idogho, P. O. (2014). Refocusing teacher education for Nigeria's national development: Issues and policies for implementation. *International Studies in Education Administration, 42*(3), 103.

Ambe-Uva, T. N. (2007). National Open University of Nigeria (NOUN): A historical perspective and challenges. *Turkish Online Journal of Distance Education (TOJDE), 1*(January), 1302–6488.

Arowosegbe, J. O. (2009). Violence and national development in Nigeria: The political economy of youth restiveness in the Niger Delta. *Review of African Political Economy, 36*(122), 575–594.

Asiedu-Akrofi, D. (1989). Judicial recognition and adoption of customary law in Nigeria. *The American Journal of Comparative Law, 37*, 571–593.

Awanbor, D. (1995). Ten years of the national policy on education in Nigeria: An assessment of policy on special education. *International Journal of Disability, Development and Education, 42*, 171–176.

Ayo, C. K., Odukoya, J. A., & Azeta, A. (2014). A review of open and distance education and human development in Nigeria. *International Journal of Emerging Technologies in Learning (iJET), 9*(6), 63–67.

Bell, D. A., Jr. (1980). *Brown v board of education* and the interest-convergence dilemma. *Harvard Law Review, 518*, 1979–1980.

Case, A., & Deaton, A. (1999). School inputs and educational outcomes in South Africa. *Quarterly Journal of Economics, 114*, 1047–1084.

Chapman, D. W., & Quijada, J. J. (2009). An analysis of USAID assistance to basic education in the developing world, 1990–2005. *International Journal of Educational Development, 29*, 268–280.

Cheong Cheng, Y., & Wai Ming, T. (1997). Multi-models of quality in education. *Quality Assurance in Education, 5*, 202–213.

Christiansen, E. C. (2008). Using constitutional adjudication to remedy socio-economic injustice: Comparative lessons from South Africa. *UCLA Journal of International Law and Foreign Affairs, 13,* 369–402.

Chukwuemeka, E., Ugwuanyi, B. J., & Ewuim, N. (2012). Curbing corruption in Nigeria: The imperatives of good leadership. *African Research Review, 6*(3), 338–358.

Constitution of the Federal Republic of Nigeria. (1999).

Cranstone, M. (1983). Are there any human rights? *Daedalus, 12,* 1–17.

Deva, S. (2009). Public interest litigation in India: A critical review. *Civil Justice Quarterly, 28*(1), 19–40.

Durojaye, E., & Foley, E. A. (2012). Making a first impression: An assessment of the decision of the committee of experts of the African children's charter in the Nubian children communication. *African Human Rights Law Journal, 12,* 567–578.

Duze, C. O. (2011). Falling standards of education in Nigeria: An empirical evidence in delta State of Nigeria. *LWATI: A Journal of Contemporary Research, 8*(3), 1–12.

Ejidike, O. M. (1999). Human rights in the cultural traditions and social practice of the Igbo of South-Eastern Nigeria. *Journal of African Law, 43,* 71–98.

Eleri, N. O. E. (2013). Teaching effectiveness in elements of special education in NCE—Awarding institutions in Nigeria: Influence of teacher qualifications and experience. *IOSR Journal of Research & Method, 2*(2), 7–22.

Emeh, I. E. J., Eluwa, I. J., & Ukah, F. O. (2012). A rural-community development in Nigeria; group dynamics perspective. *Interdisciplinary Journal of Contemporary Research, 4*(5), 1090–1107.

Etuk, G. R., Ering, S. O., & Ajake, U. E. (2012). Nigeria's universal basic education (UBE) policy: A sociological analysis. *American International Journal of Contemporary Research, 2,* 179–183.

Fabunmi, M. (2005). Historical analysis of educational policy formulation in Nigeria: Implications for educational planning and policy. *International Journal of African and African American Studies, 4*(2), 1–7.

Fowoyo, J. T. (2013). Transforming the Almajiri education for the benefit of the Nigerian society. *Journal of Educational and Social Research, 3,* 67–71.

George, R. P. (2007). Natural law. *Harvard Journal of Law & Public Policy, 31,* 171–196.

Gyang, T. S. (2011). Human resources development in Nigeria: The roadmap for vision 20:2020. *International Journal of Economic Development Research and Investment, 2,* 70–79.

Holmes, O. W. (1918). Natural law. *Harvard Law Review, 20*(2), 40.

Ibrahim, I. A., & Buba, A. (2013). Successive failure of democracy in Nigeria: The way out. *Mediterranean Journal of Social Sciences, Rome–Italy, 4*(12), 119–123.

Ijaiya, G. T. (1998). Alleviating poverty in Nigeria: Investing in education as a necessary recipe. *Ilorin Journal of Education, 18*, 125–131.

Imam, I. (1999). The myth of judicial activism in Nigeria: Making sense of Supreme Court judgments. *International Journal of African and Asian Studies-An Open Access International Journal, 4*, 99–106.

Jagusah, O. I. W. (2001). Educational policy in Africa and the issues(s) of context: The case of Nigeria and South Africa. *International Education Journal, 2*, 113–125.

Kaunga, J. O. (2005). Indigenous peoples' experiences with the formal education system: The case of a Kenya pastoralist. *Indigenous Affairs, IWGIA, 35*, 33–41.

Klaaren, J., Dugard, J., & Handmaker, J. (2011). Public interest litigation: Introduction. *South African Journal on Human Rights 27*, 1–7.

Kpolovie, P. J., & Obilor, I. E. (2013). Adequacy–Inadequacy: Education funding in Nigeria. *Universal Journal of Education and General Studies, 2*(8) 239–254.

Labo-Popoola, S. O., et al. (2009). Universal basic education in Nigeria: Challenges and way forward. *The Social Sciences, Medwell Journals, 4*(6), 636–649.

Lee, V. E., & Smith, J. B. (1996). Collective responsibility for learning and its effects on gains in achievement for early secondary school students. *American Journal of Education, 104*(2), 103–147.

McConnachie, C., & McConnachie, C. (2012). Concretising the right to a basic education. *South African Law Journal, 129*, 544–590.

McNeely, C. L. (1995). Prescribing national education policies: The role of international organisations. *Comparative Education Review, 39*, 483–507.

Ndiyo, N. A. (2007). A dynamic analysis of education and economic growth in Nigeria. *The Journal of Developing Areas, 41*(1), 1–16.

Nkata, M. (2011). The duty to provide basic education for children with severe and profound intellectual disabilities. Case review. *ESR Review: Economic and Social Rights in South Africa, 12*(3), 10–12.

Oba, A. A. (2004). The African charter on human and peoples' rights and ouster clauses under the military regimes in Nigeria: Before and after September 11. *African Human Rights Law Journal, 4*, 275–302.

Obidike, N. D., & Onwuka, L. N. (2013). Enhancing the implementation of Universal Basic Education in Nigeria. *Research Journal in Organizational Psychology & Educational Studies, 2*(4), 185–190.

Obakhedo, N. O. (2011). Curbing electoral violence in Nigeria: The imperative of political education. *International Multidisciplinary Journal, Ethiopia, 5*(5), 99–110.

Ofulue, C. I. (2011). Literacy at a distance in multilingual contexts: Issues and challenges. *International Review of Open and Distance Learning, 12*(6), 84–101.

Okeke, C. N. (1996–1997). International law in the Nigerian legal system. *California Western International Law Journal, 27,* 312–355.

Okorie, E. U., & Akubuilo, F. (2013). Towards improving quality of education in chemistry: An investigation into chemistry teachers' knowledge of chemistry curriculum. *International Journal of Emerging Science and Engineering (IJESE), 1*(9), 30–34.

Oloruntegbe, K. O. (2011). Teachers' involvement, commitment and innovativeness in curriculum development and implementation. *Journal of Emerging Trends in Educational Research and Policy Studies (JETERAPS), 2*(6), 443–449.

Oni, J. O. (2009). Management of primary education in Nigeria: Trends, constraints and solutions. *Medwell Journal, 4,* 286–290.

Oseni, M. (2012). Adequacy of budgetary allocation to educational institutions in Nigeria. *Pakistan Journal of Business and Economic Review, 3,* 143–157.

Rose, P. (2005). Is there a "fast-track" to achieving education for all? *International Journal of Educational Development, 25,* 381–398.

Rosencranz, A., & Jackson, M. (2003). The Delhi pollution case: The Supreme Court of India and the limits of judicial power. *Environmental Policy and Law, 33,* 88–91.

Salamone, F. A. (1987). The Social Construction of Colonial reality: Yauri Emirate. *Journal of Legal Pluralism, 19,* 47–70.

Sifuna, D. N. (2001). African education in the twenty first century: The challenge of change. *Journal of International Cooperation in Education, 4*(1), 21–38.

Simbo, C. (2012). Defining the term basic education in the South African Constitution: An international law approach. *Law, Democracy and Development, 20*(2), 162–184.

Singal, N. (2006). Inclusive education in India: International concept, national interpretation. *International Journal of Disability, Development and Education, 53*(93), 351–369.

Skelton, A. (2012). How far will the courts go in ensuring the right to a basic education? *Southern African Public Law, 27,* 398–408.

Skelton, A. (2013). The role of the courts in ensuring the right to a basic education in a democratic South Africa: A critical evaluation of recent education case law. *De Jure, 46,* 1–23.

Skelton, A. (2014). Leveraging funds for school infrastructure: The South African 'mud schools' case study. *International Journal of Educational Development, 39,* 59–63.

Smith, J. (2004). Exploring connections between global integration and political mobilisation. *Journal of World System Research, X*(1), 255–285.

Spreen, C. A., & Vally, S. (2006). Education rights, education policies and inequality in South Africa. *International Journal of Educational Development, 26,* 353–362.

Ssenyonjo, M. (2011). The economic, social and cultural rights jurisprudence of the African Commission: 30 years since the adoption of the African Charter. *Netherlands Quarterly of Human Rights, 29*, 358–397.

The Constitution of the Republic of South Africa. (1996).

Tom, E. J., & Attai, A. J. (2014). The legislature and national development: The Nigerian experience. *Global Journal of Arts Humanities and Social Sciences, 2*(9), 63–78.

Tomasevski, K. (2005). Globalising what: Education as a human right or as a traded service? *Indiana Journal of Global Legal Studies, 12*(1), 1–78.

Tsafe, A. K. (2013). A critical analysis of universal basic education on its implementation so far. *Scientific Journal of Pure and Applied Sciences, 2*(1), 15–22.

Turrent, V., & Oketch, M. (2009). Financing universal primary education: An analysis of official development assistance in fragile states. *International Journal of Educational Development, 29*, 357–365.

Internet Sources and Articles

Adelabu, M. A. (2005). *Teacher motivation and incentives in Nigeria*. https://www.eldis.org/vfile/upload/1/document/0709/Teacher_motivation_Nigeria.pdf. Accessed 31 Oct 2017.

Adesulu, D. (2003). *Nigeria @ 50: Milestones of Nigerian education*. https://www.vanguardngr.com/2010/09/nigeria-50-milestones-of-nigeria-education/. Accessed 17 Sept 2017.

Adeyemi, B. A., Oribabor, O. A., & Adeyemi, B. B. (2003). *An overview of educational issues in Nigeria: Thoughts and reflections*. Available at https://nau.edu/uploadedFiles/Academic/COE/About/Projects/An%20Overview%20of%20Educational%20Issues%20in%20Nigeria.pdf. Accessed 30 July 2017.

Afe, J. O. (2003). *Reflections on becoming a teacher and the challenges of teacher education*. Available at https://www.nuc.edu.ng/nucsite/File/ILS%202002/ILS-69.pdf. Accessed 22 Oct 2014.

Ajayi, S. A. (2003). *The development of free primary education scheme in Western Nigeria, 1952–1966: An analysis*. Available at https://www.ajol.info/index.php/og/article/download/52320/4044. Accessed 21 Oct 2017.

Aristotle Human Rights Theories, Classical Perspectives. (2003). https://www.mtholyoke.edu/~gerla22f/classweb/Human%20Rights%20Theories%20-%20Classic%20Perspectives.html. Accessed 10 Mar 2017.

Asibuo Sam, K. (2003). *The role of the commission on human rights and administrative justice (CHRAJ) in promoting public service accountability under Ghana's fourth republic*. https://unpan1.un.org/intradoc/groups/public/documents/CAFRAD/UNPAN017693.pdf. Accessed 18 Jan 2018.

Assefa, A. G. (2003). *Will Nubian children have to go to the African Court?* https://africlaw.com/2012/04/13/will-nubian-children-have-to-go-to-the-african-court/. Accessed 25 Apr 2017.

Atoyebi, J. A. (2003). *A critique of the five main objectives of the philosophy of Nigerian education in the contemporary socio-economic and political trends in the country.* https://www.unilorin.edu.ng/publications/atoyebi/J.A.%20ATOYEBI.htm. Accessed 23 Sept 2017.

Barakat, B., & Urdal, H. (2009). *Breaking the waves? Does education mediate the relationship between youth bulges and political violence?* Available at https://papers.ssrn.com. Accessed 21 Oct 2017.

Betcherman, G., Fares, J., Luinstra, A., & Prouty, R. (2004). 'Child labour, education, and children's rights': Social Protection Discussion Paper Series, 18. https://www.ilocarib.org.tt/projects/childlabour/library/educationchildrenrights.pdf. Accessed 14 Apr 2017.

Brown v Board of Education of Topeka; *Briggs v Elliot*, *Davis v Board of Education of Prince Edward County (VA)*, *Boiling v Sharper and Gebhart* v *Ethel*. https://www.uscourts.gov/educational-resources/get-involved/federal-court-activities/brown-board-education-re-enactment/history.aspx. Accessed 9 Apr 2017.

Brown, G. (2003). *On the road to education for all in Nigeria*.https://gordonandsarahbrown.com/2013/09/on-the-road-to-education-for-all-in-nigeria/. *Accessed 10 Sept 2017.*

Calderhead, V. (2011). *The right to an "adequate" and "equal" education in South Africa: An analysis of s 29(1) (a) of the South African Constitution and the right to equality as applied to basic education. Section 27 and equal education*, 13. Available at https://www.section27.org.za/wp-content/uploads/2011/04/The-Right-to-a-BasicEducation.pdf. Accessed 2 Apr 2017.

Colonialism and the African experience. (2003). Available at https://www.pearsonhighered.com/assets/hip/us/hip_us_pearsonhighered/samplechapter/0205208606.pdf. Accessed 26 Oct 2017.

Dausab, Y. (2003). *The best interest of the child.* Available at https://www.kas.de/upload/auslandshomepages/namibia/Children_Rights/Children_h.pdf. Accessed 13 Oct 2017.

Educrisis. (2003). https://educationincrisis.net/country-profiles/africa/item/558-nigeria. Accessed 31 Mar 2017.

Ejizu, C. I. (2003). *African traditional religions and the promotion of community-living in Africa.* Available at https://www.afrikaworld.net/afrel/community.htm. Accessed 21 Oct 2017.

Fredriksson, U. (2003). *Quality education: The teachers' key role.* Workshop 4, Education International. https://www.ibe.unesco.org. Accessed 30 Dec 2017.

Gillard, D. (2011) *Education in England: A brief history.* https://www.educationengland.org.uk/history/chapter10.html. Accessed 30 Apr 2017.

Gusau, B. U. (2008). *Educational reforms in Nigeria: Successive years of inconsistencies and confusions.* Gusau Educational Development Association (GEDA), interactive session. Available at https://www.gamji.com/article6000/NEWS7831.htm. Accessed 30 July 2013.

Hammarberg, T. (2003). *The principles of the best interest of the child-what it means and what it demands from adults.* Available at https://wcd.coe.int/ViewDoc.jsp?id=1304019. Accessed 13 Oct 2017.

Hansungule, M. (2003). *African courts and the African commission on human and peoples.* Rights 250. https://www.kas.de/upload/auslandshomepages/namibia/Human_Rights_in_Africa/8_Hansungule.pdf. Accessed 24 Apr 2017.

Hansungule, M., & Onuora-Oguno, A. C. (2003). *Making the path by walking: Education as a human right or human capital.* Paper presented at the World Congress of Constitutional Lawyers, University of Oslo, June 2014. Available at https://www.jus.uio.no/english/research/news-and-events/events/conferences/2014/wccl-cmdc/wccl/papers/ws4/w4-hansungule&azubike.pdf.

Heard, A. (2003). *Human rights: Chimeras in sheep's clothing.* https://www.sfu.ca/~aheard/intro.html. Accessed 10 Mar 2013.

Hill, K. E., & Gindiri, G. M. C. H. (2003). *Problems encountered by visually handicapped Nigerian candidates in schools and public examinations and some strategies to overcome them.* https://www.icevi.org/publications/educator/winter_99/nigeria.htm. Accessed 23 Oct 2017.

Hodgson, D. C. (2003). *The role and purposes of public schools and religious fundamentalism: An international human rights law perspective.* Available at https://files.eric.ed.gov/fulltext/EJ979441.pdf. Accessed 7 July 2017.

https://www.disability.wa.gov.au/understanding-disability1/understanding-disability/what-is-disability/. Accessed 23 Oct 2017.

https://www.dwa.org.au/whatisadisability.htm. Accessed 23 Oct 2017.

https://hudoc.echr.coe.int/sites/eng/pages/search.aspx?i=001-59454#{'itemid':['001-59454'. Accessed 31 Oct 2017.

https://www.eldis.org/vfile/upload/1/document/0709/Teacher_motivation_Nigeria.pdf. Accessed 31 Oct 2013.

https://www.equalrightstrust.org/ertdocumentbank/Microsoft%20Word%20-%20Mandla.pdf. Accessed 30 Apr 2017.

https://www.hrcr.org/safrica/equality/Mandla_DowellLee.htm. Accessed 30 Apr 2017.

https://www.irinnews.org/report/98878/boko-haram-violence-takes-toll-on-education. Accessed 21 Oct 2017.

https://www.premiumtimesng.com/news/139547-nigeria-plans-census-of-out-of-school-children.html. Accessed 26 May 2017.

https://www.un.org/disabilities/documents/convention/convoptprot-e.pdf. Accessed 29 May 2017.

https://www.vanguardngr.com/2012/04/building-a-literate-nigerian-community/. Accessed 13 Nov 2017.

https://www.who.int/topics/disabilities/en/. Accessed 23 Oct 2017.

https://www.worldbank.org/education/edstats. Accessed 8 Apr 2017.

Juneja, N. (2003). *Constitutional amendment to make education a fundamental right issue for follow up legislation*, 23–24. https://www.nuepa.org/Download/Publications/Occasional%20Paper-33njuneja.pdf. Accessed 8 Apr 2017.

Kenyan National Human Rights Commission. (2003). *An identity crisis? A study on the issuance of national identity cards in Kenya*. https://citizenshiprightsin-africa.org/docs/KNHRC-ID-Report-2007.pdf. Accessed 25 Apr 2017.

Laure-Helene, P. (2003). *Rights-based approaches to social protection*. https://www.gsdrc.org/go/display/document/legacyid/1617. Accessed 10 Mar 2013.

Leif, W. (2011). Rights. In E. N. Zalta (Ed.), *The Stanford encyclopaedia of philosophy* (Fall ed.). Available at https://plato.stanford.edu/archives/fall2011/entries/rights/. Accessed 21 May 2013.

Mkpa, M. A. (2003). *Overview of educational development: Pre-colonial to present*. https://www.onlinenigeria.com/education/?blurb=534. Accessed 23 Oct 2013.

Molokwu, N. (2010). *The challenges of reducing poverty in Nigeria: Repositioning home economics for sustainable education*. https://educationforsustainablede-velopment.org/papers/202.doc. Accessed 25 Apr 2014.

Mondos linguistic dictionary. (2003). https://mondoslinguisticdictionary.blog-spot.com/2008/03/endogeous-and-exogenous-language.html. Accessed 31 Oct 2013.

National University Commission Bulletin. (2003). *8*(9). https://www.nuc.edu.ng/nucsite/File/Monday%20Bulletin/MB%202013/11%20March.pdf. Accessed 11 Mar 2013.

Nigeria: 'Keep away from schools or we'll kill you': Right to education under attack in Nigeria. (2003). https://www.amnesty.org/en/library/info/AFR44/019/2013/en. Accessed 21 Oct 2013.

Nkwopara, C., & Alozie, C. (2003). *FG downgrades Alvan Ikoku University of Education*. Available at https://www.vanguardngr.com/2015/09/fg-down-grades-alvan-ikoku-university-of-education/. Accessed 13 Oct 2015.

Obi, B. (2003). *Equalising education opportunity for the Nigerian-Ghanaian blind girl child*. https://wecando.wordpress.com/2007/11/11/paper-equal-izing-educational-opportunity-for-the-nigerian-ghanaian-blind-girl-child/. Accessed 23 Oct 2013.

Ofoha, D. (2013) *Gender stereotypes and girl-child education in Nigeria*. Available at https://pcfpapers.colfinder.org/bitstream/handle/5678/11/Paper%20 19%20%20(Supplementary%20File).pdf?sequence=1. Accessed 15 Oct 2017.

Ogungbure, A. A. (2003). *Legal positivism and immorality of law: Implications for the Nigeria*. Available at https://www.authorsden.com/visit/viewarticle.asp?id=58469. Accessed 4 July 2015.

Onuora-Oguno, A. C. (2013). *Constitutionalising the violation of the right of the girl child in Nigeria: Exploring constitutional safeguards and pitfalls*. https://ohrh.law.ox.ac.uk/?p=2362. Accessed 30 Oct 2017.

Public interest litigation and social change in South Africa: Strategies, tactics and lessons. (2013). Available at https://www.atlanticphilanthropies.org/sites/default/files/uploads/Public-interest-litigation-and-social-change-in-South-Africa.pdf. Accessed 15 Oct 2017.

Ribadu, N. (2013). *Obstacles to effective prosecution of corrupt practices and financial crime cases in Nigeria.* https://www.nigerianlawguru.com/articles/criminal%20law%20and%20procedure/OBSTACLES%20TO%20EFFECTIVE%20PROSECUTION%20OF%20CORRUPT%20%20PRACTICES%20&%20FINANCIAL%20CRIMES%20IN%20NIGERIA.pdf. Accessed 26 May 2017.

Right to education. https://mhrd.gov.in/rte. Accessed 8 Apr 2017.

Right to education: Human rights education associates. https://www.hrea.org/index.php?doc_id=402. Accessed 21 Mar 2017.

Schools achieving success Cm 5230. http://planipolis.iiep.unesco.org/upload/UK/UK_Schools_achieving_success.pdf. Accessed 30 Apr 2017.

Selby, D., & Kagawa, F. (2013). *Disaster risk reduction in school curricula: Case studies from thirty countries 190.* UNICEF. https://www.unicef.org/education/files/DRRinCurricula-Mapping30countriesFINAL.pdf. Accessed 24 Sept 2017.

Sen, A. (2013). *Elements of a theory of human rights.* https://humanright-ias.com/cmslogin/news/file1/file1-1311.pdf. Accessed 10 Mar 2017.

Skillbeck, M. (2013). *Education for all—Global synthesis.* https://www.unesco.org/education/wef/en-docs/findings/globsynt.pdf. Accessed 21 May 2014.

Sote, A., Aramide, K. A., & Gbotoso, A. (2013). *Evaluation of State Universal Basic Education Board (SUBEB) Libraries in selected States in South-West Nigeria.* Available at https://www.webpages.uidaho.edu/~mbolin/sote-aramide-gbotoso.htm. Accessed 5 June 2017.

Tsiga, M. I. (2013). *Killing of NYSC members. My worst moment.* https://leadership.ng/news/111013/killing-nysc-members-my-worst-moment-tsiga. Accessed 31 Oct 2017.

Udo, G. O., & Chuks, A. P. (2013). *Effect of design, layout and management of primary school facilities on performance of pupils.* https://www.aibuma.org/archive/proceedings/.../Chukwu,%20Nigeria.doc. Accessed 24 Sept 2017.

UNICEF. (2013). *Working with traditional rulers to achieve the rights of children.* Available at https://www.unicef.org/nigeria/media_3328.html. Accessed 21 Oct 2017.

Van der Berg, V., Taylor, S., & Gustafsson, V. (2013). *Improving education quality in South Africa Report for the National Planning Commission September 2011.* https://resep.sun.ac.za/wp-content/uploads/2012/10/2011-Report-for-NPC.pdf. Accessed 26 Feb 2017.

Nigerian Legislation

National Human Rights Commission Act. (1995). Supplement to Official Gazette Extraordinary No. 28, Vol. 82, 6 October 1995—Part A.

Universal Basic Education Act. (2004).

Nigerian Policy Documents

Nigerian National Policy on Education. (2004).

United Nations Resolutions

United Nations General Assembly Resolution A/RES/61/266.

General Comments

General Comment 7 (CRC/C/GC/7/Rev.1 20 September 2006 (Implementing children's rights in early childhood) (paragraph 4).

General Comment 9 of the CRC.

UN Committee on Economic, Social and Cultural Rights, General Comment 4: The Right to Adequate Housing (art 11(1) of the Covenant), 13 December 1991, E/1992/23. https://www.refworld.org/docid/47a7079a1.html.

Treaties

African Charter on the Rights and Welfare of the Child. https://acerwc.org/acrwc-charter-full-text/. Accessed June 2017.

African Cultural Charter adopted at the 13th ordinary session of the Organisation of African Unity 1976. https://au.int/en/sites/default/files/CULTURAL_CHARTER_AFRICA.pdf. Accessed 29 May 2017.

Convention on the Right of the Child.

Optional Protocol to the International Covenant on Civil and Political Rights, adopted by General Assembly Resolution 2200 (XXI) of 16 December 1966. https://www.un-documents.net/iccpr-op.htm. Accessed 21 Mar 2017.

Protocol No. 1 of the European Convention for the Protection of Human Rights and Fundamental Freedoms.

Protocol of the African Charter on Human and Peoples' Rights on the Rights of Women in Africa.

UNESCO Constitution. https://portal.unesco.org/en/ev.php-URL_ID=15244&URL_DO=DO_TOPIC&URL_SECTION=201.html.

UNESCO, Convention against Discrimination in Education.

Declarations and Statements

Dakar Framework for Action World Education Forum. (2000).
E/CN.4/2001/52 of 11 January 2001.
Jomtien Declaration.
The Salamanca Statement and Framework for Action on Special Needs Education adopted by The World Conference on Special Needs Education: Access and Quality Salamanca, Spain, 7–10 June 1994.
UNESCO Round Table on Constitutional and Legal Bases of the Right to Education as a Fundamental Human Right, 5 December 2002, 12.
World Education Forum. (2000).

South African Instruments

South African Constitution. (1996).
South African Human Rights Commission Act 54 of 1994.
South African Promotion of Administrative Justice Act. https://www.justice.gov.za/legislation/acts/2000-003.pdf. Accessed 30 Apr 2017.
South African Schools Act 84 of 1996. https://www.education.gov.za/LinkClick.aspx?fileticket=808cFmkP8U4=. Accessed 26 Feb 2017.

Indian Instruments

Indian Human Rights Act. (1993).
Indian National Policy on Education. (1986). https://www.ncert.nic.in/oth_anoun/npe86.pdf. Accessed 30 Apr 2017.
The Right of Children to Free and Compulsory Education in India (RTE ACT) Act 2009 No. 35 of 2009.

Cases

Augusto v Electoral Commission 1999 (3) SA 1 (CC).
Avinash Mehrotra vs Union of India & Ors (2009) 6 SCC 398.
Belgian Linguistic Case (No. 1) (1967), Series A, No. 5 (1979–1980) 1 EHRR 241 (No. 2) (1968), Series A, No. 6 (1979–1980) 1 EHRR 252.
Berea Township case Case CCT 24/07.
Brown v Board of Education 347 US 483, 1954.
Campbell & Cosans v The United Kingdom (Application 7511/76; 7743/76.
Cyprus v Turkey Application 25781/94.
Free Legal Assistance Group & OthersvZaire (2000) AHRLR 74 (ACHPR 1995).
Gani v Abacha (2000) 6 NWLR (Pt.660) 228.
Jeldsen, Busk Madsen & Pedersen v Denmark Application 5095/71; 5920/72; 5926/72.

Juma Musjid Primary School & Others v Essay No & Others 2011 8 BCLR 761 (CC).

Kevin Mgwanga Gumne et al v Cameroon Communication 266/2003 (2009).

Mandla v Dowell Lee (1983) 2 AC 548.

MEC for Education: KwaZulu-Natal and Others v Navaneethum Pillay and Others Case CCT 51/06.

Member of the Executive Council for Education in Gauteng Province, Head of Department: Gauteng Department of Education, District Director Johannesburg East D9: Gauteng Department of Education v Governing Body of the Rivonia Primary School Ms Cele, Mr Mackenzie Ms Drysdale (Rivonia case) Case CCT 135/12 [2013] ZACC 34.

Mohini Jain v State of Karnataka 1992 AIR 1858, 1992 SCR (3) 658.

Nubian Minors v Kenya Communication 002/2009.

Nwabudike v Southwark LondonBorough [1997] ELR 35.

Premier Mpumalange v Executive Committee of State-Aided Schools, Eastern Transvaal 1999 (2) SA 91; 1999 BCLR 151.

Purohit & Another v The Gambia (2003) AHRLR 96 (ACHPR 2003).

Re Certification of the Constitution of the Republic of South Africa 1996 (4) SA 744 (CC).

Soobramoney v Minister of Health (KwaZulu-Natal) (CCT32/97) [1997] ZACC 17; 1998 (1) SA 765 (CC); 1997 12 BCLR 1696 (27 November 1997).

Society for Un-Aided Private Schools of Rajasthan v UOI & Another Writ Petition (C) No. 95 of 2010.

The Centre for Child Law & Others v The Minister of Basic Education & Others Case 1749/2012.

The Centre for Human Rights (University of Pretoria) and La Rencontre Africaine Pour La Defense Des Droits De L'homme (Senegal) v Government of Senegal Communication 001/Com/001/2012.

The Governing Body of the Juma Musjid Primary School v Essay (Centre for Child Law as amicus curiae*)* 2011 7 BCLR 651 (CC) para 37.

The Head of Department: Department of Education, Free State Province v Welkom High School & Harmony High Case 766 & 767/2011.

The Registered Trustee of the Socio-Economic Rights and Accountability Project (SERAP) v The Federal Republic of Nigeria and Universal Basic Education Commission (UBEC) Suit ECW/CCJ/APP/12/07; Judgment ECW/CCJ/JUD/07/10.

UnniKrishnan JP v State of Andhra Pradesh & Ords SC 2178 (1993).

Unnikrishnan JP v State of Andhra Pradesh 1993 AIR 217, 1993 SCR (1) 594.

Wandsworth London Borough Council v A (2000) RLR 257.

Zimbabwe Lawyers for Human Rights, Human Rights Trust of Southern Africa v The Government of Zimbabwe Forced Evictions Hopley-Porta Farm & Hatcliffe Communities Communication 314/05.

E-mail and Personal Interactions

Dr. Ajoku, MOU Department of Education Psychology, Abia State University, Uturu, Abia State, Focus Group Discussion, 26 August, Owerri.

Adetokunbo Mumuni, Executive Director SERAP, conversation during the session on Nigerian National Human Rights Commission, Nigerian Bar Association annual national conference, 24–29 August, Owerri, 2014.

Adetokunbo Mumuni, interview granted to Silver Bird Television Nigeria 10 August 2014.

Beredugu, A. J. A doctoral candidate with a particular interest in the functioning of the NHRC and a special assistant to the Minister for State for Education in Nigeria.

Gov Babatunde Fashola (Support Our Schools Initiative seminar reported by channels TV Nigeria on 9 February 2014.

Dr. Jude Manu, Department of Early Childhood Care and Education, Alvan Ikoku Federal College of Education Focus Group Discussion, 26 August, Owerri.

Labaran Maku, Reaction of the Minister for Information during the presentation of education score card by the present government of Dr. Ebele Goodluck Jonathan monitored on Channels TV Nigeria, 3 July 2014.

Malala Yousafazi, 17th birthday celebration visit to Nigeria, monitored on Channels TV, Nigeria, 14 July 2014.

Olateju, M. Executive Director The Education Partnership (TEP).

Olatoke, J. (Senior Advocate of Nigeria) conversation during the session on Nigerian National Human Rights Commission, Nigerian Bar Association annual national conference, 24–29 August, Owerri, 2014.

Ojukwu, T. Director Monitoring National Human Rights Commission speaking during a session titled 'Is the National Human Rights Commission another court—A review of the scope of the National Human Rights Act' Nigerian Bar Association annual national conference, 24–29 August Owerri, 2014.

Unpublished Theses and Conference Presentations

Badwaza, Y. M. *Public interest litigation as practiced by South African human rights NGOS: any lessons for Ethiopia?* Unpublished LLM dissertation submitted to the University of Pretoria. Available at https://repository.up.ac.za/bitstream/handle/2263/1135/badwaza_ym_1.pdf?sequence=1. Accessed 15 Oct 2017.

Chigbu, V. M. C. *Morale and motivation of teachers in Nigeria*. Unpublished PhD thesis. Available at https://bura.brunel.ac.uk/bitstream/2438/3869/1/FulltextThesis.pdf. Accessed 7 July 2017.

Hansungule, M., & Onuora-Oguno, A. C. *African perspective of education: A catalyst for the desired Africa of tomorrow?* Paper presented at the Thabo Mbeki Leadership Institute symposium on finding solutions to Africa's development, University of South Africa.

Kamga, S. D. (2013). *The right to education of persons living with disability.* Lecture delivered during the Advanced Human Rights Courses, Centre for Human Rights, University of Pretoria, March 2013.

Onuora-Oguno, A. C. (2008). *Assessing the right of the indigenous child to education: Case study of the Batwa.* https://repository.up.ac.za/bitstream/handle/2263/8005/azubike.pdf?sequence=1. Accessed 21 May 2014.

Salman, K. R. *The effectiveness of the Nigerian National Human Rights Commission in human rights protection.* Unpublished PhD thesis. https://www.rksalman.com.ng/publications/RK_Salman_PhD_Thesis_Abstract.pdf. Accessed 1 May 2014.

Sen, Y. (2010). *Challenges and prospects of Nigeria's development at 50.* 9 Golden Jubilee Symposium Paper at Carleton University, Ottawa, Canada.

Taiwo, E. A. *Implementation of the right to education in South Africa and Nigeria.* Unpublished LLD thesis, Faculty of Law, Nelson Mandela Metropolitan University. https://dspace.nmmu.ac.za:8080/jspui/bitstream/10948/1392/1/ELIJAH%20ADEWALE%20TAIWO.pdf. Accessed 10 Mar 2017.

Uzoukwu, L. I. *Constitutionalism, human rights and the judiciary in Nigeria.* Unpublished LLD thesis. Available at https://uir.unisa.ac.za/bitstream/handle/10500/3561/thesis_ozoukwu_1.pdf?sequence=1. (July 3 2017).

Reports

African Peer Review Mechanism Report. (2008). No. 8 Para 104.

Bamgbose, A., & Akere, F. (Eds.). (2013). *Summary of Recommendations from the Seminar on the Implementation of the Language Provisions of the National Policy on Education.* Abuja, Nigeria: Nigerian Educational Research and Development Council, Federal Ministry of Education.

Bray, W. (2008). *Human rights in education, centre for education law and policy* (CLEP).

Daudet, Y., & Eisemann, P. M. (2005). *Right to education—Commentary.* UNESCO. https://unesdoc.unesco.org/images/0014/001412/141286e.pdf. Accessed 14 Oct 2014.

Fredriksen, B. (2002). *Education for all African children by 2015: What will it take to keep the promise?* 4 Paper prepared for the Forum on Cost and Financing of Education in Nigeria.

General Comment 13 *The Right to Education (Art 13)* adopted at the 21st session of the Committee on Economic, Social and Cultural Rights, 8 December 1999 (obtained in Document E/C.12/1999/10).

Gloppen, S. (2013). *New Frontiers of Social Policy.* Conference paper on Public Interest Litigation, Social Rights and Social Policy, Arusha, 12–15 December 2005.

Govinda, R., & Bandyopadhyay, M. (2008). Access to elementary education in India. Country analytical review. *National University of Educational Planning and Administration*, 1–64.

Gusau, B. U. (2008). *Educational reforms in Nigeria: Successive years of inconsistencies and confusions.* Gusau educational development association (GEDA), interactive session. Available at https://www.gamji.com/article6000/NEWS7831.htm. Accessed 30 July 2017.

Jjuuko, F., & Kabonesa, C. (2007). *Universal Primary Education (UPE) in contemporary Uganda. Right or privilege?* (HURIPEC Working Paper 8).

Ladan, M. T. (2013). *The Child Rights Act, 2003 and the challenges of its adoption by state governments in the 19 Northern states.* Paper presented at a one-day interactive forum for Sokoto State House of Assembly Legislators, organised by the Sokoto State Ministry of Women Affairs and UNICEF, 23 July 2007.

Lauglo, J. (2013). *World Bank Africa Regional Office Human Development Sector 2001, Engaging with adults: The case for increased support to adult basic education in sub-Saharan Africa.* Africa region human development working paper series, World Bank, Washington, https://siteresources.worldbank.org/AFRICAEXT/Resources/engage_adults.pdf. Accessed 23 Apr 2014.

Madonsela, T. N. (2010). *Corruption and governance challenges: The South African experience.* CLEEN Foundation Monograph Series No. 7, 1–67.

Mbazira, C. (2008). *You are the "weakest link" in realising socio-economic rights: Goodbye strategies for effective implementation of court orders in South Africa.* Socio-Economic Rights Project Community Law Centre, University of the Western Cape, 1–63.

Moja, T. (2013). *Nigeria education sector analysis: An analytical synthesis of performance and main issues* 10, produced for the World Bank 2000. https://siteresources.worldbank.org/NIGERIAEXTN/Resources/ed_sec_analysis.pdf. Accessed 24 Sept 2013.

Monitoring the implementation of the Standard Rules on the Equalisation of Opportunities for Persons with Disabilities [A/52/56—Report on First Mandate of the Special Rapporteur]—Part 2, https://www.un.org/disabilities/default.asp?id=59. Accessed 22 May 2017.

National basement of education series developed by the World Bank. Available at https://web.worldbank.org/WBSITE/EXTERNAL/TOPICS/EXTEDUCATION/0,,contentMDK:22301663~menuPK:5495844~pagePK:148956~piPK:216618~theSitePK:282386~isCURL:Y,00.html (October 14 2017).

National Population Commission (Nigeria) and RTI International. (2011). *Nigeria Demographic and Health Survey (DHS) EdData Profile 1990, 2003, and 2008: Education Data for Decision-Making.* Washington, DC, USA: National Population Commission and RTI International.

Nelson, C. L., & Wilson, K. A. (Eds.). (1998). *Seeding the process of multicultural education—An Anthology*. Minnesota Inclusiveness Programme Plymouth.

Nigeria corruption busters. Available at https://www.unodc.org/unodc/en/frontpage/nigerias-corruption-busters.html. Accessed 15 Oct 2017.

Nuhu Ya'u, P., & Muhammad, U. M. (2010). *Funding and the challenge of teacher education in Nigeria*. 9 paper presented at the 3rd zonal conference of the Colleges of Education Academic Staff Union held at FCE (T) Gombe.

Obanya, P. (2013). *The place of languages in literacy and basic education programmes: An overview*. In A. Ouane (Ed.), *Towards a multilingual culture of education*, 121. UNESCO Institute for Education.

Okebukola, P. (2005). *Quality assurance in teacher education: The role of faculties of education in Nigerian universities*. Committee of Deans of Education of Nigerian Universities.

Onuora-Oguno, A. C. (2013). 'Protecting the rights of same sex relationships in Nigeria: Case note on *Teriah Joseph Ebah v Federal Government of Nigeria*' presented at the Centre for human rights sexual orientation seminar, December 2014.

Osafo-Kwako, P., & Apampa, S. (2009). *Nigeria: Country Assessment Research Background Paper on the political economy of the budget process*. Center for Study of the Economics of Africa (CSEA) Nigeria.

Laure-Helene, P. (2004). *Rights-based approaches to social protection*. Overseas Development Institute London, https://www.sed.manchester.ac.uk/research/events/conferences/documents/Winners%20and%20Losers%20Papers/Piron.pdf. Accessed 10 Mar 2013.

Sarelin, A. L. (2006). *The right to education from a developing country perspective* 11 KIOS Thematical reports.

Singh, K. Report of the Special Rapporteur on the Right to Education, normative action for quality education, 2 May 2012, A/HRC/20/21. https://www.ohchr.org/Documents/HRBodies/HRCouncil/RegularSession/Session20/A-HRC-20-21_en.pdf. Accessed 13 Sept 2017.

The report, Nigeria's path to sustainable development through green economy country report to the Rio + 20 Summit June 2012, 39. https://sustainabledevelopment.un.org/content/documents/1023nigerianationalreport.pdf. Accessed 13 Sept 2017.

The Standard Rules on the Equalisation of Opportunities for Persons with Disabilities, Adopted by the United Nations General Assembly, 48th session, Resolution 48/96, annex, 20 December 1993.

Tomasevski, K. (2001). *Free and compulsory education for all children: The gap between promise and performance Right to Education Primers No. 2*.https://www.campanaderechoeducacion.org/justiciabilidad/downloads/documentosCLAVE/documentosanaliticos/free_and_compulsory_education_tomasevski.pdf.

Tomasevski, K. (2001). *Removing obstacles in the way of the right to education Primers No. 1.*

Tomasevski, K. (2002). *The right to education report* submitted in accordance with Commission Resolution 2002/23, mission to Indonesia, 1–7 July 2002. E/CN.4/2003/9/Add.1 4.

Tomasevski, K. (2002). *The right to education report, mission to United States of America* 24 September–10 October 2001E/CN.4/2002/60/Add.1 January 17.

Tomasevski, K. (2013). *Six reasons why the World Bank should be debarred from education.*https://www.brettonwoodsproject.org/2006/09/art-542516/. *Accessed 21 May 2014.*

Tomasevski, K. (2009). *Human Rights Report* 2009/9, E/CN.4/2001/52.

UIS Fact Sheet. (2013, June). https://www.uis.unesco.org/Education/Documents/fs-25-out-ofschool-children-en.pdf. Accessed 21 Feb 2017.

UNESCO. (2013). *Languages are the most powerful instruments of preserving and developing our tangible and intangible heritage.* https://www.un.org/en/events/motherlanguageday/. Accessed 25 Sept 2017.

UNICEF Fact sheet on the rights of a child. (2007). https://www.unicef.org/wcaro/WCARO_Nigeria_Factsheets_CRA.pdf. Accessed 25 Sept 2017.

UNICEF Statistics. (2013). https://www.uis.unesco.org/Education/Documents/fs-25-out-of-school-childrenen.pdf. Accessed 8 Apr 2017.

Universal Basic Education Commission (UBEC) Communiqué issued at the end of the 12th quarterly meeting of UBEC management with Executive Chairmen of State Universal Basic Education Boards (SUBEBs) held from 28 April to 1 May 2014 at Disney Hotels and Resorts, Onitsha Road, Owerri, Imo State https://ubeconline.com/Pre/COMMUNIQUE%20ISSUED%20AT%20THE%20END%20OF%20TWELFTH%20QUARTERLY%20MEETING%20AT%20OWERRI.pdf. Accessed 4 June 2017.

UN Committee on the Rights of the Child: Concluding Observations: Nigeria. https://www.refworld.org/docid/43f3053c0.html. Accessed 17 Sept 2017.

UNESCO. (2008). Inclusive Dimensions of the Right to Education: Normative Bases Concept Paper. Prepared for the Eighth and Ninth Meetings of the Joint Expert Group UNESCO (CR)/ECOSOC (CESCR) on the Monitoring of the Right to Education.

UNHCR Guidelines on Formal Determination of the Best Interests of the Child Provisional Release, May 2006.

Waziri, F. (2010). 'Chairman's opening remarks' CLEEN Foundation 1 Monograph Series 7.

White Paper on Education and Training Notice 196 of 1995 Department of Education Parliament of the Republic of South Africa, Cape Town, 15 March 1995, WPJ/1995.

Wouter, P. (1996). International human rights law and its relation with national law: Monism, dualism and the self-executing character of human rights. In E. Verhellen (Ed.), *Understanding children's rights* 299 Collected papers presented at the first International Interdisciplinary Course on Children's Rights: University of Ghent.

Newspaper Reports

Chibok abductions: Nigeria girls taken abroad. Available at https://www.bbc.com/news/world-africa-27206449.

Ezekwesili, O. (2013, May 22). Governors diverted UBE funds to hire thugs, praise singers for 2007 polls. *ThisDay Nigeria.*

Issues in the Chibok school girls' abduction. https://nigeriamasterweb.com/paperfrmes.html. Accessed 30 Apr 2017.

Nigeria and Global Partnership for Education have boosted educational development in the country with $500 million to serve as additional resources to support the development of universal basic education in Nigeria. https://sunnewsonline.com/new/cover/nigeria-global-partnership-boost-education-with-500m-2/. Accessed 13 Sept 2013.

No going back on primary school teachers strike in Kogi—NUT. https://www.vanguardngr.com/2013/07/no-going-back-on-primary-school-teachers-strike-in-kogi-nut/. Accessed 31 Oct 2013.

Non-implementation of policy major challenge to Nigeria's education system. Agency Report. https://leadership.ng/news/270613/non-implementation-policy-major-challenge-nigerias-education-system-minister. Accessed 23 Oct 2017.

Primary school teachers end strike in Edo. https://www.vanguardngr.com/2013/07/primary-school-teachers-end-strike-in-edo/. Accessed 31 Oct 2013.

Index

A. C. Onuora-Oguno, *Development and the Right to Education in Africa*,
https://doi.org/10.1007/978-3-319-90335-4

The manufacturer's authorised representative in the EU is Springer Nature Customer Service Centre GmbH, Europaplatz 3, 69115 Heidelberg, Germany. If you have any concerns regarding our products, please contact ProductSafety@springernature.com

Printed and bound by CPI Group (UK) Ltd, Croydon, CR0 4YY
22/09/2026
02220950-0006